The Oxford School Spelling Dictionary

Robert Allen
Education consultant Michele Chapman

OXFORD
UNIVERSITY PRESS

OXFORD
UNIVERSITY PRESS

Great Clarendon Street, Oxford OX2 6DP

Oxford University Press is a department of the University of Oxford.
It furthers the University's objective of excellence in research, scholarship,
and education by publishing worldwide in

Oxford New York

Athens Auckland Bangkok Bogatá Buenos Aires
Cape Town Chennai Dar es Salaam Delhi Florence Hong Kong Istanbul
Karachi Kolkata Kuala Lumpur Madrid Melbourne Mexico City Mumbai
Nairobi Paris São Paulo Shanghai Singapore Taipei Tokyo Toronto Warsaw

with associated companies in Berlin Ibadan

First published 2001

British Library cataloguing in Publication Data available

Hardback ISBN 0-19-910713-0
Paperback ISBN 0-19-910714-9

1 3 5 7 9 10 8 6 4 2

Typeset in Gill Sans
Printed in Italy

Introduction

The Oxford School Spelling Dictionary is a special dictionary designed to help students with their spelling. Generally speaking there are three main areas of spelling difficulty for users of English whatever their age.

- Some words are difficult because they have unusual or unpredictable features. **Eighth**, **guard**, and **niece** are often spelt wrongly because they have awkward letter sequences. **Disappear** and **embarrass** are confusing because some letters are doubled while others are not. Words such as **desperate** and **separate** seem inconsistent because one has an **e** in the middle where the other has an **a** for no apparent reason.

- Then there are words that are easily confused. **Vain**, **vein**, and **vane** sound the same but have different meanings. Some words change their spelling according to how they are used. For example, **dependant** as a *noun* is spelt with an **a**, but as an *adjective*, it is spelt with an **e**.

- The third type of difficulty arises when suffixes and endings are added to words. It is not easy to remember to keep an **e** in **changeable**, to replace **y** with **i** in **happily**, and not to double the **p** in **galloping**.

With increased interest in spelling, reading, and writing in schools today we hope that *The Oxford School Spelling Dictionary* will provide a valuable tool offering useful strategies for dealing with spelling difficulties. We also hope that it will support teachers and parents whose task is to enable young writers to become confident, accurate spellers and to express themselves with a voice of their own.

How to use
The Oxford School Spelling Dictionary

Entries

Words are listed alphabetically in **blue** and the part of speech (e.g. *noun*, *verb*, *adjective*) follows in black. If the word has endings (called inflections), these are also listed in black below the headword.

Decide on the first sound of the word you are looking for. Some first sounds can be confusing. If you cannot find the word you are looking for, use the **Try also** tips which will guide you to other possible spellings.

Footnotes

Some words have footnotes attached to them. These identify words when you need to check that you have the right one. For example, at **bite** you will find a footnote to tell you that there is another word that sounds like it but is spelt a different way, **! byte**. Words that sound the same but are spelt differently are called homophones. Some footnotes also give extra information on usage and grammar.

Panels

There are about 250 panels which highlight particular problems. For example, you may want to know which words are spelt **-able** like **bendable**, and which are spelt **-ible** like **accessible**. Or you may want to know how you form plurals of nouns ending in **-f** such as **calf** or **roof**. Use these information panels to build your knowledge of spelling rules and practices.

It may be useful to keep a spelling jotter for new words. When using a new word, say it aloud several times before you write it down. When you go on to use it in your writing, try not to copy it but to write the word from memory.

Try also

Entry word

Panel

Inflections

Part of speech

se Try also words beginning with **ce-**, **ci-**, **cy-**, **ps-**, or **sc-** 216

selfishness
selfless *adjective*
selflessly
self-service
★ **sell** *verb*
sells
selling
sold
semaphore
semen

semi-
semi- makes words meaning 'half', e.g. **semi-automatic**, **semi-skimmed**. A few words are spelt joined up, e.g. **semicircle**, **semicolon**, but most of them have hyphens.

semibreve *noun*
semibreves
semicircle *noun*
semicircles
semicircular
semicolon *noun*
semicolons
semi-detached
semi-final *noun*
semi-finals
semi-finalist *noun*
semi-finalists
semitone *noun*
semitones
semolina
senate
senator *noun*
senators
send *verb*
sends
sending
sent
senior *adjective* and *noun*
seniors
seniority
sensation *noun*
sensations
sensational *adjective*
sensationally
sense *noun*
senses
sense *verb*
senses
sensing
sensed
senseless *adjective*
senselessly
sensible *adjective*
sensibly
sensitive *adjective*
sensitively
sensitivity *noun*
sensitivities
sensitize *verb*
sensitizes
sensitizing
sensitized
sensor *noun*
sensors
☆ **sent** see **send**
sentence *noun*
sentences
sentence *verb*
sentences
sentencing
sentenced
sentiment *noun*
sentiments
sentimental *adjective*
sentimentally
sentimentality
sentinel *noun*
sentinels
sentry *noun*
sentries
separable
separate *adjective*
separately
separate *verb*
separates
separating
separated
separation *noun*
separations
September *noun*
Septembers
septic
sequel *noun*
sequels
sequence *noun*
sequences
sequin *noun*
sequins
serene *adjective*
serenely
serenity
sergeant *noun*
sergeants
sergeant major *noun*
sergeant majors
✪ **serial** *noun*
serials
series *noun*
series
serious *adjective*
seriously

★ To **sell** something means 'to exchange it for money'. ! **cell**.
☆ You use **sent** in e.g. *he was sent home*. ! **cent**, **scent**.
✪ A **serial** is a story or programme in separate parts. ! **cereal**.

Footnote

Do not confuse with

Aa

-a
Most nouns ending in -*a*, e.g. **amoeba**, **gala**, have plurals ending in -*as*, e.g. **amoebas**, **galas**. A few technical words have plurals ending in -*ae*, e.g. **antennae**.

aback
abacus *noun*
abacuses
abandon *verb*
abandons
abandoning
abandoned
abbey *noun*
abbeys
abbot *noun*
abbots
abbreviate *verb*
abbreviates
abbreviating
abbreviated
abbreviation *noun*
abbreviations
abdomen *noun*
abdomens
abdominal
abduct *verb*
abducts
abducting
abducted
abide *verb*
abides
abiding
abided
ability *noun*
abilities
ablaze
able *adjective*
abler
ablest

-able and -ible
You add -*able* to a verb to make an adjective that means 'able to be done', e.g. **bendable** means 'able to be bent'. Some adjectives that have this meaning end in -*ible*, e.g. **accessible**, **convertible** and **incredible**. You cannot use -*ible* to make new words as you can with -*able*.

ably
abnormal
abnormally
abnormality *noun*
abnormalities
aboard
abode *noun*
abodes
abolish *verb*
abolishes
abolishing
abolished
abolition
abominable
aboriginal
Aborigines
abort *verb*
aborts
aborting
aborted
abortion *noun*
abortions
abound *verb*
abounds
abounding
abounded
about
above
abrasive
abreast
abroad
abrupt
abscess *noun*
abscesses
abseil *verb*
abseils
abseiling
abseiled
absence *noun*
absences
absent
absentee *noun*
absentees
absent-minded
absent-mindedly
absolute
absolutely
absorb *verb*
absorbs
absorbing
absorbed
absorbent
absorption
abstract *adjective* and *noun*
abstracts
abstract *verb*
abstracts
abstracting
abstracted

absurd
absurdly
absurdity *noun*
absurdities
abundance
abundant
abuse *verb*
abuses
abusing
abused
abuse *noun*
abuses
abusive
abusively
abysmal
abyss *noun*
abysses
academic
academy *noun*
academies
accelerate *verb*
accelerates
accelerating
accelerated
acceleration
accelerator *noun*
accelerators
accent *noun*
accents
accent *verb*
accents
accenting
accented
★ **accept** *verb*
accepts
accepting
accepted
acceptable
acceptance
access *noun*
accesses
access *verb*
accesses
accessing
accessed
accessibility
accessible
accession *noun*
accessions
accessory *noun*
accessories
accident *noun*
accidents
accidental
accidentally
acclaim *verb*
acclaims
acclaiming
acclaimed
accommodate *verb*
accommodates
accommodating
accommodated
accommodation
accompaniment *noun*
accompaniments
accompanist *noun*
accompanists
accompany *verb*
accompanies
accompanying
accompanied
accomplish *verb*
accomplishes
accomplishing
accomplished
accomplished
accomplishment *noun*
accomplishments
accord *noun*
accords
according
accordingly
accordion *noun*
accordions
account *noun*
accounts
account *verb*
accounts
accounting
accounted
accountancy
accountant *noun*
accountants
accumulate *verb*
accumulates
accumulating
accumulated
accumulation
accuracy
accurate
accurately
accusation *noun*
accusations
accuse *verb*
accuses
accusing
accused
accustomed
ace *noun*
aces
ache *noun*
aches
ache *verb*
aches
aching
ached
achieve *verb*
achieves
achieving
achieved

★ To **accept** something is to take it. ! **except**.

achievement
achievements
acid *noun*
acids
acidic
acidity *noun*
acknowledge *verb*
acknowledges
acknowledging
acknowledged
acknowledgement *noun*
acknowledgements
acne
acorn *noun*
acorns
acoustic
acoustics
acquaint *verb*
acquaints
acquainting
acquainted
acquaintance *noun*
acquaintances
acquire *verb*
acquires
acquiring
acquired
acquisition *noun*
acquisitions
acquit *verb*
acquits
acquitting
acquitted
acquittal *noun*
acquittals
acre *noun*
acres
acrobat *noun*
acrobats
acrobatic *adjective*
acrobatically
acrobatics
acronym *noun*
acronyms
across *adverb* and *preposition*
act *noun*
acts
act *verb*
acts
acting
acted
action *noun*
actions
activate *verb*
activates
activating
activated
active
activity *noun*
activities
actor *noun*
actors
actress *noun*
actresses
actual
actually
acupuncture
acute
Adam's apple *noun*
Adam's apples
adapt *verb*
adapts
adapting
adapted
adaptable
adaptation
adaptor *noun*
adaptors
add *verb*
adds
adding
added
adder *noun*
adders
addict *noun*
addicts
addicted
addiction *noun*
addictions
addictive
addition *noun*
additions
additional
additive *noun*
additives
address *noun*
addresses
address *verb*
addresses
addressing
addressed
adenoids
adequate
adhere *verb*
adheres
adhering
adhered
adhesive *noun*
adhesives
adhesion
adhesive
Adi Granth
adjacent
adjective *noun*
adjectives

adjourn *verb*
adjourns
adjourning
adjourned
adjournment
adjudicate *verb*
adjudicates
adjudicating
adjudicated
adjudication
adjudicator
adjust *verb*
adjusts
adjusting
adjusted
adjustment *noun*
adjustments
administer *verb*
administers
administering
administered
administration *noun*
administrations
administrative
administrator
admirable
admirably
admiral *noun*
admirals
admiration
admire *verb*
admires
admiring
admired
admirer *noun*
admirers
admission *noun*
admissions
admit *verb*
admits
admitting
admitted
admittance
admittedly
ado
adolescence
adolescent *noun*
adolescents
adopt *verb*
adopts
adopting
adopted
adoption
adoptive
adorable
adorably
adoration
adore *verb*
adores
adoring
adored
adorn *verb*
adorns
adorning
adorned
adornment
adrenalin
adrift
adult *noun*
adults
adulterer
adultery
advance *noun*
advances
advance *verb*
advances
advancing
advanced
advanced
advantage *noun*
advantages
advantageous
★ **Advent**
adventure *noun*
adventures
adventurous *adjective*
adventurously
adverb *noun*
adverbs
adversary *noun*
adversaries
adverse
adversity *noun*
adversities
advertise *verb*
advertises
advertising
advertised
advertisement *noun*
advertisements
advice
advisable
advise *verb*
advises
advising
advised
adviser *noun*
advisers
advisory
advocate *noun*
advocates
advocate *verb*
advocates
advocating
advocated
aerial *adjective* and *noun*
aerials

★ Use a capital A when you mean the period before Christmas.

aero-
You use *aero-* to make words to do with the air or aircraft, e.g. **aerobatics**. If the word is a long one you spell it with a hyphen, e.g. **aero-engineering**.

aerobatic
aerobatics
aerobics
aeronautical
aeronautics
aeroplane *noun*
aeroplanes
aerosol *noun*
aerosols
aesthetic
aesthetically
affair *noun*
affairs
★ **affect** *verb*
affects
affecting
affected
affection *noun*
affections
affectionate
affectionately
afflict *verb*
afflicts
afflicting
afflicted
affliction
afflictions
affluence
affluent
afford *verb*
affords
affording
afforded
afforestation
afloat *adjective* and *adverb*
afraid
afresh
African *adjective* and *noun*
Africans
aft
after
afternoon *noun*
afternoons
afterwards
again
against
age *noun*
ages
age *verb*
ages
ageing
aged
aged
agency *noun*
agencies
agenda *noun*
agendas
agent *noun*
agents
aggravate *verb*
aggravates
aggravating
aggravated
aggravation
aggression
aggressive
aggressively
aggressor
aggressors
agile
agility
agitate *verb*
agitates
agitating
agitated
agitation
agitator *noun*
agitators
agnostic *noun*
agnostics
ago
agonizing
agony *noun*
agonies
agree *verb*
agrees
agreeing
agreed
agreeable
agreement *noun*
agreements
agriculture
agricultural
aground
ahead
ahoy
aid *noun*
aids
aid *verb*
aids
aiding
aided
☆ **Aids**
ailing
ailment *noun*
ailments
aim *verb*
aims
aiming
aimed

★ **Affect** means 'to make something change'. ! **effect**.
☆ Use a capital A when you mean the disease.

aim *noun*
aims
aimless
aimlessly
★ **air** *noun*
airs
air *verb*
airs
airing
aired
airborne
air-conditioned
air-conditioning
aircraft *noun*
aircraft
Airedale *noun*
Airedales
airfield *noun*
airfields
air force *noun*
air forces
airgun *noun*
airguns
airline *noun*
airlines
airlock *noun*
airlocks
airmail
airman *noun*
airmen
airport *noun*
airports
airship *noun*
airships
airstream *noun*
airstreams
airtight
airy *adjective*
airier
airiest
airily
☆ **aisle** *noun*
aisles
ajar
✪ **akela** *noun*
akelas
alarm *verb*
alarms
alarming
alarmed
alarm *noun*
alarms
alas
albatross *noun*
albatrosses
album *noun*
albums
alcohol
alcoholic *adjective* and *noun*
alcoholics
alcoholism
alcove *noun*
alcoves
✲ **ale** *noun*
ales
alert *verb*
alerts
alerting
alerted
alert *adjective* and *noun*
alerts
algebra
algebraic
alias *noun*
aliases
alibi *noun*
alibis
alien *adjective* and *noun*
aliens
alienate *verb*
alienates
alienating
alienated
alienation
alight
alike
alive
alkali *noun*
alkalis
alkaline
alkalinity
Allah
allegation *noun*
allegations
allege *verb*
alleges
alleging
alleged
allegedly
allegiance *noun*
allegiances
allegorical
allegory *noun*
allegories
allergic
allergy *noun*
allergies
alley *noun*
alleys
alliance *noun*
alliances
allied
alligator *noun*
alligators

★ You can use a plural in the phrase *to put on airs*.
☆ An **aisle** is a passage in a church or cinema. **! isle**.
✪ **Akela** is a Scout leader.
✲ You can use a plural when you mean 'different types of ale'.

allot *verb*
allots
allotting
allotted
allotment *noun*
allotments
allow *verb*
allows
allowing
allowed
allowance *noun*
allowances
alloy *noun*
alloys
all right
all-round
all-rounder
ally *noun*
allies
ally *verb*
allies
allying
allied
almighty
almond *noun*
almonds
almost
aloft
alone
along
alongside
★ **aloud**
alphabet *noun*
alphabets
alphabetical
alphabetically
alpine
already
Alsatian *noun*
Alsatians
also
☆ **altar** *noun*
altars
✪ **alter** *verb*
alters
altering
altered
alteration
alternate
alternately
alternate *verb*
alternates
alternating
alternated
alternation
alternating current
alternative *noun*
alternatives
alternative
alternator *noun*
alternators
although *conjunction*
altitude *noun*
altitudes
altogether
aluminium
always
amalgamate *verb*
amalgamates
amalgamating
amalgamated
amalgamation
amateur *adjective* and *noun*
amateurs
amateurish
amaze *verb*
amazes
amazing
amazed
amazement
ambassador *noun*
ambassadors
amber
ambiguity
ambiguities
ambiguous
ambiguously
ambition *noun*
ambitions
ambitious
ambitiously
amble *verb*
ambles
ambling
ambled
ambulance *noun*
ambulances
ambush *noun*
ambushes
ambush *verb*
ambushes
ambushing
ambushed
amen
amend *verb*
amends
amending
amended
amendment
amenity *noun*
amenities
American *adjective* and *noun*
Americans
amiable
amiably
amicable
amicably
✲ **amid**

★ **Aloud** means 'in a voice that can be heard'. ! **allowed**.
☆ An **altar** is a raised surface in religious ceremonies. ! **alter**.
✪ **Alter** means to change something. ! **altar**.
✲ You can also spell this word *amidst*.

amidships
ammonia
ammunition
amnesty *noun*
amnesties
amoeba *noun*
amoebas
★ **among**
amount *noun*
amounts
amount *verb*
amounts
amounting
amounted
amphibian *adjective* and *noun*
amphibians
amphibious
ample *adjective*
ampler
amplest
amply
amplification
amplifier *noun*
amplifiers
amplify *verb*
amplifies
amplifying
amplified
amputate *verb*
amputates
amputating
amputated
amputation
amuse *verb*
amuses
amusing
amused
amusement *noun*
amusements
amusing
☆ **an**
anaemia
anaemic
anaesthetic *noun*
anaesthetics
anaesthetist
anaesthetize *verb*
anaesthetizes
anaesthetizing
anaesthetized
anagram *noun*
anagrams
analogous
✪ **analogue**
analogy *noun*
analogies
analyse *verb*
analyses
analysing
analysed
analysis *noun*
analyses
analytical
anarchism
anarchist *noun*
anarchists
anarchy
anatomical
anatomy

-ance and -ence
Most nouns ending in *-ance* come from verbs, e.g. **disturbance**, **endurance**. Some nouns end in *-ence*, e.g. **dependence**, **obedience**, and you need to be careful not to misspell these.

ancestor *noun*
ancestors
ancestral
ancestry *noun*
ancestries
anchor *noun*
anchors
anchorage *noun*
anchorages
ancient
anemone *noun*
anemones
angel *noun*
angels
angelic
anger
angle *noun*
angles
angle *verb*
angles
angling
angled
angler *noun*
anglers
Anglican *adjective* and *noun*
Anglicans
Anglo-Saxon *adjective* and *noun*
Anglo-Saxons
angry *adjective*
angrier
angriest
angrily
anguish
angular
animal *noun*
animals
animated
animation

★ You can also spell this word *amongst*.
☆ You use *an* instead of *a* before a word beginning with a vowel, e.g. *an apple*, or before an abbreviation that sounds as though it begins with a vowel, e.g. *an MP*.
✪ You will sometimes see the spelling *analog*, especially when it is about computers.

animosity *noun*
animosities
aniseed
ankle *noun*
ankles
annex *verb*
annexes
annexing
annexed
annexation
annexe *noun*
annexes
annihilate *verb*
annihilates
annihilating
annihilated
annihilation
anniversary *noun*
anniversaries
announce *verb*
announces
announcing
announced
announcer
announcement *noun*
announcements
annoy *verb*
annoys
annoying
annoyed
annoyance *noun*
annoyances
annual *adjective*
annually
annual *noun*
annuals
★ **anonymity**
anonymous
anonymously
anorak *noun*
anoraks
anorexia
anorexic
another
answer *noun*
answers
answer *verb*
answers
answering
answered

-ant and -ent
Many adjectives end in *-ant*, e.g. **abundant**, **important**. Some adjectives end in *-ent*, e.g. **dependent** (**dependant** is a noun), **permanent**, and you need to be careful not to misspell these.

antagonism
antagonistic
antagonize *verb*
antagonizes
antagonizing
antagonized
Antarctic *adjective* and *noun*
anteater *noun*
anteaters
☆ **antelope** *noun*
antelope *or* antelopes
antenna *noun*
antelopes
anthem *noun*
anthems
anthill *noun*
anthills
anthology *noun*
anthologies
anthracite
anthropologist
anthropology

anti-
anti- at the beginning of a word makes a word meaning 'against something' or 'stopping something', e.g. **antifreeze** means 'a liquid that stops water from freezing'. If the word you are adding *anti-* to begins with a vowel, you use a hyphen, e.g. **anti-aircraft**.

antibiotic *noun*
antibiotics
anticipate *verb*
anticipates
anticipating
anticipated
anticipation
anticlimax *noun*
anticlimaxes
anticlockwise *adverb* and *adjective*
anticyclone *noun*
anticyclones
antidote *noun*
antidotes
antifreeze
✪ **antipodes**
antiquated
antique *adjective* and *noun*
antiques
antiseptic *noun*
antiseptics

★ The noun from **anonymous**.
☆ You use **antelope** when you mean a lot of animals and **antelopes** when you mean several you are thinking about separately.
✪ A word Europeans use for Australia and New Zealand.

antler *noun*
antlers
anus *noun*
anuses
anvil *noun*
anvils
anxiety *noun*
anxieties
anxious
anxiously
anybody
anyhow
anyone
anything
anyway
anywhere
apart
apartment *noun*
apartments
apathetic
apathy
ape *noun*
apes
aphid *noun*
aphids
apiece
apologetic
apologetically
apologize *verb*
apologizes
apologizing
apologized
apology *noun*
apologies
apostle *noun*
apostles
apostrophe *noun*
apostrophes
appal *verb*
appals
appalling
appalled
appalling
apparatus *noun*
apparatuses
apparent
apparently
appeal *verb*
appeals
appealing
appealed
appeal *noun*
appeals
appear *verb*
appears
appearing
appeared
appearance *noun*
appearances
appease *verb*
appeases
appeasing
appeased
appeasement
appendicitis
★ **appendix**
appendixes *or*
appendices
appetite *noun*
appetites
appetizing
applaud *verb*
applauds
applauding
applauded
applause
apple *noun*
apples
appliance *noun*
appliances
applicable
applicant *noun*
applicants
application *noun*
applications
applied
apply *verb*
applies
applying
applied
appoint *verb*
appoints
appointing
appointed
appointment *noun*
appointments
appraisal
appraisals
appraise *verb*
appraises
appraising
appraised
appreciate *verb*
appreciates
appreciating
appreciated
appreciation
appreciative
apprehension *noun*
apprehensive
apprentice *noun*
apprentices
apprenticeship
approach *verb*
approaches
approaching
approached
approach *noun*
approaches
approachable
appropriate

★ You use **appendixes** when you mean organs of the body and **appendices** when you mean parts of a book.

approval
approve *verb*
approves
approving
approved
approximate
approximately
apricot *noun*
apricots
April
apron *noun*
aprons
aptitude *noun*
aptitudes
aquarium *noun*
aquariums
aquatic
aqueduct *noun*
aqueducts
★ **Arab** *noun*
Arabs
★ **Arabian** *adjective*
☆ **Arabic**
☆ **arabic**
arable
arbitrary
arbitrate *verb*
arbitrates
arbitrating
arbitrated
arbitration
arbitrator
✪ **arc** *noun*
arcs
arcade *noun*
arcades
arch *noun*
arches
arch *verb*
arches
arching
arched
archaeology
archaeological
archaeologist
archbishop *noun*
archbishops
archer *noun*
archers
archery
architect *noun*
architects
architecture

-archy
-archy at the end of a word means 'rule or government', e.g. **anarchy** (= a lack of rule) and **monarchy** (= rule by a king or queen). The plural forms is *-archies*, e.g. **monarchies**.

Arctic
are
area *noun*
areas
arena *noun*
arenas
aren't *abbreviation*
argue *verb*
argues
arguing
argued
argument *noun*
arguments
arid
aridity
arise *verb*
arises
arising
arose
arisen
aristocracy *noun*
aristocracies
aristocrat *noun*
aristocrats
aristocratic
arithmetic
arithmetical
✲ **ark** *noun*
arks
arm *noun*
arms
arm *verb*
arms
arming
armed
armada *noun*
armadas
armadillo *noun*
armadillos
armaments
armchair *noun*
armchairs
armful *noun*
armfuls
armistice *noun*
armistices
armour
armoured
armpit *noun*
armpits
army *noun*
armies
aroma *noun*
aromas
aromatic
arose see **arise**
around

★ You use **Arab** when you mean a person or the people, and **Arabian** when you mean the place, e.g. *the Arabian desert.*
☆ You use **Arabic** when you mean the language, and **arabic** when you mean numbers, e.g. *arabic numerals.*
✪ **Arc** means a curve. ! **ark**.
✲ **Ark** means a boat. ! **arc**.

arouse *verb*
arouses
arousing
aroused
arrange *verb*
arranges
arranging
arranged
arrangement
array *noun*
arrays
arrears
arrest *verb*
arrests
arresting
arrested
arrest *noun*
arrests
arrival
arrive *verb*
arrives
arriving
arrived
arrogance
arrogant
arrow *noun*
arrows
arsenal *noun*
arsenals
arsenic
arson
artefact *noun*
artefacts
artery *noun*
arteries
artful
artfully
arthritic
arthritis
article *noun*
articles
articulate *adjective*
articulate *verb*
articulates
articulating
articulated
artificial
artificially
artillery *noun*
artilleries
artist *noun*
artists
artiste *noun*
artistes
artistic
artistry
asbestos
ascend *verb*
ascends
ascending
ascended
ascent *noun*
ascents
★ **ash** *noun*
ashes
ashamed
ashen
ashore
ashtray *noun*
ashtrays
Asian *adjective* and *noun*
Asians
aside
ask *verb*
asks
asking
asked
asleep
aspect *noun*
aspects
☆ **asphalt**
aspirin *noun*
aspirins
ass *noun*
asses
assassin *noun*
assassins
assassinate *verb*
assassinates
assassinating
assassinated
assassination *noun*
assassinations
assault *verb*
assaults
assaulting
assaulted
assault *noun*
assaults
assemble *verb*
assembles
assembling
assembled
assembly *noun*
assemblies
assent
assert *verb*
asserts
asserting
asserted
assertion
assertive
assess *verb*
assesses
assessing
assessed
assessment
assessor

★ The tree and the burnt powder.
☆ Note that this word is not spelt *ash-*.

asset *noun*
assets
assign *verb*
assigns
assigning
assigned
assignment *noun*
assignments
assist *verb*
assists
assisting
assisted
assistance
assistant *noun*
assistants
associate *verb*
associates
associating
associated
associate *noun*
associates
association *noun*
associations
assorted
assortment
assume *verb*
assumes
assuming
assumed
assumption *noun*
assumptions
assurance *noun*
assurances
assure *verb*
assures
assuring
assured
asterisk *noun*
asterisks
asteroid *noun*
asteroids
asthma
asthmatic *adjective* and *noun*
asthmatics
astonish *verb*
astonishes
astonishing
astonished
astonishment
astound *verb*
astounds
astounding
astounded
astride
astrologer
astrological
astrology
astronaut *noun*
astronauts
astronomer
astronomical
astronomy

-asy
Not many words end in *-asy*. The most important are **ecstasy**, **fantasy**, **idiosyncrasy**. There are a lot of words ending in *-acy*, however, e.g. **accuracy**.

★ **ate** see **eat**
atheist *noun*
atheists
atheism
athlete *noun*
athletes
athletic
athletics
atlas *noun*
atlases
atmosphere *noun*
atmospheres
atmospheric
atoll *noun*
atolls
atom *noun*
atoms
atomic
atrocious
atrociously
atrocity *noun*
atrocities
attach *verb*
attaches
attaching
attached
attached
attachment *noun*
attachments
attack *verb*
attacks
attacking
attacked
attack *noun*
attacks
attain *verb*
attains
attaining
attained
attainment
attempt *verb*
attempts
attempting
attempted
attempt *noun*
attempts

★ **Ate** is the past tense of eat e.g. *I ate an apple*. ! **eight**.

attend *verb*
attends
attending
attended
attendance *noun*
attendances
attendant *noun*
attendants
attention
attentive
attic *noun*
attics
attitude *noun*
attitudes
attract *verb*
attracts
attracting
attracted
attraction *noun*
attractions
attractive
auburn
auction *noun*
auctions
auctioneer
audibility
audible
audience *noun*
audiences

> **audio-**
> *audio-* makes words with 'sound' or 'hearing' in their meaning. Some of them have hyphens, e.g. **audio-visual** (= to do with hearing and seeing).

audiovisual
audition *noun*
auditions
auditorium *noun*
auditoriums
August
aunt *noun*
aunts
★ **auntie** *noun*
aunties
☆ **au pair** *noun*
au pairs
✪ **aural**
austere
austerity
Australian *adjective* and *noun*
Australians
authentic
authentically
authenticity
author *noun*
authors
authority *noun*
authorities
authorize *verb*
authorizes
authorizing
authorized
autistic

> **auto-**
> *auto-* at the beginning of a word means 'self', e.g. **autobiography** (= a biography of yourself), **automatic** (= done by itself). But some words beginning with *auto-* are to do with cars, e.g. **autocross** (= car racing across country).

autobiography *noun*
autobiographies
autograph *noun*
autographs
automate *verb*
automates
automating
automated
automatic
automatically
automation
automobile *noun*
automobiles
autumn *noun*
autumns
autumnal
auxiliary *adjective* and *noun*
auxiliaries
availability
available
avalanche *noun*
avalanches
avenue *noun*
avenues
average *adjective* and *noun*
averages
average *verb*
averages
averaging
averaged
avert *verb*
averts
averting
averted
aviary *noun*
aviaries
aviation
avid

★ You can also spell this word *aunty*.
☆ **Au pair** means a young person from another country who works in your house.
✪ **Aural** means 'to do with hearing'. ! **oral**.

avoid *verb*
avoids
avoiding
avoided
avoidance
await *verb*
awaits
awaiting
awaited
awake *adjective*
awake *verb*
awakes
awaking
awoke
awoken
awaken *verb*
awakens
awakening
awakened
award *noun*
awards
award *verb*
awards
awarding
awarded
aware
awareness
awash
away
awe
awed
awful
awfully
★ **awhile**
awkward
awoke see **awake**
awoken see **awake**
axe *noun*
axes
axe *verb*
axes
axing
axed
axis *noun*
axes
axle *noun*
axles
Aztec *noun*
Aztecs
azure *adjective*

Bb

babble *verb*
babbles
babbling
babbled
baboon *noun*
baboons
baby *noun*
babies
babyish
babysit *verb*
babysits
babysitting
babysat
babysitter *noun*
babysitters
bachelor *noun*
bachelors
back *noun*
backs
back *verb*
backs
backing
backed
backache *noun*
backaches
backbone *noun*
backbones
background *noun*
backgrounds
backing
backlash *noun*
backlashes
backlog *noun*
backlogs
backside *noun*
backsides
backstroke
backward *adjective* and *adverb*
backwards *adverb*
backwater *noun*
backwaters
backyard *noun*
backyards
bacon
bacteria
bacterial
bad *adjective*
worse
worst
badly
baddy *noun*
baddies
badge *noun*
badges
badger *noun*
badgers
badger *verb*
badgers
badgering
badgered
badminton

★ **Awhile** means 'for a short time', e.g. *Wait here awhile*. You spell it as two words in e.g. *a short while*.

baffle *verb*
baffles
baffling
baffled
bag *noun*
bags
bag *verb*
bags
bagging
bagged
bagel *noun*
bagels
baggage
baggy *adjective*
baggier
baggiest
bagpipes
★ **bail** *noun*
bails
☆ **bail** *verb*
bails
bailing
bailed
Bairam *noun*
Bairams
Baisakhi
bait *noun*
bait *verb*
baits
baiting
baited
bake *verb*
bakes
baking
baked
baker *noun*
bakers
bakery *noun*
bakeries
baking powder
balance *noun*
balances
balance *verb*
balances
balancing
balanced
balcony *noun*
balconies
bald *adjective*
balder
baldest
✪ **bale** *noun*
bales
✲ **bale** *verb*
bales
baling
baled
ballad *noun*
ballads
ballerina *noun*
ballerinas
ballet *noun*
ballets
ballistic *adjective*
balloon *noun*
balloons
ballot *noun*
ballots
ballpoint *noun*
ballpoints
ballroom *noun*
ballrooms
balsa
bamboo *noun*
bamboos
ban *verb*
bans
banning
banned
banana *noun*
bananas
band *noun*
bands
band *verb*
bands
banding
banded
bandage *noun*
bandages
bandit *noun*
bandits
bandstand *noun*
bandstands
bandwagon *noun*
bandwagons
bandy *adjective*
bandier
bandiest
bang *noun*
bangs
bang *verb*
bangs
banging
banged
banger *noun*
bangers
banish *verb*
banishes
banishing
banished
banishment
banisters
banjo *noun*
banjos
bank *noun*
banks
bank *verb*
banks
banking
banked
banknote *noun*
banknotes

★ **Bail** means 'money paid to let a prisoner out of prison' and 'a piece of wood put on the stumps in cricket'. ! **bale**.
☆ **Bail** means 'to pay money to let a prisoner out of prison' and 'to scoop water out of a boat'. ! **bale**.
✪ **Bale** means 'a large bundle'. ! **bail**.
✲ **Bale** means 'to jump out of an aircraft'. ! **bail**.

bankrupt
bankruptcy
banner *noun*
banners
banquet *noun*
banquets
baptism *noun*
baptisms
★ **Baptist** *noun*
Baptists
baptize *verb*
baptizes
baptizing
baptized
bar *noun*
bars
bar *verb*
bars
barring
barred
barb *noun*
barbs
barbarian *noun*
barbarians
barbaric
barbarism
barbarity *noun*
barbarities
barbarous *adjective*
barbecue *noun*
barbecues
barber *noun*
barbers
bar code *noun*
bar codes
bard *noun*
bards
☆ **bare** *adjective*
barer
barest
bareback
barely
bargain *noun*
bargains
bargain *verb*
bargains
bargaining
bargained
barge *noun*
barges
barge *verb*
barges
barging
barged
baritone *noun*
baritones
bark *noun*
barks
bark *verb*
barks
barking
barked
barley
barman *noun*
barmen
bar mitzvah *noun*
bar mitzvahs
barnacle *noun*
barnacles
barnyard *noun*
barnyards
barometer *noun*
barometers
barometric
baron *noun*
barons
baroness *noun*
baronesses
baronial
barrack *verb*
barracks
barracking
barracked
✪ **barracks** *plural noun*
barrage *noun*
barrages
barrel *noun*
barrels
barren
barricade *noun*
barricades
barricade *verb*
barricades
barricading
barricaded
barrier *noun*
barriers
barrister *noun*
barristers
barrow *noun*
barrows
barter *verb*
barters
bartering
bartered
✲ **base** *noun*
bases
base *verb*
bases
basing
based
baseball *noun*
baseballs
basement *noun*
basements
bash *verb*
bashes
bashing
bashed
bash *noun*
bashes
bashful
bashfully

★ You use a capital B when you mean a member of the Christian Church.
☆ **Bare** means 'naked' or 'not covered'. ! **bear**.
✪ Barracks is plural but sometimes has a singular verb, e.g. *The Barracks is over there.*
✲ **Base** means 'a place where things are controlled'. ! **bass**.

basic
basically
basin *noun*
basins
basis *noun*
bases
bask *verb*
basks
basking
basked
basket *noun*
baskets
basketball *noun*
basketballs
basketful *noun*
basketfuls
★ **bass** *noun*
basses
bassoon *noun*
bassoons
bastard *noun*
bastards
bat *noun*
bats
bat *verb*
bats
batting
batted
batch *noun*
batches
bath *noun*
baths
bath *verb*
baths
bathing
bathed
bathe *verb*
bathes
bathing
bathed
bathroom *noun*
bathrooms

☆ **baton** *noun*
batons
batsman *noun*
batsmen
battalion *noun*
battalions
✪ **batten** *noun*
battens
batter *verb*
batters
battering
battered
batter *noun*
battery *noun*
batteries
battle *noun*
battles
battlefield *noun*
battlefields
battlements
battleship *noun*
battleships
bawl *verb*
bawls
bawling
bawled
bay *noun*
bays
bayonet *noun*
bayonets
bazaar *noun*
bazaars
✲ **beach** *noun*
beaches
beacon *noun*
beacons
bead *noun*
beads
beady *adjective*
beadier
beadiest

beagle *noun*
beagles
beak *noun*
beaks
beaker *noun*
beakers
beam *noun*
beams
beam *verb*
beams
beaming
beamed
✹ **bean** *noun*
beans
❄ **bear** *verb*
bears
bearing
bore
borne
❄ **bear** *noun*
bears
bearable
beard *noun*
beards
bearded
bearing *noun*
bearings
beast *noun*
beasts
beastly
beat *verb*
beats
beating
beat
beaten
beat *noun*
beats
beautiful
beautifully

★ **Bass** means 'a singer with a low voice'. ! **base.**
☆ A **baton** is a stick used by a conductor in an orchestra. ! **batten.**
✪ A **batten** is a flat strip of wood. ! **baton.**
✲ **Beach** means 'sandy part of the seashore'. ! **beech.**
✹ A **bean** is a vegetable. ! **been.**
❄ To **bear** something is to carry it and a **bear** is an animal. ! **bare.**

beautify *verb*
beautifies
beautifying
beautified
beauty *noun*
beauties
beaver *noun*
beavers
becalmed
became see **become**
because
beckon *verb*
beckons
beckoning
beckoned
become *verb*
becomes
becoming
became
become
bedclothes
bedding
bedlam
bedraggled
bedridden
bedroom *noun*
bedrooms
bedside
bedspread *noun*
bedspreads
bedstead *noun*
bedsteads
bedtime
bee *noun*
bees
★ **beech** *noun*
beeches
beef
beefburger *noun*
beefburgers
beefeater *noun*
beefeaters
beefy *adjective*
beefier
beefiest
beehive *noun*
beehives
beeline
☆ **been** see **be**
beer *noun*
beers
beet *noun*
beet *or* beets
beetle *noun*
beetles
beetroot *noun*
beetroot
before
beforehand
beg *verb*
begs
begging
begged
began see **begin**
beggar *noun*
beggars
begin *verb*
begins
beginning
began
begun
beginner *noun*
beginners
beginning *noun*
beginnings
begrudge *verb*
begrudges
begrudging
begrudged
begun see **begin**
behalf
behave *verb*
behaves
behaving
behaved
behaviour
behead *verb*
beheads
beheading
beheaded
behind *adverb* and *preposition*
behind *noun*
behinds
beige *noun*
being *noun*
beings
belch *verb*
belches
belching
belched
belch *noun*
belches
belfry *noun*
belfries
belief *noun*
beliefs
believe *verb*
believes
believing
believed
believable
believer
bellow *verb*
bellows
bellowing
bellowed
bellows
belly *noun*
bellies

★ **Beech** means 'a tree'. ! **beach**.
☆ You use **been** in e.g. *I've been to the zoo.* ! **bean**.

belong *verb*
belongs
belonging
belonged
belongings
beloved
below
belt *noun*
belts
belt *verb*
belts
belting
belted
bench *noun*
benches
bend *verb*
bends
bending
bent
bend *noun*
bends
beneath
benefaction
benefactor *noun*
benefactors
benefit *noun*
benefits
beneficial
beneficially
benevolence
benevolent
bent see **bend**
bequeath *verb*
bequeaths
bequeathing
bequeathed
bequest
★ **bereaved**
bereavement
☆ **bereft**
beret *noun*
berets
berry *noun*
berries
berserk
berth *noun*
berths
beside
besides
besiege *verb*
besieges
besieging
besieged
bestseller *noun*
bestsellers
bet *noun*
bets
bet *verb*
bets
betting
bet
betted
betray *verb*
betrays
betraying
betrayed
betrayal
better *adjective* and *adverb*
better *verb*
betters
bettering
bettered
between
✪ **beware** *verb*
bewilder *verb*
bewilders
bewildering
bewildered
bewilderment
bewitch *verb*
bewitches
bewitching
bewitched
beyond

bi-
bi- at the beginning of a word means 'two', e.g. **bicycle** (= a machine with two wheels), **bilateral** (= having two sides).

bias *noun*
biases
biased
bib *noun*
bibs
Bible *noun*
Bibles
biblical
bicycle *noun*
bicycles
bid *noun*
bids
bid *verb*
bids
bidding
bid
bide *verb*
bides
biding
bided
big *adjective*
bigger
biggest
bigamist
bigamous
bigamy
bike *noun*
bikes
bikini *noun*
bikinis

★ You use **bereaved** when you mean a person with a close relative who has died.
! **bereft**.
☆ You use **bereft** when you mean 'deprived of something', e.g. *bereft of hope*.
! **bereaved**.
✪ **Beware** has no other forms.

bile
bilge *noun*
bilges
bilingual
billiards
billion *noun*
billions
billionth
billow *noun*
billows
billow *verb*
billows
billowing
billowed
billy goat *noun*
billy goats
binary
bind *verb*
binds
binding
bound
bingo
binoculars

bio-
bio- at the beginning of a word means 'life', e.g. **biography** (= a story of a person's life), **biology** (= the study of living things).

biodegradable
biographer
biographical
biography *noun*
biographies
biological
biologist
biology
bionic
biosphere
birch *noun*
birches
bird *noun*
birds
birdseed
Biro *noun*
Biros
birth *noun*
births
birth control
birthday *noun*
birthdays
birthmark *noun*
birthmarks
birthplace *noun*
birthplaces
biscuit *noun*
biscuits
bisect *verb*
bisects
bisecting
bisected
bishop *noun*
bishops
bison *noun*
bison
bit *noun*
bits
bit see **bite**
bitch *noun*
bitches
bitchy *adjective*
bitchier
bitchiest
bite *verb*
bites
biting
bit
bitten
★ **bite** *noun*
bites
bitter
black *adjective*
blacker
blackest
black *noun*
blacks
blackberry *noun*
blackberries
blackbird *noun*
blackbirds
blackboard *noun*
blackboards
blacken *verb*
blackens
blackening
blackened
blackmail *verb*
blackmails
blackmailing
blackmailed
blackout *noun*
blackouts
blacksmith *noun*
blacksmiths
bladder *noun*
bladders
blade *noun*
blades
blame *verb*
blames
blaming
blamed
blame *noun*
blancmange *noun*
blancmanges
blank *adjective* and *noun*
blanks
blanket *noun*
blankets

★ A **bite** is an act of biting. ! **byte**.

blare *verb*
blares
blaring
blared
blaspheme *verb*
blasphemes
blaspheming
blasphemed
blasphemous
blasphemy
blast *noun*
blasts
blast *verb*
blasts
blasting
blasted
blast-off
blaze *noun*
blazes
blaze *verb*
blazes
blazing
blazed
blazer *noun*
blazers
bleach *noun*
bleaches
bleach *verb*
bleaches
bleaching
bleached
bleak *adjective*
bleaker
bleakest
bleary *adjective*
blearier
bleariest
blearily
bleat *noun*
bleats
bleat *verb*
bleats
bleating
bleated
bleed *verb*
bleeds
bleeding
bled
bleep *noun*
bleeps
blemish *noun*
blemishes
blend *verb*
blends
blending
blended
blend *noun*
blends
bless *verb*
blesses
blessing
blessed
blessing *noun*
blessings
★ **blew** see **blow**
blight *noun*
blights
blind *adjective*
blinder
blindest
blind *verb*
blinds
blinding
blinded
blind *noun*
blinds
blindfold *noun*
blindfolds
blindfold *verb*
blindfolds
blindfolding
blindfolded
blindfold
blink *verb*
blinks
blinking
blinked
bliss
blissful
blissfully
blister *noun*
blisters
blitz *noun*
blitzes
blizzard *noun*
blizzards
bloated
block *noun*
blocks
block *verb*
blocks
blocking
blocked
blockade *noun*
blockades
blockage *noun*
blockages
blond *adjective*
blonder
blondest
☆ **blonde** *noun*
blondes
blood
bloodhound *noun*
bloodhounds
bloodshed
bloodshot
bloodstream
bloodthirsty *adjective*
bloodthirstier
bloodthirstiest

★ You use **blew** in e.g. *the wind blew hard.* ! **blue**.
☆ You use **blonde** when you are talking about a girl or woman.

bloody *adjective*
bloodier
bloodiest
bloom *verb*
blooms
blooming
bloomed
bloom *noun*
blooms
blossom *noun*
blossoms
blossom *verb*
blossoms
blossoming
blossomed
blot *noun*
blots
blot *verb*
blots
blotting
blotted
blotch *noun*
blotches
blotchy *adjective*
blotchier
blotchiest
blouse *noun*
blouses
blow *noun*
blows
blow *verb*
blows
blowing
blew
blown
blowlamp *noun*
blowlamps
blowtorch *noun*
blowtorches
blue *adjective*
bluer
bluest
★ **blue** *noun*
blues
bluebell *noun*
bluebells
bluebottle *noun*
bluebottles
blueprint *noun*
blueprints
bluff *verb*
bluffs
bluffing
bluffed
bluff *noun*
bluffs
blunder *verb*
blunders
blundering
blundered
blunder *noun*
blunders
blunt *adjective*
blunter
bluntest
blur *verb*
blurs
blurring
blurred
blur *noun*
blurs
blush *verb*
blushes
blushing
blushed
bluster *verb*
blusters
blustering
blustered
blustery
boa constrictor
noun
boa constrictors
☆ **boar** *noun*
boars
✪ **board** *noun*
boards
board *verb*
boards
boarding
boarded
boarder *noun*
boarders
board game *noun*
board games
boast *verb*
boasts
boasting
boasted
boastful
boastfully
boat *noun*
boats
boating
bob *verb*
bobs
bobbing
bobbed
bobble *noun*
bobbles
bobsled *noun*
bobsleds
bobsleigh *noun*
bobsleighs
bodice *noun*
bodices
bodily
body *noun*
bodies
bodyguard *noun*
bodyguards

★ **Blue** is the colour. ! **blew**.
☆ A **boar** is a wild pig. ! **bore**.
✪ A **board** is a piece of wood. ! **bored**.

boggy *adjective*
boggier
boggiest
bogus
boil *verb*
boils
boiling
boiled
boil *noun*
boils
boiler *noun*
boilers
boisterous
boisterously
bold *adjective*
bolder
boldest
bollard *noun*
bollards
bolster *verb*
bolsters
bolstering
bolstered
bolster *noun*
bolsters
bolt *noun*
bolts
bolt *verb*
bolts
bolting
bolted
bomb *noun*
bombs
bomb *verb*
bombs
bombing
bombed
bombard *verb*
bombards
bombarding
bombarded
bombardment
bomber *noun*
bombers
bond *noun*
bonds
bondage
bone *noun*
bones
bonfire *noun*
bonfires
bonnet *noun*
bonnets
bonus *noun*
bonuses
bony *adjective*
bonier
boniest
boo *verb*
boos
booing
booed
booby *noun*
boobies
book *noun*
books
book *verb*
books
booking
booked
bookcase *noun*
bookcases
booklet *noun*
booklets
bookmaker *noun*
bookmakers
bookmark *noun*
bookmarks
boom *noun*
booms
boom *verb*
booms
booming
boomed
boomerang *noun*
boomerangs
boost *verb*
boosts
boosting
boosted
booster *noun*
boosters
boot *noun*
boots
boot *verb*
boots
booting
booted
booth *noun*
booths
border *noun*
borders
borderline
bore *verb*
bores
boring
bored
★ **bore** *noun*
bores
boredom
boring
☆ **born**
✪ **borne** see **bear**
borough *noun*
boroughs
borrow *verb*
borrows
borrowing
borrowed
bosom *noun*
bosoms

★ **Bore** means 'something boring'. ! **boar**.
☆ You use **born** in e.g. *He was born in June*. ! **borne**.
✪ You use **borne** in e.g. *She has borne three children* and *The cost is borne by the government*. ! **born**.

boss *noun*
bosses
boss *verb*
bosses
bossing
bossed
bossy *adjective*
bossier
bossiest
botanical
botanist
botany
both
bother *verb*
bothers
bothering
bothered
bother *noun*
bottle *noun*
bottles
bottle *verb*
bottles
bottling
bottled
bottleneck *noun*
bottlenecks
bottom *noun*
bottoms
bottomless
★ **bough** *noun*
boughs
bought
boulder *noun*
boulders
bounce *verb*
bounces
bouncing
bounced
bounce *noun*
bounces
bouncing
bouncy *adjective*
bouncier
bounciest
bound *verb*
bounds
bounding
bounded
bound *adjective* and *noun*
bounds
bound see **bind**
boundary *noun*
boundaries
bounds
bouquet *noun*
bouquets
bout *noun*
bouts
boutique *noun*
boutiques
☆ **bow** *noun*
bows
✪ **bow** *verb*
bows
bowing
bowed
bowels
bowl *noun*
bowls
bowl *verb*
bowls
bowling
bowled
bow-legged
bowler *noun*
bowlers
bowling
bowls
bow tie *noun*
bow ties
box *noun*
boxes
box *verb*
boxes
boxing
boxed
boxer *noun*
boxers
Boxing Day *noun*
boy *noun*
boys
boycott *verb*
boycotts
boycotting
boycotted
boyfriend *noun*
boyfriends
boyhood
boyish
bra *noun*
bras
brace *noun*
braces
bracelet *noun*
bracelets
braces
bracken
bracket *noun*
brackets
bracket *verb*
brackets
bracketing
bracketed
brag *verb*
brags
bragging
bragged

★ A **bough** is a part of a tree. ! **bow**.
☆ A **bow** is a knot with loops and rhymes with 'go'. A **bow** is also the front of a ship or a bending of the body and rhymes with 'cow'.
✪ To **bow** is to bend the body and rhymes with 'cow'.

braid *noun*
braids
braille
brain *noun*
brains
brainy *adjective*
brainier
brainiest
★ **brake** *noun*
brakes
bramble *noun*
brambles
branch *noun*
branches
branch *verb*
branches
branching
branched
brand *noun*
brands
brand *verb*
brands
branding
branded
brandish *verb*
brandishes
brandishing
brandished
brand-new
brandy *noun*
brandies
brass
brassière *noun*
brassières
brassy *adjective*
brassier
brassiest
brave *adjective*
braver
bravest
brave *noun*
braves
bravery
brawl *noun*
brawls
brawn
brawny *adjective*
brawnier
brawniest
bray *verb*
brays
braying
brayed
brazen
brazier *noun*
braziers
☆ **breach** *noun*
breaches
bread
breadth *noun*
breadths
breadwinner *noun*
breadwinners
✪ **break** *verb*
breaks
breaking
broke
broken
break *noun*
breaks
breakable
breakage *noun*
breakages
breakdown *noun*
breakdowns
breaker *noun*
breakers
breakfast *noun*
breakfasts
breakneck
breakthrough *noun*
breakthroughs
breakwater *noun*
breakwaters
breast *noun*
breasts
breaststroke
breath *noun*
breaths
breathalyse
breathalyses
breathalysing
breathalysed
breathalyser *noun*
breathalysers
breathe *verb*
breathes
breathing
breathed
breather *noun*
breathers
breathless
breathtaking
bred see **breed**
✲ **breech** *noun*
breeches
breeches
breed *verb*
breeds
breeding
bred
breed *noun*
breeds
breeder *noun*
breeders
breeze *noun*
breezes
breezy *adjective*
breezier
breeziest
brethren

★ A **brake** is what makes a car stop. ! **break**.
☆ A **breach** is a gap or a breaking of a rule. ! **breech**.
✪ To **break** something is to make it go into pieces. ! **brake**.
✲ A **breech** is a part of a gun. ! **breach**.

brevity
brew *verb*
brews
brewing
brewed
brewer *noun*
brewers
brewery *noun*
breweries
★ **briar** *noun*
briars
bribe *noun*
bribes
bribe *verb*
bribes
bribing
bribed
bribery
brick *noun*
bricks
bricklayer *noun*
bricklayers
bride *noun*
brides
☆ **bridal**
bridegroom *noun*
bridegrooms
bridesmaid *noun*
bridesmaids
bridge *noun*
bridges
✪ **bridle** *noun*
bridles
brief *adjective*
briefer
briefest
brief *noun*
briefs
brief *verb*
briefs
briefing
briefed
briefcase *noun*
briefcases
brigade *noun*
brigades
brigadier *noun*
brigadiers
brigand *noun*
brigands
bright *adjective*
brighter
brightest
brighten *verb*
brightens
brightening
brightened
brilliance
brilliant
brim *noun*
brims
brimming
brine
bring *verb*
brings
bringing
brought
brink
brisk *adjective*
brisker
briskest
bristle *noun*
bristles
bristly
bristlier
bristliest
British
Briton *noun*
Britons
brittle *adjective*
brittler
brittlest
✲ **broach** *verb*
broaches
broaching
broached
broad *adjective*
broader
broadest
broadly
broadcast *noun*
broadcasts
broadcast *verb*
broadcasts
broadcasting
broadcast
broadcaster
broaden *verb*
broadens
broadening
broadened
broad-minded
broadside *noun*
broadsides
brochure *noun*
brochures
brogue *noun*
brogues
broke see **break**
broken see **break**
bronchitis
bronze
✹ **brooch** *noun*
brooches
brood *noun*
broods
brood *verb*
broods
brooding
brooded

★ **Briar** means 'a prickly bush' and 'a pipe'. You will sometimes see it spelt *brier*.
☆ **Bridal** means 'to do with a **bride**'. ! **bridle**.
✪ A **bridle** is part of a horse's harness. ! **bridal**.
✲ **Broach** means 'to mention something'. ! **brooch**.
✹ A **brooch** is an ornament you wear. ! **broach**.

broody *adjective*
broodier
broodiest
brook *noun*
brooks
broom *noun*
brooms
broomstick *noun*
broomsticks
broth *noun*
broths
brother *noun*
brothers
brotherly
brother-in-law *noun*
brothers-in-law
brought see **bring**
brow *noun*
brows
brown *adjective*
browner
brownest
★ **brownie** *noun*
brownies
☆ **Brownie** *noun*
Brownies
browse *verb*
browses
browsing
browsed
bruise *noun*
bruises
bruise *verb*
bruises
bruising
bruised
brunette *noun*
brunettes
brush *noun*
brushes
brush *verb*
brushes
brushing
brushed
Brussels sprout *noun*
Brussels sprouts
brutal
brutally
brutality
brutalities
brute *noun*
brutes
bubble *noun*
bubbles
bubble *verb*
bubbles
bubbling
bubbled
bubble gum
bubbly *adjective*
bubblier
bubbliest
buccaneer *noun*
buccaneers
buck *noun*
bucks
buck *verb*
bucks
bucking
bucked
bucket *noun*
buckets
bucketful *noun*
bucketfuls
buckle *noun*
buckles
buckle *verb*
buckles
buckling
buckled
bud *noun*
buds
Buddhism
Buddhist
budding
budge *verb*
budges
budging
budged
budgerigar *noun*
budgerigars
budget *noun*
budgets
budget *verb*
budgets
budgeting
budgeted
budgie *noun*
budgies
buff
buffalo *noun*
buffalo or
buffaloes
buffer *noun*
buffers
buffet *noun*
buffets
bug *noun*
bugs
bug *verb*
bugs
bugging
bugged
bugle *noun*
bugles
bugler
build *verb*
builds
building
built

★ A **brownie** is a chocolate cake.
☆ A **Brownie** is a junior Guide.

builder *noun*
builders
building *noun*
buildings
built-in
built-up
bulb *noun*
bulbs
bulge *noun*
bulges
bulge *verb*
bulges
bulging
bulged
bulk
bulky *adjective*
bulkier
bulkiest
bull *noun*
bulls
bulldog *noun*
bulldogs
bulldoze *verb*
bulldozes
bulldozing
bulldozed
bulldozer *noun*
bulldozers
bullet *noun*
bullets
bulletin *noun*
bulletins
bulletproof
bullfight *noun*
bullfights
bullfighter
bullion
bullock *noun*
bullocks
bull's-eye *noun*
bull's-eyes
bully *verb*
bullies
bullying
bullied
bully *noun*
bullies
bulrush *noun*
bulrushes
★ **bulwark** *noun*
bulwarks
☆ **bulwarks** *plural noun*
bum *noun*
bums
bumble-bee *noun*
bumble-bees
bump *verb*
bumps
bumping
bumped
bump *noun*
bumps
bumper *adjective* and *noun*
bumpers
bumpy *adjective*
bumpier
bumpiest
bunch *noun*
bunches
bundle *noun*
bundles
bundle *verb*
bundles
bundling
bundled
bung *verb*
bungs
bunging
bunged
bung *noun*
bungs
bungalow *noun*
bungalows
bungle *verb*
bungles
bungling
bungled
bungler
bunk *noun*
bunks
bunk bed *noun*
bunk beds
bunker *noun*
bunkers
bunny *noun*
bunnies
bunsen burner *noun*
bunsen burners
buoy *noun*
buoys
buoyancy
buoyant
burden *noun*
burdens
burdensome
✪ **bureau** *noun*
bureaux
burglar *noun*
burglars
burglary *noun*
burglaries
burgle *verb*
burgles
burgling
burgled
burial *noun*
burials
burly *adjective*
burlier
burliest

★ A **bulwark** is a strong wall.
☆ **Bulwarks** are the sides of a ship.
✪ **Bureau** is a French word used in English. It means 'a writing desk' or 'an office'.

★ **burn** *verb*
burns
burning
burnt *or* burned
burn *noun*
burns
burner *noun*
burners
burning
burp *noun*
burps
burp *verb*
burps
burping
burped
burr *noun*
burrs
burrow *noun*
burrows
burrow *verb*
burrows
burrowing
burrowed
burst *verb*
bursts
bursting
burst
burst *noun*
bursts
bury *verb*
buries
burying
buried
bus *noun*
buses
bus stop *noun*
bus stops
bush *noun*
bushes
bushy *adjective*
bushier
bushiest
busily
business *noun*
businesses
businesslike
busker *noun*
buskers
bust *verb*
busts
busting
bust
bust *noun*
busts
bust *adjective*
bustle *verb*
bustles
bustling
bustled
busy *adjective*
busier
busiest
busybody *noun*
busybodies
☆ **but**
butcher *noun*
butchers
butchery
butler *noun*
butlers
✪ **butt** *noun*
butts
✲ **butt** *verb*
butts
butting
butted
butter
buttercup *noun*
buttercups
butterfingers *noun*
butterfingers
butterfly *noun*
butterflies
butterscotch *noun*
butterscotches
buttocks
button *noun*
buttons
button *verb*
buttons
buttoning
buttoned
buttonhole *noun*
buttonholes
buttress *noun*
buttresses
buy *verb*
buys
buying
bought
buy *noun*
buys
buyer
buzz *noun*
buzzes
buzz *verb*
buzzes
buzzing
buzzed
buzzard *noun*
buzzards
buzzer *noun*
buzzers
✹ **by** *preposition*
❄ **bye** *noun*
byes
bye-bye
by-election *noun*
by-elections
by-law *noun*
by-laws

★ You use **burned** in e.g. *I burned the cakes*. You use **burnt** in e.g. *I can smell burnt cakes*. You use **burned** or **burnt** in e.g. *I have burned/burnt the cakes*.
☆ You use **but** in e.g. *I like fish but I'm not hungry*. **! butt**.
✪ A **butt** is a barrel or part of a gun. **! but**.
✲ **Butt** means 'to hit with your head'. **! but**.
✹ You use **by** in e.g. *a book by J. K. Rowling*. **! bye**.
❄ You use **bye** in e.g *bye for now*. **! by**.

bypass *noun*
bypasses
by-product *noun*
by-products
bystander *noun*
bystanders
★ **byte** *noun*

Cc

CAB *abbreviation*
cab *noun*
cabs
cabaret *noun*
cabarets
cabbage *noun*
cabbages
cabin *noun*
cabins
cabinet *noun*
cabinets
cable *noun*
cables
cackle *verb*
cackles
cackling
cackled
cackle *noun*
cackles
cactus *noun*
cacti
☆ **caddie** *noun*
caddies
✪ **caddy** *noun*
caddies
cadet *noun*
cadets
cadge *verb*
cadges
cadging
cadged
café *noun*
cafés
cafeteria *noun*
cafeterias
caffeine
caftan *noun*
caftans use **kaftan**
cage *noun*
cages
cagey *adjective*
cagier
cagiest
cagoule *noun*
cagoules
cake *noun*
cakes
caked
calamine
calamitous
calamity *noun*
calamities
calcium
calculate *verb*
calculates
calculating
calculated
calculation
calculator *noun*
calculators
calendar *noun*
calendars
✲ **calf** *noun*
calves
calico
call *noun*
calls
call *verb*
calls
calling
called
calling *noun*
callings
callipers
callous
calm *adjective*
calmer
calmest
calmly
calmness
calorie *noun*
calories
✸ **calves** see **calf**
calypso *noun*
calypsos
camcorder *noun*
camcorders
came see **come**
camel *noun*
camels
camera *noun*
cameras
cameraman
camouflage
camp *noun*
camps
camp *verb*
camps
camping
camped
campaign *noun*
campaigns
camper *noun*
campers

★ A **byte** is a unit in computing. ! **bite**.
☆ A **caddie** is a person who helps a golfer. ! **caddy**.
✪ A **caddy** is a container for tea. ! **caddie**.
✲ **Calf** means 'a young cow' and 'a part of your leg'.
✸ **Calves** is the plural of calf. ! **carves**.

campaign *verb*
campaigns
campaigning
campaigned
campsite *noun*
campsites
campus *noun*
campuses
can *verb*
could
★ **can** *verb*
cans
canning
canned
can *noun*
cans
canal *noun*
canals
canary *noun*
canaries
cancel *verb*
cancels
cancelling
cancelled
cancellation *noun*
cancellations
cancer *noun*
cancers
candidate *noun*
candidates
candle *noun*
candles
candlelight
candlestick *noun*
candlesticks
candy *noun*
candies
candyfloss
cane *noun*
canes
cane *verb*
canes
caning
caned
canine
cannabis
canned music
cannibal *noun*
cannibals
cannibalism
☆ **cannon** *noun*
cannon *or*
cannons
cannonball *noun*
cannonballs
cannot
canoe *noun*
canoes
canoe *verb*
canoes
canoeing
canoed
canoeist
✪ **canon** *noun*
canons
canopy *noun*
canopies
can't *verb*
canteen *noun*
canteens
canter *verb*
canters
cantering
cantered
canton *noun*
cantons
✲ **canvas** *noun*
canvases
✸ **canvass** *verb*
canvasses
canvassing
canvassed
canyon *noun*
canyons
cap *verb*
caps
capping
capped
cap *noun*
caps
capable
capably
capability
capacity *noun*
capacities
cape *noun*
capes
caper *verb*
capers
capering
capered
caper *noun*
capers
capital *noun*
capitals
capitalism
capitalist
capsize *verb*
capsizes
capsizing
capsized
capsule *noun*
capsules
captain *noun*
captains
caption *noun*
captions
captivating
captive *adjective* and *noun*
captives

★ This verb **can** means 'to put food in a can', and it has normal forms.
☆ A **cannon** is a gun. ! **canon**. You use **cannons** in e.g. *There are ten cannons on the walls* and **cannon** in e.g. *They use all their cannon.*
✪ A **canon** is a member of the clergy. ! **cannon**.
✲ **Canvas** means 'a strong cloth'. ! **canvass**.
✸ **Canvass** means 'to ask people for their support'. ! **canvas**.

captivity
captor *noun*
captors
capture *verb*
captures
capturing
captured
capture *noun*
car *noun*
cars
caramel *noun*
caramels
carat *noun*
carats
caravan *noun*
caravans
carbohydrate *noun*
carbohydrates
carbon
car-boot sale *noun*
car-boot sales
carburettor *noun*
carburettors
carcass *noun*
carcasses
card *noun*
cards
cardboard
cardigan *noun*
cardigans
cardinal *noun*
cardinals
cardphone *noun*
cardphones
care *noun*
cares
care *verb*
cares
caring
cared
career *noun*
careers
career *verb*
careers
careering
careered
carefree
careful *adjective*
carefully
careless *adjective*
carelessly
carelessness
caress *verb*
caresses
caressing
caressed
caress *noun*
caresses
caretaker *noun*
caretakers
cargo *noun*
cargoes
Caribbean
caricature *noun*
caricatures
carnation *noun*
carnations
carnival *noun*
carnivals
carnivore *noun*
carnivores
carnivorous
carol *noun*
carols
caroller
carolling
carp *noun*
carp
carpenter *noun*
carpenters
carpentry
carpet *noun*
carpets
carriage *noun*
carriages
carriageway *noun*
carriageways
carrier *noun*
carriers
carrot *noun*
carrots
carry *verb*
carries
carrying
carried
cart *noun*
carts
cart *verb*
carts
carting
carted
carthorse *noun*
carthorses
cartilage
carton *noun*
cartons
cartoon *noun*
cartoons
cartoonist
cartridge *noun*
cartridges
cartwheel *noun*
cartwheels
★ **carve** *verb*
carves
carving
carved
cascade *noun*
cascades
case *noun*
cases

★ You use **carves** in e.g. *He carves the meat with a knife.* ! **calves**.

cash *verb*
cashes
cashing
cashed
cash *noun*
cashier *noun*
cashiers
cash register *noun*
cash registers
cask *noun*
casks
casket *noun*
caskets
casserole *noun*
casseroles
cassette *noun*
cassettes
cast *verb*
casts
casting
cast
cast *noun*
casts
castanets *plural noun*
castaway *noun*
castaways
castle *noun*
castles
castor *noun*
castors
castor sugar
casual *adjective*
casually
casualty *noun*
casualties
cat *noun*
cats
catalogue *noun*
catalogues
catalyst *noun*
catalysts
catamaran *noun*
catamarans
catapult *noun*
catapults
catastrophe *noun*
catastrophes
catastrophic
catch *verb*
catches
catching
caught
catch *noun*
catches
catching
catchphrase *noun*
catchphrases
catchy *adjective*
catchier
catchiest
category *noun*
categories
cater *verb*
caters
catering
catered
caterer *noun*
caterers
caterpillar *noun*
caterpillars
cathedral *noun*
cathedrals
Catherine wheel *noun*
Catherine wheels
cathode *noun*
cathodes
Catholic *adjective and noun*
Catholics
catkin *noun*
catkins
Cat's-eye *noun*
Cat's-eyes
cattle
caught see **catch**
cauldron *noun*
cauldrons
cauliflower *noun*
cauliflowers
cause *verb*
causes
causing
caused
cause *noun*
causes
caution *noun*
cautions
cautious *adjective*
cautiously
cavalier *noun*
cavaliers
cavalry *noun*
cavalries
cave *noun*
caves
cave *verb*
caves
caving
caved
caveman *noun*
cavemen
cavern *noun*
caverns
cavity *noun*
cavities
CD
CD-ROM *noun*

cease *verb*
ceases
ceasing
ceased
ceasefire *noun*
ceasefires
ceaseless *adjective*
ceaselessly
cedar *noun*
cedars
ceiling *noun*
ceilings
celebrate *verb*
celebrates
celebrating
celebrated
celebration *noun*
celebrations
celebrity *noun*
celebrities
celery
★ **cell** *noun*
cells
cellar *noun*
cellars
cello *noun*
cellos
cellular
celluloid
cellulose
Celsius
Celt *noun*
Celts
Celtic
cement
cemetery *noun*
cemeteries
censor *verb*
censors
censoring
censored
☆ **censor** *noun*
censors
censorship
censure *verb*
censures
censured
censuring
✪ **censure** *noun*
census *noun*
censuses
✲ **cent** *noun*
cents
centenary *noun*
centenaries
centigrade
centimetre *noun*
centimetres
centipede *noun*
centipedes
central *adjective*
centrally
centre *noun*
centres
centrifugal force
centurion *noun*
centurions
century *noun*
centuries
ceramic *adjective*
ceramics *plural noun*
✹ **cereal** *noun*
cereals
ceremony *noun*
ceremonies
ceremonial *adjective*
ceremonially
certain
certainly
certainty *noun*
certainties
certificate *noun*
certificates
certify *verb*
certifies
certifying
certified
chaffinch *noun*
chaffinches
chain *noun*
chains
chair *noun*
chairs
chairlift *noun*
chairlifts
chairman *noun*
chairmen
chairperson *noun*
chairpersons
chalet *noun*
chalets
chalk *noun*
chalks
chalky *adjective*
chalkier
chalkiest
challenge *verb*
challenges
challenging
challenged
challenge *noun*
challenges
challenger *noun*
challengers
chamber *noun*
chambers
champagne
champion *noun*
champions
championship *noun*
championships

★ A **cell** is a small room or a part of an organism. ! **sell**.
☆ A **censor** is someone who makes sure books and films are suitable for people to see. ! **censure**.
✪ **Censure** means 'harsh criticism'. ! **censor**.
✲ A **cent** is a coin used in America. ! **scent**, **sent**.
✹ A **cereal** is something you eat. ! **serial**.

chance *noun*
chances
chancel *noun*
chancels
chancellor *noun*
chancellors
Chancellor of the Exchequer
chandelier *noun*
chandeliers
change *verb*
changes
changing
changed
change *noun*
changes
changeable
channel *noun*
channels
chant *noun*
chants
chant *verb*
chants
chanting
chanted
chaos
chaotic *adjective*
chaotically
chap *noun*
chaps
chapatti *noun*
chapattis
chapel *noun*
chapels
chapped
chapter *noun*
chapters
char *verb*
chars
charring
charred
character *noun*
characters
characteristic *adjective*
characteristically
characteristic *noun*
characteristics
characterize *verb*
characterizes
characterizing
characterized
charades *plural noun*
charcoal
charge *verb*
charges
charging
charged
charge *noun*
charges
chariot *noun*
chariots
charioteer *noun*
charioteers
charitable *adjective*
charitably
charity *noun*
charities
charm *verb*
charms
charming
charmed
charm *noun*
charms
charming
chart *noun*
charts
charter *noun*
charters
charter *verb*
charters
chartering
chartered
charwoman *noun*
charwomen
chase *verb*
chases
chasing
chased
chase *noun*
chases
chasm *noun*
chasms
chassis *noun*
chassis
chat *verb*
chats
chatting
chatted
chat *noun*
chats
chatty *adjective*
chattier
chattiest
★ **château** *noun*
châteaux
chatter *verb*
chatters
chattering
chattered
chauffeur *noun*
chauffeurs
chauvinism
chauvinist
☆ **cheap** *adjective*
cheaper
cheapest
cheat *verb*
cheats
cheating
cheated
cheat *noun*
cheats

★ **Château** is a French word used in English. It means 'a castle or large house'.
☆ **Cheap** means 'not costing much'. ! **cheep**.

check *verb*
checks
checking
checked
check *noun*
checks
checkmate *noun*
checkmates
checkout *noun*
checkouts
check-up *noun*
check-ups
cheek *noun*
cheeks
cheek *verb*
cheeks
cheeking
cheeked
cheeky *adjective*
cheekier
cheekiest
cheekily
★ **cheep** *verb*
cheeps
cheeping
cheeped
cheer *verb*
cheers
cheering
cheered
cheer *noun*
cheers
cheerful *adjective*
cheerfully
cheerio
cheese *noun*
cheeses
cheesy *adjective*
cheesier
cheesiest
cheetah *noun*
cheetahs

chef *noun*
chefs
chemical *adjective*
chemically
chemical *noun*
chemicals
chemist *noun*
chemists
chemistry
cheque *noun*
cheques
chequebook *noun*
chequebooks
chequered
cherish *verb*
cherishes
cherishing
cherished
cherry *noun*
cherries
chess
chest *noun*
chests
chestnut *noun*
chestnuts
chest of drawers *noun*
chests of drawers
chew *verb*
chews
chewing
chewed
chewy *adjective*
chewier
chewiest
☆ **chic**
chick *noun*
chicks
chicken *noun*
chickens

chicken *verb*
chickens
chickening
chickened
chickenpox
chief *adjective*
chiefly
chief *noun*
chiefs
chieftain *noun*
chieftains
chilblain *noun*
chilblains
child *noun*
children
childhood *noun*
childhoods
childish
childminder *noun*
childminders
childproof
chill *noun*
chills
chill *verb*
chills
chilling
chilled
✪ **chilli** *noun*
chillies
✲ **chilly** *adjective*
chillier
chilliest
chime *noun*
chimes
chime *verb*
chimes
chiming
chimed
chimney *noun*
chimneys

★ **Cheep** is the noise a bird makes. ! **cheap**.
☆ Chic is a French word and means 'smart or elegant'. There is no word *chicly*.
✪ A **chilli** is a type of hot pepper, added to meat or vegetable dishes. ! **chilly**.
✲ You use **chilly** to describe cold, bleak weather or atmosphere. ! **chilli**.

chimpanzee *noun*
chimpanzees
chin *noun*
chins
china
chink *noun*
chinks
chip *noun*
chips
chip *verb*
chips
chipping
chipped
chirp *verb*
chirps
chirping
chirped
chirpy *adjective*
chirpier
chirpiest
chisel *noun*
chisels
chisel *verb*
chisels
chiselling
chiselled
chivalrous *adjective*
chivalrously
chivalry
chlorine
chlorophyll
choc ice *noun*
choc ices
chock-a-block
chock-full
chocolate *noun*
chocolates
choice *noun*
choices
choir *noun*
choirs
choirboy *noun*
choirboys
choirgirl *noun*
choirgirls
choke *verb*
chokes
choking
choked
choke *noun*
chokes
cholera
cholesterol
choose *verb*
chooses
choosing
chose
chosen
choosy *adjective*
choosier
choosiest
chop *verb*
chops
chopping
chopped
chop *noun*
chops
chopper *noun*
choppers
choppy *adjective*
choppier
choppiest
chopsticks
choral
★ **chord** *noun*
chords
chore *noun*
chores
chorister *noun*
choristers
chorus *noun*
choruses
chose see **choose**
chosen see **choose**
christen *verb*
christens
christening
christened
christening
Christian *adjective*
and *noun*
Christians
Christianity
Christmas *noun*
Christmases
chrome
chromium
chromosome *noun*
chromosomes
chronic *adjective*
chronically
chronicle *noun*
chronicles
chronological
adjective
chronologically
chronology
chrysalis *noun*
chrysalises
chrysanthemum
noun
chrysanthemums
chubby *adjective*
chubbier
chubbiest
chuck *verb*
chucks
chucking
chucked
chuckle *verb*
chuckles
chuckling
chuckled

★ A **chord** is a number of musical notes played together. ! **cord**.

chuckle *noun*
chuckles
chug *verb*
chugs
chugging
chugged
chum *noun*
chums
chummy *adjective*
chummier
chummiest
chunk *noun*
chunks
chunky *adjective*
chunkier
chunkiest
church *noun*
churches
churchyard *noun*
churchyards
churn *noun*
churns
churn *verb*
churns
churning
churned
★ **chute** *noun*
chutes
chutney *noun*
chutneys
cider *noun*
ciders
cigar *noun*
cigars
cigarette *noun*
cigarettes
cinder *noun*
cinders
cine camera *noun*
cine cameras
cinema *noun*
cinemas
cinnamon
circle *noun*
circles
circle *verb*
circles
circling
circled
circuit *noun*
circuits
circular *adjective*
and *noun*
circulars
circulate *verb*
circulates
circulating
circulated
circulation *noun*
circulations
circumference *noun*
circumferences
circumstance *noun*
circumstances
circus *noun*
circuses
cistern *noun*
cisterns
citizen *noun*
citizens
citizenship
citric acid
citrus
city *noun*
cities
civic
civil
civilian *noun*
civilians
civilization *noun*
civilizations
civilize *verb*
civilizes
civilizing
civilized
clad
claim *verb*
claims
claiming
claimed
claim *noun*
claims
claimant *noun*
claimants
clam *noun*
clams
clamber *verb*
clambers
clambering
clambered
clammy *adjective*
clammier
clammiest
clamp *noun*
clamps
clamp *verb*
clamps
clamping
clamped
clan *noun*
clans
clang *verb*
clangs
clanging
clanged
clanger *noun*
clangers
clank *verb*
clanks
clanking
clanked

★ A **chute** is a funnel for sending things down. ! **shoot**.

clap *verb*
claps
clapping
clapped
clap *noun*
claps
clapper *noun*
clappers
clarification
clarify *verb*
clarifies
clarifying
clarified
clarinet *noun*
clarinets
clarinettist
clarity
clash *verb*
clashes
clashing
clashed
clash *noun*
clashes
clasp *verb*
clasps
clasping
clasped
clasp *noun*
clasps
class *noun*
classes
class *verb*
classes
classing
classed
classic *noun*
classics
classic
classical *adjective*
classically
classification
classified
classify *verb*
classifies
classifying
classified
classmate *noun*
classmates
classroom *noun*
classrooms
clatter *noun*
clatter *verb*
clatters
clattering
clattered
★ **clause** *noun*
clauses
☆ **claw** *noun*
claws
✪ **claw** *verb*
claws
clawing
clawed
clay
clayey
clean *adjective*
cleaner
cleanest
cleanly
clean *verb*
cleans
cleaning
cleaned
cleaner *noun*
cleaners
cleanliness
cleanse *verb*
cleanses
cleansing
cleansed
cleanser
clear *adjective*
clearer
clearest
clearly
clear *verb*
clears
clearing
cleared
clearance *noun*
clearances
clearing *noun*
clearings
clef *noun*
clefs
clench *verb*
clenches
clenching
clenched
clergy
clergyman *noun*
clergymen
clergywoman *noun*
clergywomen
clerical
clerk *noun*
clerks
clever *adjective*
cleverer
cleverest
cliché *noun*
clichés
click *noun*
clicks
client *noun*
clients
cliff *noun*
cliffs
cliffhanger *noun*
cliffhangers
climate *noun*
climates

★ A **clause** is a part of a sentence or contract. ! **claws**.
☆ **Claws** are the hard sharp nails that some animals have on their feet. ! **clause**.
✪ To **claw** is to scratch, maul, or pull a person or thing.

climatic
climax *noun*
climaxes
climb *verb*
climbs
climbing
climbed
climb *noun*
climbs
climber *noun*
climbers
cling *verb*
clings
clinging
clung
clingfilm
clinic *noun*
clinics
clink *verb*
clinks
clinking
clinked
clip *verb*
clips
clipping
clipped
clip *noun*
clips
clipboard *noun*
clipboards
clipper *noun*
clippers
clippers *plural noun*
clipping *noun*
clippings
cloak *noun*
cloaks
cloakroom *noun*
cloakrooms
clobber *verb*
clobbers
clobbering
clobbered
clock *noun*
clocks
clockwise
clockwork
clog *verb*
clogs
clogging
clogged
clog *noun*
clogs
cloister *noun*
cloisters
clone *noun*
clones
clone *verb*
clones
cloning
cloned
close *verb*
closes
closing
closed
close *adjective* and *noun*
closer
closest
closely
close *noun*
closes
close-up *noun*
close-ups
closure *noun*
closures
clot *noun*
clots
clot *verb*
clots
clotting
clotted
cloth *noun*
cloths
clothe *verb*
clothes
clothing
clothed
clothes
clothing
cloud *noun*
clouds
cloud *verb*
clouds
clouding
clouded
cloudless
cloudy *adjective*
cloudier
cloudiest
clout *verb*
clouts
clouting
clouted
clove *noun*
cloves
clover
clown *noun*
clowns
clown *verb*
clowns
clowning
clowned
club *noun*
clubs
club *verb*
clubs
clubbing
clubbed
cluck *verb*
clucks
clucking
clucked

clue *noun*
clues
clueless
clump *noun*
clumps
clumsiness
clumsy *adjective*
clumsier
clumsiest
clumsily
clung see **cling**
cluster *noun*
clusters
clutch *verb*
clutches
clutching
clutched
clutch *noun*
clutches
clutter *verb*
clutters
cluttering
cluttered
clutter *noun*

co-
co- makes words meaning 'together', e.g. a **co-pilot** is another pilot who sits together with the chief pilot. You often need a hyphen, e.g. **co-author**, **co-driver**, but some words are spelt joined up, e.g. **cooperate**, **coordinate**.

coach *verb*
coaches
coaching
coached
coach *noun*
coaches
coal
★ **coarse** *adjective*
coarser
coarsest
coarsely
coast *noun*
coasts
coast *verb*
coasts
coasting
coasted
coastal
coastguard *noun*
coastguards
coastline
coat *noun*
coats
coat *verb*
coats
coating
coated
coating *noun*
coatings
coax *verb*
coaxes
coaxing
coaxed
cobalt
cobbled
cobbler *noun*
cobblers
cobbles *plural noun*
cobblestone *noun*
cobblestones
cobra *noun*
cobras
cobweb *noun*
cobwebs
cock *noun*
cocks
cock *verb*
cocks
cocking
cocked
cockerel *noun*
cockerels
cocker spaniel *noun*
cocker spaniels
cockle *noun*
cockles
cockney *noun*
cockneys
cockpit *noun*
cockpits
cockroach *noun*
cockroaches
cocky *adjective*
cockier
cockiest
cocoa *noun*
cocoas
coconut *noun*
coconuts
cocoon *noun*
cocoons
☆ **cod** *noun*
cod
code *noun*
codes
code *verb*
codes
coding
coded
coeducation
coeducational
coffee *noun*
coffees
coffin *noun*
coffins

★ **Coarse** means 'rough' or 'crude'. ! **course**.
☆ You use **cod** for the plural: *The sea is full of cod.*

cog *noun*
cogs
cohort *noun*
cohorts
coil *verb*
coils
coiling
coiled
coil *noun*
coils
coin *noun*
coins
coin *verb*
coins
coining
coined
coinage *noun*
coinages
coincide *verb*
coincides
coinciding
coincided
coincidence *noun*
coincidences
coincidentally
coke
cola *noun*
colas
colander *noun*
colanders
cold *adjective*
colder
coldest
coldly
cold *noun*
colds
cold-blooded
coldness
coleslaw
collaborate *verb*
collaborates
collaborating
collaborated
collaboration
collaborator
collage *noun*
collages
collapse *verb*
collapses
collapsing
collapsed
collapse *noun*
collapses
collapsible
collar *noun*
collars
collate *verb*
collates
collating
collated
colleague *noun*
colleagues
collect *verb*
collects
collecting
collected
collection *noun*
collections
collective
collector
college *noun*
colleges
collide *verb*
collides
colliding
collided
collie *noun*
collies
collision *noun*
collisions
colloquial *adjective*
colloquially
colon *noun*
colons
★ **colonel** *noun*
colonels
colonial
colonist *noun*
colonists
colony *noun*
colonies
colossal *adjective*
colossally
colour *noun*
colours
colour *verb*
colours
colouring
coloured
colour-blind
coloured
colourful *adjective*
colourfully
colouring
colourless
colt *noun*
colts
column *noun*
columns
coma *noun*
comas
comb *noun*
combs
comb *verb*
combs
combing
combed
combat *noun*
combats
combat *verb*
combats
combating
combated

★ A **colonel** is an army officer. ! **kernel**.

combatant *noun*
combatants
combination *noun*
combinations
combine *verb*
combines
combining
combined
combine *noun*
combines
combustion
come *verb*
comes
coming
came
comeback *noun*
comebacks
comedian *noun*
comedians
comedy *noun*
comedies
comet *noun*
comets
comfort *verb*
comforts
comforting
comforted
comfort *noun*
comforts
comfortable *adjective*
comfortably
comic *adjective* and *noun*
comics
comical *adjective*
comically
comma *noun*
commas
command *verb*
commands
commanding
commanded
command *noun*
commands
commander *noun*
commanders
commandment *noun*
commandments
commando *noun*
commandos
commemorate *verb*
commemorates
commemorating
commemorated
commemoration
commence *verb*
commences
commencing
commenced
commencement
commend *verb*
commends
commending
commended
commendable
commendation
comment *verb*
comments
commenting
commented
comment *noun*
comments
commentary *noun*
commentaries
commentate
commentator *noun*
commentators
commerce
commercial *adjective*
commercially
commercial *noun*
commercials
commercialized
commit *verb*
commits
committing
committed
commitment *noun*
commitments
committee *noun*
committees
commodity *noun*
commodities
common *adjective*
commoner
commonest
common *noun*
commons
commonplace
commonwealth *noun*
commonwealths
commotion *noun*
commotions
communal *adjective*
communally
commune *noun*
communes
communicate *verb*
communicates
communicating
communicated
communication *noun*
communications
communicative
communion *noun*
communions
communism

communist *noun*
communists
community *noun*
communities
commute
commuter *noun*
commuters
compact *adjective*
compactly
compact *noun*
compacts
compact disc *noun*
compact discs
companion *noun*
companions
companionship
company *noun*
companies
comparable *adjective*
comparably
comparative *adjective*
comparatively
comparative *noun*
comparatives
compare *verb*
compares
comparing
compared
comparison *noun*
comparisons
compartment *noun*
compartments
compass *noun*
compasses
compassion
compassionate *adjective*
compassionately
compatible *adjective*
compatibly
compel *verb*
compels
compelling
compelled
compensate *verb*
compensates
compensating
compensated
compensation *noun*
compensations
compère *noun*
compères
compete *verb*
competes
competing
competed
competence
competent *adjective*
competently
competition *noun*
competitions
competitive *adjective*
competitively
competitor *noun*
competitors
compilation *noun*
compilations
compile *verb*
compiles
compiling
compiled
compiler *noun*
compilers
complacent *adjective*
complacently
complain *verb*
complains
complaining
complained
complaint *noun*
complaints
★ **complement** *noun*
complements
☆ **complementary**
complete *adjective*
completely
complete *verb*
completes
completing
completed
completion
complex *adjective* and *noun*
complexes
complexion *noun*
complexions
complexity *noun*
complexities
complicated
complication *noun*
complications
✪ **compliment** *noun*
compliments
✲ **complimentary**
component *noun*
components
compose *verb*
composes
composing
composed
composer *noun*
composers
composition *noun*
compositions
compost
compound *noun*
compounds

★ A **complement** is a thing that completes something. ! **compliment**.
☆ Something **complementary** completes something. ! **complimentary**.
✪ A **compliment** is something good you say about someone. ! **complement**.
✲ Something **complimentary** praises someone. ! **complementary**.

comprehend *verb*
comprehends
comprehending
comprehended
comprehension *noun*
comprehensions
comprehensive *adjective*
comprehensively
comprehensive *noun*
comprehensives
compress *verb*
compresses
compressing
compressed
compression
comprise *verb*
comprises
comprising
comprised
compromise *noun*
compromises
compromise *verb*
compromises
compromising
compromised
compulsory
computation
compute *verb*
computes
computing
computed
computer *noun*
computers
comrade *noun*
comrades
comradeship
con *verb*
cons
conning
conned
concave
conceal *verb*
conceals
concealing
concealed
concealment
conceit
conceited
conceive *verb*
conceives
conceiving
conceived
concentrate *verb*
concentrates
concentrating
concentrated
concentrated
concentration *noun*
concentrations
concentric
concept *noun*
concepts
conception *noun*
conceptions
concern *verb*
concerns
concerning
concerned
concern *noun*
concerns
concerning
concert *noun*
concerts
concertina *noun*
concertinas
concerto *noun*
concertos
concession *noun*
concessions
concise *adjective*
concisely
conclude *verb*
concludes
concluding
concluded
conclusion *noun*
conclusions
concrete *adjective* and *noun*
concussion
condemn *verb*
condemns
condemning
condemned
condemnation
condensation
condense *verb*
condenses
condensing
condensed
condition *noun*
conditions
condom *noun*
condoms
conduct *verb*
conducts
conducting
conducted
conduct *noun*
conduction
conductor *noun*
conductors
cone *noun*
cones
confectioner *noun*
confectioners
confectionery

confer *verb*
confers
conferring
conferred
conference *noun*
conferences
confess *verb*
confesses
confessing
confessed
confession *noun*
confessions
confetti
confide *verb*
confides
confiding
confided
confidence *noun*
confidences
confident *adjective*
confidently
confidential *adjective*
confidentially
confine *verb*
confines
confining
confined
confinement
confirm *verb*
confirms
confirming
confirmed
confirmation
confiscate *verb*
confiscates
confiscating
confiscated
confiscation *noun*
confiscations
conflict *verb*
conflicts
conflicting
conflicted
conflict *noun*
conflicts
conform *verb*
conforms
conforming
conformed
conformity
confront *verb*
confronts
confronting
confronted
confrontation *noun*
confrontations
confuse *verb*
confuses
confusing
confused
confusion *noun*
confusions
congested
congestion
congratulate *verb*
congratulates
congratulating
congratulated
congratulations *plural noun*
congregation *noun*
congregations
congress *noun*
congresses
congruence
congruent
conical
conifer *noun*
conifers
coniferous
conjunction *noun*
conjunctions
conjure *verb*
conjures
conjuring
conjured
conjuror *noun*
conjurors
★ **conker** *noun*
conkers
connect *verb*
connects
connecting
connected
connection *noun*
connections
conning tower *noun*
conning towers
☆ **conquer** *verb*
conquers
conquering
conquered
conqueror *noun*
conquerors
conquest *noun*
conquests
conscience
conscientious *adjective*
conscientiously
conscious *adjective*
consciously
consciousness
conscription
consecutive *adjective*
consecutively
consensus
consent *verb*
consents
consenting
consented

★ A **conker** is the fruit of a horse chestnut tree. ! **conquer**.
☆ To **conquer** means 'to invade or take over'. ! **conker**.

consent *noun*
consequence *noun*
consequences
consequently
conservation
conservationist
conservative
★ **Conservative** *noun*
Conservatives
conservatory *noun*
conservatories
conserve *verb*
conserves
conserving
conserved
consider *verb*
considers
considering
considered
considerable *adjective*
considerably
considerate *adjective*
considerately
consideration *noun*
considerations
consist *verb*
consists
consisting
consisted
consistency *noun*
consistencies
consistent *adjective*
consistently
consolation *noun*
consolations
console *verb*
consoles
consoling
consoled
consonant *noun*
consonants
conspicuous *adjective*
conspicuously
conspiracy *noun*
conspiracies
conspirator
conspire *verb*
conspires
conspiring
conspired
constable *noun*
constables
constancy
constant *adjective*
constantly
constant *noun*
constants
constellation *noun*
constellations
constipated
constipation
constituency *noun*
constituencies
constituent *noun*
constituents
constitute *verb*
constitutes
constituting
constituted
constitution *noun*
constitutions
constitutional
construct *verb*
constructs
constructing
constructed
construction *noun*
constructions
constructive
consul *noun*
consuls
consult *verb*
consults
consulting
consulted
consultant *noun*
consultants
consultation *noun*
consultations
consume *verb*
consumes
consuming
consumed
consumer *noun*
consumers
consumption
contact *noun*
contacts
contact *verb*
contacts
contacting
contacted
contagious
contain *verb*
contains
containing
contained
container *noun*
containers
contaminate *verb*
contaminates
contaminating
contaminated
contamination
contemplate *verb*
contemplates
contemplating
contemplated
contemplation

★ Use a capital C when you mean a member of the political party.

contemporary *adjective* and *noun*
contemporaries
contempt
contemptible *adjective*
contemptibly
contemptuous *adjective*
contemptuously
contend *verb*
contends
contending
contended
contender *noun*
contenders
content *adjective* and *noun*
contented *adjective*
contentedly
contentment
contents *plural noun*
contest *verb*
contests
contesting
contested
contest *noun*
contests
contestant *noun*
contestants
context *noun*
contexts
continent *noun*
continents
continental
continual *adjective*
continually
continuation
continue *verb*
continues
continuing
continued
continuous *adjective*
continuously
continuity
contour *noun*
contours
contraception
contraceptive *noun*
contraceptives
contract *verb*
contracts
contracting
contracted
contract *noun*
contracts
contraction *noun*
contractions
contractor *noun*
contractors
contradict *verb*
contradicts
contradicting
contradicted
contradiction *noun*
contradictions
contradictory
contraflow *noun*
contraflows
contraption *noun*
contraptions
contrary *adjective* and *noun*
contrast *verb*
contrasts
contrasting
contrasted
contrast *noun*
contrasts
contribute *verb*
contributes
contributing
contributed
contribution *noun*
contributions
contributor *noun*
contributors
contrivance *noun*
contrivances
contrive *verb*
contrives
contriving
contrived
control *verb*
controls
controlling
controlled
control *noun*
controls
controller *noun*
controllers
controversial *adjective*
controversially
controversy *noun*
controversies
conundrum *noun*
conundrums
convalescence
convalescent
convection
convector *noun*
convectors
convenience *noun*
conveniences
convenient *adjective*
conveniently
convent *noun*
convents
convention *noun*
conventions

conventional *adjective*
conventionally
converge *verb*
converges
converging
converged
conversation *noun*
conversations
conversational *adjective*
conversationally
converse *verb*
converses
conversing
conversed
converse *noun*
conversion *noun*
conversions
convert *verb*
converts
converting
converted
convert *noun*
converts
convertible
convex
convey *verb*
conveys
conveying
conveyed
conveyor belt *noun*
conveyor belts
convict *verb*
convicts
convicting
convicted
convict *noun*
convicts
conviction *noun*
convictions
convince *verb*
convinces
convincing
convinced
convoy *noun*
convoys
cook *verb*
cooks
cooking
cooked
cook *noun*
cooks
cooker *noun*
cookers
cookery
cool *adjective*
cooler
coolest
coolly
cool *verb*
cools
cooling
cooled
cooler
coolness
coop *noun*
coops
cooperate *verb*
cooperates
cooperating
cooperated
cooperation
cooperative
coordinate *verb*
coordinates
coordinating
coordinated
coordinate *noun*
coordinates
coordination
coordinator *noun*
coordinators
coot *noun*
coots
cop *verb*
cops
copping
copped
cop *noun*
cops
cope *verb*
copes
coping
coped
copier *noun*
copiers
copper *noun*
coppers
copper sulphate
copy *verb*
copies
copying
copied
copy *noun*
copies
coral
★ **cord** *noun*
cords
cordial *adjective*
cordially
cordial *noun*
cordials
cordiality
corduroy
core *noun*
cores
corgi *noun*
corgis
cork *noun*
corks
corkscrew *noun*
corkscrews

★ A **cord** is a piece of thin rope. ! **chord**.

cormorant *noun*
cormorants
corn *noun*
corns
corned beef
corner *noun*
corners
corner *verb*
corners
cornering
cornered
cornet *noun*
cornets
cornfield *noun*
cornfields
cornflakes
cornflour
cornflower *noun*
cornflowers
Cornish
Cornish pasty *noun*
Cornish pasties
corny *adjective*
cornier
corniest
coronation *noun*
coronations
coroner *noun*
coroners
corporal *noun*
corporals
corporal *adjective*
corporation *noun*
corporations
★ **corps** *noun*
corps
☆ **corpse** *noun*
corpses
corpuscle *noun*
corpuscles
corral *noun*
corrals
correct *adjective*
correctly
correct *verb*
corrects
correcting
corrected
correction *noun*
corrections
correctness
correspond *verb*
corresponds
corresponding
corresponded
correspondence
correspondent *noun*
correspondents
corridor *noun*
corridors
corrode *verb*
corrodes
corroding
corroded
corrosion
corrosive
corrugated
corrupt
corruption
corset *noun*
corsets
cosmetics *plural noun*
cosmic
cosmonaut *noun*
cosmonauts
cost *verb*
costs
costing
cost
cost *noun*
costs
costly *adjective*
costlier
costliest
costume *noun*
costumes
cosy *adjective*
cosier
cosiest
cosy *noun*
cosies
cot *noun*
cots
cottage *noun*
cottages
cotton
couch *noun*
couches
cough *verb*
coughs
coughing
coughed
cough *noun*
coughs
could see **can**
couldn't
✪ **council** *noun*
councils
✲ **councillor** *noun*
councillors
✹ **counsel** *noun*
counsels
counsel *verb*
counsels
counselling
counselled
❄ **counsellor** *noun*
counsellors

★ A **corps** is a unit of soldiers. ! **corpse**.
☆ A **corpse** is a dead body. ! **corps**.
✪ A **council** is a group of people who run the affairs of a town. ! **counsel**.
✲ A **councillor** is a member of a council. ! **counsellor**.
✹ **Counsel** means 'advice'. ! **council**.
❄ A **counsellor** is someone who gives advice. ! **councillor**.

count *verb*
counts
counting
counted
count *noun*
counts
countdown *noun*
countdowns
countenance *noun*
countenances

counter-
counter- makes words meaning 'opposite', e.g. a **counter-claim** is a claim someone makes in response to a claim from someone else. You often need a hyphen, but some words are spelt joined up, e.g. **counteract**, **counterbalance**.

counter *noun*
counters
counterfeit
countess *noun*
countesses
countless
country *noun*
countries
countryman *noun*
countrymen
countryside
countrywoman *noun*
countrywomen
county *noun*
counties
couple *noun*
couples
couple *verb*
couples
coupling
coupled
coupling *noun*
couplings
coupon *noun*
coupons
courage
courageous *adjective*
courageously
courgette *noun*
courgettes
courier *noun*
couriers
★ **course** *noun*
courses
court *noun*
courts
court *verb*
courts
courting
courted
courteous *adjective*
courteously
courtesy *noun*
courtesies
court martial *noun*
courts martial
courtship
courtyard *noun*
courtyards
cousin *noun*
cousins
cove *noun*
coves
cover *verb*
covers
covering
covered
cover *noun*
covers
coverage
cover-up *noun*
cover-ups
cow *noun*
cows
coward *noun*
cowards
cowardice
cowardly
cowboy *noun*
cowboys
cowslip *noun*
cowslips
cox *noun*
coxes
coxswain *noun*
coxswains
coy *adjective*
coyly
coyness
crab *noun*
crabs
crack *verb*
cracks
cracking
cracked
crack *noun*
cracks
cracker *noun*
crackers
crackle *verb*
crackles
crackling
crackled
crackling
cradle *noun*
cradles
craft *noun*
crafts

★ You use **course** in e.g. *a French course*. ! **coarse**.

craftsman *noun*
craftsmen
craftsmanship
crafty *adjective*
craftier
craftiest
craftily
craftiness
crag *noun*
crags
craggy *adjective*
craggier
craggiest
cram *verb*
crams
cramming
crammed
cramp *verb*
cramps
cramping
cramped
cramp *noun*
cramps
crane *noun*
cranes
crane *verb*
cranes
craning
craned
crane-fly *noun*
crane-flies
crank *verb*
cranks
cranking
cranked
crank *noun*
cranks
cranky *adjective*
crankier
crankiest
cranny *noun*
crannies
crash *verb*
crashes
crashing
crashed
crash *noun*
crashes
crate *noun*
crates
crater *noun*
craters
crave *verb*
craves
craving
craved
crawl *verb*
crawls
crawling
crawled
crawl *noun*
crawls
crayon *noun*
crayons
craze *noun*
crazes
craziness
crazy *adjective*
crazier
craziest
crazily
creak *verb*
creaks
creaking
creaked
creak *noun*
creaks
creaky *adjective*
creakier
creakiest
cream *noun*
creams
creamy *adjective*
creamier
creamiest
crease *verb*
creases
creasing
creased
crease *noun*
creases
create *verb*
creates
creating
created
creation *noun*
creations
creative *adjective*
creatively
creativity
creator *noun*
creators
creature *noun*
creatures
crèche *noun*
crèches
credibility
credible *adjective*
credibly
credit *verb*
credits
crediting
credited
credit *noun*
creditable *adjective*
creditably
creditor *noun*
creditors
creed *noun*
creeds
creek *noun*
creeks

creep *verb*
creeps
creeping
crept
creep *noun*
creeps
creeper *noun*
creepers
creepy *adjective*
creepier
creepiest
cremate *verb*
cremates
cremating
cremated
cremation *noun*
cremations
crematorium *noun*
crematoria
creosote
crêpe *noun*
crêpes
crept see **creep**
crescendo *noun*
crescendos
crescent *noun*
crescents
cress
crest *noun*
crests
crevice *noun*
crevices
crew *noun*
crews
crib *verb*
cribs
cribbing
cribbed
crib *noun*
cribs
★ **cricket** *noun*
crickets
cricketer *noun*
cricketers
cried see **cry**
crime *noun*
crimes
criminal *adjective* and *noun*
criminals
crimson
crinkle *verb*
crinkles
crinkling
crinkled
crinkly *adjective*
crinklier
crinkliest
cripple *verb*
cripples
crippling
crippled
cripple *noun*
cripples
crisis *noun*
crises
crisp *adjective*
crisper
crispest
crisp *noun*
crisps
criss-cross *adjective*
critic *noun*
critics
critical *adjective*
critically
criticism *noun*
criticisms
criticize *verb*
criticizes
criticizing
criticized
croak *verb*
croaks
croaking
croaked
croak *noun*
croaks
☆ **crochet**
crock *noun*
crocks
crockery
crocodile *noun*
crocodiles
crocus *noun*
crocuses
croft *noun*
crofts
crofter
croissant *noun*
croissants
crook *noun*
crooks
crook *verb*
crooks
crooking
crooked
crooked
croon *verb*
croons
crooning
crooned
crop *noun*
crops
crop *verb*
crops
cropping
cropped

★ **Cricket** means 'a game' and 'an insect like a grasshopper'.
☆ **Crochet** is a kind of needlework. ! **crotchet**.

cross-
cross- makes words meaning 'across', e.g. a *cross-channel ferry* is one that goes across the English Channel. You usually need a hyphen, but some words are spelt joined up, e.g. **crossroads** and **crosswind**.

cross *adjective*
crossly
cross *verb*
crosses
crossing
crossed
cross *noun*
crosses
crossbar *noun*
crossbars
crossbow *noun*
crossbows
cross-country
cross-examine *verb*
cross-examines
cross-examining
cross-examined
cross-examination *noun*
cross-examinations
cross-eyed
crossing *noun*
crossings
cross-legged
crossness
crossroads *noun*
crossroads
cross-section *noun*
cross-sections
crosswise
crossword *noun*
crosswords
★ **crotchet** *noun*
crotchets
crouch *verb*
crouches
crouching
crouched
crow *noun*
crows
crow *verb*
crows
crowing
crowed
crowbar *noun*
crowbars
crowd *noun*
crowds
crowd *verb*
crowds
crowding
crowded
crown *noun*
crowns
crown *verb*
crowns
crowning
crowned
crow's-nest *noun*
crow's-nests
crucial *adjective*
crucially
crucifix *noun*
crucifixes
☆ **crucifixion** *noun*
crucifixions
crucify *verb*
crucifies
crucifying
crucified
crude *adjective*
cruder
crudest
cruel *adjective*
crueller
cruellest
cruelly
cruelty *noun*
cruelties
cruise *verb*
cruises
cruising
cruised
cruise *noun*
cruises
cruiser *noun*
cruisers
crumb *noun*
crumbs
crumble *verb*
crumbles
crumbling
crumbled
crumbly *adjective*
crumblier
crumbliest
crumpet *noun*
crumpets
crumple *verb*
crumples
crumpling
crumpled
crunch *noun*
crunches
crunch *verb*
crunches
crunching
crunched
crunchy *adjective*
crunchier
crunchiest

★ A **crotchet** is a note in music. ! **crochet**.
☆ Use a capital C when you are talking about Christ.

crusade *noun*
crusades
crusader *noun*
crusaders
crush *verb*
crushes
crushing
crushed
crush *noun*
crushes
crust *noun*
crusts
crustacean *noun*
crustaceans
crutch *noun*
crutches
cry *verb*
cries
crying
cried
cry *noun*
cries
crypt *noun*
crypts
crystal *noun*
crystals
crystalline
crystallize *verb*
crystallizes
crystallizing
crystallized
cub *noun*
cubs
cubbyhole *noun*
cubbyholes
cube *noun*
cubes
cube *verb*
cubes
cubing
cubed
cubic
cubicle *noun*
cubicles
cuboid *noun*
cuboids
cuckoo *noun*
cuckoos
cucumber *noun*
cucumbers
cud
cuddle *verb*
cuddles
cuddling
cuddled
cuddly
★ **cue** *noun*
cues
cuff *verb*
cuffs
cuffing
cuffed
cuff *noun*
cuffs
cul-de-sac *noun*
cul-de-sacs *or*
culs-de-sac
culminate *verb*
culminates
culminating
culminated
culmination
culprit *noun*
culprits
cult *noun*
cults
cultivate *verb*
cultivates
cultivating
cultivated
cultivation
cultivated
culture *noun*
cultures
cultural *adjective*
culturally
cultured
cunning
cup *noun*
cups
cup *verb*
cups
cupping
cupped
cupboard *noun*
cupboards
cupful *noun*
cupfuls
curate *noun*
curates
curator *noun*
curators
☆ **curb** *verb*
curbs
curbing
curbed
curd *noun*
curds
curdle *verb*
curdles
curdling
curdled
cure *verb*
cures
curing
cured
cure *noun*
cures
curfew *noun*
curfews

★ A **cue** is a signal for action or a stick used in snooker. ! **queue**.
☆ To **curb** a feeling is to restrain it. ! **kerb**.

curiosity *noun*
curiosities
curious *adjective*
curiously
curl *verb*
curls
curling
curled
curl *noun*
curls
curly *adjective*
curlier
curliest
★ **currant** *noun*
currants
currency *noun*
currencies
☆ **current** *noun*
currents
current *adjective*
currently
curriculum *noun*
curriculums *or*
curricula
curry *verb*
curries
currying
curried
curry *noun*
curries
curse *verb*
curses
cursing
cursed
curse *noun*
curses
cursor *noun*
cursors
curtain *noun*
curtains
curtsy *verb*
curtsies
curtsying
curtsied
curtsy *noun*
curtsies
curvature *noun*
curvatures
curve *verb*
curves
curving
curved
curve *noun*
curves
cushion *noun*
cushions
cushion *verb*
cushions
cushioning
cushioned
custard
custom *noun*
customs
customary *adjective*
customarily
customer *noun*
customers
customize *noun*
customizes
customizing
customized
cut *verb*
cuts
cutting
cut
cut *noun*
cuts
cute *adjective*
cuter
cutest
cutlass *noun*
cutlasses
cutlery
cutlet *noun*
cutlets
cut-out *noun*
cut-outs
cut-price
cutter *noun*
cutters
cutting *noun*
cuttings
cycle *noun*
cycles
cycle *verb*
cycles
cycling
cycled
cyclist *noun*
cyclists
cyclone *noun*
cyclones
cyclonic
✪ **cygnet** *noun*
cygnets
cylinder *noun*
cylinders
cylindrical
cymbal *noun*
cymbals
cynic *noun*
cynics
cynical *adjective*
cynically
cynicism
cypress *noun*
cypresses

★ A **currant** is a small dried grape. ! **current**.
☆ A **current** is a flow of water, air, or electricity. ! **currant**.
✪ A **cygnet** is a young swan. ! **signet**.

Dd

dab *verb*
dabs
dabbing
dabbed
dab *noun*
dabs
dabble *verb*
dabbles
dabbling
dabbled
dachshund *noun*
dachshunds
dad *noun*
dads
daddy *noun*
daddies
daddy-long-legs *noun*
daddy-long-legs
daffodil *noun*
daffodils
daft *adjective*
dafter
daftest
dagger *noun*
daggers
dahlia *noun*
dahlias
daily *adjective* and *adverb*
daintiness
dainty *adjective*
daintier
daintiest
daintily
dairy *noun*
dairies
daisy *noun*
daisies
dale *noun*
dales
Dalmatian *noun*
Dalmatians
dam *noun*
dams
★ **dam** *verb*
dams
damming
dammed
damage *verb*
damages
damaging
damaged
damage *noun*
damages *plural noun*
☆ **Dame** *noun*
Dames
✪ **dame** *noun*
dames
✲ **damn** *verb*
damns
damning
damned
damned
damp *adjective* and *noun*
damper
dampest
dampen *verb*
dampens
dampening
dampened
damson *noun*
damsons
dance *verb*
dances
dancing
danced
dance *noun*
dances
dancer *noun*
dancers
dandelion *noun*
dandelions
dandruff
danger *noun*
dangers
dangerous *adjective*
dangerously
dangle *verb*
dangles
dangling
dangled
dappled
dare *verb*
dares
daring
dared
dare *noun*
dares
daredevil *noun*
daredevils
daring
dark *adjective* and *noun*
darker
darkest
darken *verb*
darkens
darkening
darkened
darkness
darkroom *noun*
darkrooms
darling *noun*
darlings
darn *verb*
darns
darning
darned

★ **Dam** means 'to build a dam across water'. ! **damn**.
☆ Use a capital D when it is a title, e.g. *Dame Jane Smith*.
✪ Use a small d when you mean a pantomime woman played by a man.
✲ **Damn** means 'to say that something is very bad'. ! **dam**.

dart *noun*
darts
dartboard *noun*
dartboards
dash *verb*
dashes
dashing
dashed
dash *noun*
dashes
dashboard *noun*
dashboards
★ **data** *plural noun*
database *noun*
databases
date *noun*
dates
date *verb*
dates
dating
dated
daughter *noun*
daughters
dawdle *verb*
dawdles
dawdling
dawdled
dawn *noun*
dawns
dawn *verb*
dawns
dawning
dawned
day *noun*
days
daybreak
daydream *verb*
daydreams
daydreaming
daydreamed
daylight
day-to-day
daze *verb*
dazes
dazing
dazed
daze *noun*
dazzle *verb*
dazzles
dazzling
dazzled

de-
de- makes verbs with an opposite meaning, e.g. **deactivate** means 'to stop something working'. You need a hyphen when the word begins with an e or *i*, e.g. **de-escalate**, **de-ice**.

dead
deaden *verb*
deadens
deadening
deadened
dead end *noun*
dead ends
deadline *noun*
deadlines
deadlock
deadly *adjective*
deadlier
deadliest
deaf *adjective*
deafer
deafest
deafness
deafen *verb*
deafens
deafening
deafened
deal *verb*
deals
dealing
dealt
deal *noun*
deals
dealer *noun*
dealers
dean *noun*
deans
☆ **dear** *adjective*
dearer
dearest
death *noun*
deaths
deathly
debatable
debate *noun*
debates
debate *verb*
debates
debating
debated
debris
debt *noun*
debts
debtor *noun*
debtors
debug *verb*
debugs
debugging
debugged
début *noun*
débuts
decade *noun*
decades
decay *verb*
decays
decaying
decayed

★ **Data** is strictly a plural noun, but is often used as a singular noun: *Here is the data.*
☆ **Dear** means 'loved' or 'expensive'. ! **deer**.

decay *noun*
deceased
deceit
deceitful *adjective*
deceitfully
deceive *verb*
deceives
deceiving
deceived
December
decency
decent *adjective*
decently
deception *noun*
deceptions
deceptive
decibel *noun*
decibels
decide *verb*
decides
deciding
decided
deciduous
decimal *noun*
decimals
decimalization
decimalize *verb*
decimalizes
decimalizing
decimalized
decipher *verb*
deciphers
deciphering
deciphered
decision *noun*
decisions
decisive *adjective*
decisively
deck *noun*
decks
deckchair *noun*
deckchairs
declaration *noun*
declarations
declare *verb*
declares
declaring
declared
decline *verb*
declines
declining
declined
decode *verb*
decodes
decoding
decoded
decompose *verb*
decomposes
decomposing
decomposed
decorate *verb*
decorates
decorating
decorated
decoration *noun*
decorations
decorative
decorator *noun*
decorators
decoy *noun*
decoys
decrease *verb*
decreases
decreasing
decreased
decrease *noun*
decreases
decree *noun*
decrees
decree *verb*
decrees
decreeing
decreed
decrepit
dedicate *verb*
dedicates
dedicating
dedicated
dedication
deduce *verb*
deduces
deducing
deduced
deduct *verb*
deducts
deducting
deducted
deductible
deduction *noun*
deductions
deed *noun*
deeds
deep *adjective*
deeper
deepest
deeply
deepen *verb*
deepens
deepening
deepened
deep-freeze *noun*
deep-freezes
★ **deer** *noun*
deer
deface *verb*
defaces
defacing
defaced
default *noun*
defaults

★ A **deer** is an animal. ! **dear**.

defeat *verb*
defeats
defeating
defeated
defeat *noun*
defeats
defect *noun*
defects
defect *verb*
defects
defecting
defected
defective *adjective*
defectively
defence *noun*
defences
defenceless
defend *verb*
defends
defending
defended
defendant *noun*
defendants
defender *noun*
defenders
defensible
defensive *adjective*
defensively
defer *verb*
defers
deferring
deferred
deferment
defiance
defiant *adjective*
defiantly
deficiency *noun*
deficiencies
deficient
deficit *noun*
deficits
defile *verb*
defiles
defiling
defiled
define *verb*
defines
defining
defined
definite *adjective*
definitely
definition *noun*
definitions
deflate *verb*
deflates
deflating
deflated
deflect *verb*
deflects
deflecting
deflected
deflection
deforestation
deformed
deformity *noun*
deformities
defrost *verb*
defrosts
defrosting
defrosted
deft *adjective*
defter
deftest
deftly
defuse *verb*
defuses
defusing
defused
defy *verb*
defies
defying
defied
degenerate *verb*
degenerates
degenerating
degenerated
degeneration
degradation
degrade *verb*
degrades
degrading
degraded
degree *noun*
degrees
dehydrated
dehydration
de-ice *verb*
de-ices
de-icing
de-iced
de-icer
deity *noun*
deities
dejected
dejection
delay *verb*
delays
delaying
delayed
delay *noun*
delays
delegate *noun*
delegates
delegate *verb*
delegates
delegating
delegated
delegation
delete *verb*
deletes
deleting
deleted
deletion

deliberate *adjective*
deliberately
deliberate *verb*
deliberates
deliberating
deliberated
deliberation
delicacy *noun*
delicacies
delicate *adjective*
delicately
delicatessen *noun*
delicatessens
delicious *adjective*
deliciously
delight *verb*
delights
delighting
delighted
delight *noun*
delights
delightful *adjective*
delightfully
delinquency
delinquent *noun*
delinquents
delirious *adjective*
deliriously
delirium *noun*
deliver *verb*
delivers
delivering
delivered
delivery *noun*
deliveries
delta *noun*
deltas
delude *verb*
deludes
deluding
deluded
deluge *noun*
deluges
deluge *verb*
deluges
deluging
deluged
delusion *noun*
delusions
de luxe
demand *verb*
demands
demanding
demanded
demand *noun*
demands
demanding
demerara
demist *verb*
demists
demisting
demisted
demo *noun*
demos
democracy *noun*
democracies
democrat *noun*
democrats
democratic *adjective*
democratically
demolish *verb*
demolishes
demolishing
demolished
demolition
demon *noun*
demons
demonstrate *verb*
demonstrates
demonstrating
demonstrated
demonstration *noun*
demonstrations
demonstrator *noun*
demonstrators
demoralize *verb*
demoralizes
demoralizing
demoralized
demote *verb*
demotes
demoting
demoted
den *noun*
dens
denial *noun*
denials
denim
denominator *noun*
denominators
denote *verb*
denotes
denoting
denoted
denounce *verb*
denounces
denouncing
denounced
denunciation
dense *adjective*
denser
densest
densely
density *noun*
dent *noun*
dents
dental
dentist *noun*
dentists
dentistry
denture *noun*
dentures

deny *verb*
denies
denying
denied
deodorant *noun*
deodorants
depart *verb*
departs
departing
departed
department *noun*
departments
departure *noun*
departures
depend *verb*
depends
depending
depended
dependable
★ **dependant** *noun*
dependants
dependence
☆ **dependent** *adjective*
depict *verb*
depicts
depicting
depicted
deplorable *adjective*
deplorably
deplore *verb*
deplores
deploring
deplored
deport *verb*
deports
deporting
deported
deposit *verb*
deposits
depositing
deposited
deposit *noun*
deposits
depot *noun*
depots
depress *verb*
depresses
depressing
depressed
depression *noun*
depressions
deprivation
deprive *verb*
deprives
depriving
deprived
depth *noun*
depths
deputize *verb*
deputizes
deputizing
deputized
deputy *noun*
deputies
derail *verb*
derails
derailing
derailed
derby *noun*
derbies
derelict
deride *verb*
derides
deriding
derided
derision
derive *verb*
derives
deriving
derived
derrick *noun*
derricks
derv
✪ **descant** *noun*
descants
descend *verb*
descends
descending
descended
descendant *noun*
descendants
✲ **descent**
describe *verb*
describes
describing
described
description *noun*
descriptions
descriptive *adjective*
descriptively
✹ **desert** *noun*
deserts
desert *verb*
deserts
deserting
deserted
deserter *noun*
deserters
desertion
deserve *verb*
deserves
deserving
deserved
design *verb*
designs
designing
designed
design *noun*
designs
designate *verb*
designates
designating
designated

★ **Dependant** is a noun: *She has three dependants.* ! **dependent.**
☆ **Dependent** is an adjective: *She has three dependent children.* ! **dependant.**
✪ **Descant** is a term in music. ! **descent.**
✲ **Descent** is a way down. ! **descant.**
✹ A **desert** is a very dry area of land. ! **dessert.**

designer *noun*
designers
desirable
desire *verb*
desires
desiring
desired
desire *noun*
desires
desk *noun*
desks
desktop
desolate
desolation
despair *verb*
despairs
despairing
despaired
despair *noun*
despatch *verb*
use **dispatch**
desperate *adjective*
desperately
desperation
despicable *adjective*
despicably
despise *verb*
despises
despising
despised
despite
★ **dessert** *noun*
desserts
dessertspoon *noun*
dessertspoons
destination *noun*
destinations
destined
destiny *noun*
destinies
destroy *verb*
destroys
destroying
destroyed
destroyer *noun*
destroyers
destruction
destructive
detach *verb*
detaches
detaching
detached
detachable
detached
detachment *noun*
detachments
detail *noun*
details
detain *verb*
detains
detaining
detained
detect *verb*
detects
detecting
detected
detection
detector
detective *noun*
detectives
detention *noun*
detentions
deter *verb*
deters
deterring
deterred
detergent *noun*
detergents
deteriorate *verb*
deteriorates
deteriorating
deteriorated
deterioration
determination
determine *verb*
determines
determining
determined
determined
deterrence
deterrent *noun*
deterrents
detest *verb*
detests
detesting
detested
detestable
detonate *verb*
detonates
detonating
detonated
detonation
detonator
detour *noun*
detours
☆ **deuce**
devastate *verb*
devastates
devastating
devastated
devastation
develop *verb*
develops
developing
developed
development *noun*
developments
device *noun*
devices
devil *noun*
devils

★ A **dessert** is a sweet pudding. ! **desert**.
☆ **Deuce** is a score in tennis. ! **juice**.

devilish
devilment
devious *adjective*
deviously
devise *verb*
devises
devising
devised
devolution
devote *verb*
devotes
devoting
devoted
devotee
devotion
devour *verb*
devours
devouring
devoured
devout
★ **dew**
dewy
☆ **dhoti** *noun*
dhotis
diabetes
diabetic
diabolical *adjective*
diabolically
diagnose *verb*
diagnoses
diagnosing
diagnosed
diagnosis *noun*
diagnoses
diagonal *adjective*
diagonally
diagonal *noun*
diagonals
diagram *noun*
diagrams
dial *noun*
dials
dial *verb*
dials
dialling
dialled
dialect *noun*
dialects
dialogue *noun*
dialogues
diameter *noun*
diameters
diamond *noun*
diamonds
diaphragm *noun*
diaphragms
diarrhoea
diary *noun*
diaries
dice *noun*
dice
dictate *verb*
dictates
dictating
dictated
dictation
dictator *noun*
dictators
dictatorial *adjective*
dictatorially
dictionary *noun*
dictionaries
did see **do**
diddle *verb*
diddles
diddling
diddled
didn't *verb*
die *verb*
dies
dying
died
diesel *noun*
diesels
diet *noun*
diets
diet *verb*
diets
dieting
dieted
differ *verb*
differs
differing
differed
difference *noun*
differences
different *adjective*
differently
difficult
difficulty *noun*
difficulties
dig *verb*
digs
digging
dug
dig *noun*
digs
digest *verb*
digests
digesting
digested
digestible
digestion
digestive
digger
digit *noun*
digits
digital *adjective*
digitally

★ **Dew** is moisture on grass and plants. ! **due**.
☆ A **dhoti** is a piece of clothing worn by Hindus.

dignified
dignity
dike *noun*
use **dyke**
dilemma *noun*
dilemmas
dilute *verb*
dilutes
diluting
diluted
dilution
dim *adjective*
dimmer
dimmest
dimly
dimension *noun*
dimensions
diminish *verb*
diminishes
diminishing
diminished
dimple *noun*
dimples
din *noun*
dins
dine *verb*
dines
dining
dined
★ **diner** *noun*
diners
☆ **dinghy** *noun*
dinghies
✪ **dingy** *adjective*
dingier
dingiest
✲ **dinner** *noun*
dinners
dinosaur *noun*
dinosaurs
dioxide *noun*
dioxides
dip *verb*
dips
dipping
dipped
dip *noun*
dips
diphtheria
diploma *noun*
diplomas
diplomacy
diplomat
diplomatic *adjective*
diplomatically
dire *adjective*
direr
direst
direct *adjective*
directly
direct *verb*
directs
directing
directed
direction *noun*
directions
director *noun*
directors
directory *noun*
directories
dirt
dirtiness
dirty *adjective*
dirtier
dirtiest
dirtily

dis-
dis- makes a word with an opposite meaning, e.g. **disobey** means 'to refuse to obey' and **disloyal** means 'not loyal'. These words are spelt joined up.

disability *noun*
disabilities
disabled
disadvantage *noun*
disadvantages
disagree *verb*
disagrees
disagreeing
disagreed
disagreeable *adjective*
disagreeably
disagreement *noun*
disagreements
disappear *verb*
disappears
disappearing
disappeared
disappearance *noun*
disappearances
disappoint *verb*
disappoints
disappointing
disappointed
disappointing
disappointment *noun*
disappointments
disapproval

★ A **diner** is someone who eats dinner. ! **dinner**.
☆ A **dinghy** is a small sailing boat. ! **dingy**.
✪ **Dingy** means 'dirty-looking, drab, dull-coloured'. ! **dinghy**.
✲ **Dinner** is a meal. ! **diner**.

disapprove *verb*
disapproves
disapproving
disapproved
disarm *verb*
disarms
disarming
disarmed
disarmament
disaster *noun*
disasters
disastrous *adjective*
disastrously
★ **disc** *noun*
discs
discard *verb*
discards
discarding
discarded
discharge *verb*
discharges
discharging
discharged
disciple *noun*
disciples
discipline
disc jockey *noun*
disc jockeys
disclose *verb*
discloses
disclosing
disclosed
disclosure
disco *noun*
discos
discomfort
disconnect *verb*
disconnects
disconnecting
disconnected
disconnection
discontent
discontented
discotheque *noun*
discotheques
discount *noun*
discounts
discourage *verb*
discourages
discouraging
discouraged
discouragement
discover *verb*
discovers
discovering
discovered
discovery *noun*
discoveries
discreet *adjective*
discreetly
discriminate *verb*
discriminates
discriminating
discriminated
discrimination
discus *noun*
discuses
discuss *verb*
discusses
discussing
discussed
discussion *noun*
discussions
disease *noun*
diseases
diseased
disgrace *verb*
disgraces
disgracing
disgraced
disgrace *noun*
disgraceful *adjective*
disgracefully
disguise *verb*
disguises
disguising
disguised
disguise *noun*
disguises
disgust *verb*
disgusts
disgusting
disgusted
disgust *noun*
disgusting
dish *noun*
dishes
dish *verb*
dishes
dishing
dished
dishcloth *noun*
dishcloths
dishevelled
dishonest *adjective*
dishonestly
dishonesty
dishwasher *noun*
dishwashers
disinfect *verb*
disinfects
disinfecting
disinfected
disinfectant *noun*
disinfectants
disintegrate *verb*
disintegrates
disintegrating
disintegrated
disintegration
disinterested
☆ **disk** *noun*
disks

★ A **disc** is a flat round object. ! **disk**.
☆ A **disk** is what you put in a computer. ! **disc**.

dislike *verb*
dislikes
disliking
disliked
dislike *noun*
dislikes
dislocate *verb*
dislocates
dislocating
dislocated
dislodge *verb*
dislodges
dislodging
dislodged
disloyal *adjective*
disloyally
disloyalty
dismal *adjective*
dismally
dismantle *verb*
dismantles
dismantling
dismantled
dismay
dismayed
dismiss *verb*
dismisses
dismissing
dismissed
dismissal
dismount *verb*
dismounts
dismounting
dismounted
disobedience
disobedient
disobey *verb*
disobeys
disobeying
disobeyed
disorder *noun*
disorders
disorderly
dispatch *verb*
dispatches
dispatching
dispatched
dispense *verb*
dispenses
dispensing
dispensed
dispenser *noun*
dispensers
dispersal
disperse *verb*
disperses
dispersing
dispersed
display *verb*
displays
displaying
displayed
display *noun*
displays
displease *verb*
displeases
displeasing
displeased
disposable
disposal
dispose *verb*
disposes
disposing
disposed
disprove *verb*
disproves
disproving
disproved
dispute *noun*
disputes
disqualification
disqualify *verb*
disqualifies
disqualifying
disqualified
disregard *verb*
disregards
disregarding
disregarded
disrespect
disrespectful *adjective*
disrespectfully
disrupt *verb*
disrupts
disrupting
disrupted
disruption
disruptive
dissatisfaction
dissatisfied
dissect *verb*
dissects
dissecting
dissected
dissection
dissolve *verb*
dissolves
dissolving
dissolved
dissuade *verb*
dissuades
dissuading
dissuaded
distance *noun*
distances
distant *adjective*
distantly
distil *verb*
distils
distilling
distilled
distillery *noun*
distilleries

distinct *adjective*
distinctly
distinction *noun*
distinctions
distinctive
distinguish *verb*
distinguishes
distinguishing
distinguished
distinguished
distort *verb*
distorts
distorting
distorted
distortion *noun*
distortions
distract *verb*
distracts
distracting
distracted
distraction *noun*
distractions
distress *verb*
distresses
distressing
distressed
distress *noun*
distribute *verb*
distributes
distributing
distributed
distribution
distributor
district *noun*
districts
distrust
distrustful
disturb *verb*
disturbs
disturbing
disturbed
disturbance *noun*
disturbances
disused
ditch *noun*
ditches
dither *verb*
dithers
dithering
dithered
divan *noun*
divans
dive *verb*
dives
diving
dived
diver *noun*
divers
diverse
diversify *verb*
diversifies
diversifying
diversified
diversion *noun*
diversions
diversity
divert *verb*
diverts
diverting
diverted
divide *verb*
divides
dividing
divided
dividend *noun*
dividends
dividers *plural noun*
divine *adjective*
divinely
divine *verb*
divines
divining
divined
divinity
divisible
division *noun*
divisions
divorce *verb*
divorces
divorcing
divorced
divorce *noun*
divorces
★ **Diwali**
dizziness
dizzy *adjective*
dizzier
dizziest
dizzily
do *verb*
does
doing
did
done
docile *adjective*
docilely
dock *noun*
docks
dock *verb*
docks
docking
docked
dock *noun*
docks
docker *noun*
dockers
dockyard *noun*
dockyards
doctor *noun*
doctors
doctrine *noun*
doctrines

★ **Diwali** is a Hindu festival.

document *noun*
documents
documentary *noun*
documentaries
doddery
dodge *verb*
dodges
dodging
dodged
dodge *noun*
dodges
dodgem *noun*
dodgems
dodgy *adjective*
dodgier
dodgiest
★ **doe** *noun*
does
doesn't *abbreviation*
dog *noun*
dogs
dog-eared
dogged *adjective*
doggedly
doldrums *plural noun*
dole *verb*
doles
doling
doled
dole *noun*
doll *noun*
dolls
dollar *noun*
dollars
dolly *noun*
dollies
dolphin *noun*
dolphins

-dom
-dom makes nouns, e.g. **kingdom**. Other noun suffixes are **-hood**, **-ment**, **-ness**, and **-ship**.

domain *noun*
domains
dome *noun*
domes
domestic *adjective*
domestically
domesticated
dominance
dominant *adjective*
dominantly
dominate *verb*
dominates
dominating
dominated
domination
dominion *noun*
dominions
domino *noun*
dominoes
donate *verb*
donates
donating
donated
donation *noun*
donations
done see **do**
donkey *noun*
donkeys
donor *noun*
donors
don't *abbreviation*
doodle *verb*
doodles
doodling
doodled
doodle *noun*
doodles
doom *verb*
dooms
dooming
doomed
doom *noun*
door *noun*
doors
doorstep *noun*
doorsteps
doorway *noun*
doorways
dope *noun*
dopes
dopey *adjective*
dopier
dopiest
dormitory *noun*
dormitories
dose *noun*
doses
dossier *noun*
dossiers
dot *verb*
dots
dotting
dotted
dot *noun*
dots
dottiness
dotty *adjective*
dottier
dottiest
dottily
double *adjective*
doubly
double *noun*
doubles

★ A **doe** is a female deer. ! **dough**.

double *verb*
doubles
doubling
doubled
double-cross *verb*
double-crosses
double-crossing
double-crossed
double-decker *noun*
double-deckers
doubt *verb*
doubts
doubting
doubted
doubt *noun*
doubts
doubtful *adjective*
doubtfully
doubtless
★ **dough**
doughnut *noun*
doughnuts
doughy *adjective*
doughier
doughiest
dove *noun*
doves
dowel *noun*
dowels
down
downcast
downfall *noun*
downfalls
downhill
downpour *noun*
downpours
downright *adjective*
downs *plural noun*
downstairs
downstream
downward *adjective and adverb*
downwards *adverb*
downy *adjective*
downier
downiest
doze *verb*
dozes
dozing
dozed
dozen *noun*
dozens
dozy *adjective*
dozier
doziest
drab *adjective*
drabber
drabbest
draft *verb*
drafts
drafting
drafted
draft *noun*
drafts
drag *verb*
drags
dragging
dragged
drag *noun*
dragon *noun*
dragons
dragonfly *noun*
dragonflies
drain *verb*
drains
draining
drained
drain *noun*
drains
drainage
drake *noun*
drakes
drama *noun*
dramas
dramatic *adjective*
dramatically
dramatist *noun*
dramatists
dramatization
dramatize *verb*
dramatizes
dramatizing
dramatized
drank see **drink**
drape *verb*
drapes
draping
draped
drastic *adjective*
drastically
draught *noun*
draughts
draughty *adjective*
draughtier
draughtiest
draughts *noun*
draughtsman *noun*
draughtsmen
☆ **draw** *verb*
draws
drawing
drew
drawn
draw *noun*
draws
drawback *noun*
drawbacks
drawbridge *noun*
drawbridges
✪ **drawer** *noun*
drawers

★ **Dough** is a mixture of flour and water used for baking. ! **doe**.
☆ To **draw** is to make a picture with a pencil, pen, or crayon. ! **drawer**.
✪ A **drawer** is part of a cupboard. ! **draw**.

drawing *noun*
drawings
drawl *verb*
drawls
drawling
drawled
dread *verb*
dreads
dreading
dreaded
dread *noun*
dreadful *adjective*
dreadfully
dreadlocks
dream *noun*
dreams
dream *verb*
dreams
dreaming
dreamt *or* dreamed
dreamy *adjective*
dreamier
dreamiest
dreariness
dreary *adjective*
drearier
dreariest
drearily
dredge *verb*
dredges
dredging
dredged
dredger
drench *verb*
drenches
drenching
drenched
dress *verb*
dresses
dressing
dressed
dress *noun*
dresses
dresser *noun*
dressers
dressing *noun*
dressings
dressmaker *noun*
dressmakers
drew see **draw**
dribble *verb*
dribbles
dribbling
dribbled
dried see **dry**
drier *noun*
driers
drift *verb*
drifts
drifting
drifted
drift *noun*
drifts
driftwood
drill *verb*
drills
drilling
drilled
drill *noun*
drills
drink *verb*
drinks
drinking
drank
drunk
drink *noun*
drinks
drinker *noun*
drinkers
drip *noun*
drips
drip *verb*
drips
dripping
dripped
dripping
drive *verb*
drives
driving
drove
driven
drive *noun*
drives
driver *noun*
drivers
drizzle *verb*
drizzles
drizzling
drizzled
drizzle *noun*
drone *verb*
drones
droning
droned
drone *noun*
drones
drool *verb*
drools
drooling
drooled
droop *verb*
droops
drooping
drooped
drop *verb*
drops
dropping
dropped
drop *noun*
drops
droplet *noun*
droplets

drought *noun*
droughts
drove see **drive**
drown *verb*
drowns
drowning
drowned
drowsiness
drowsy *adjective*
drowsier
drowsiest
drowsily
drug *noun*
drugs
drug *verb*
drugs
drugging
drugged
Druid *noun*
Druids
drum *noun*
drums
drum *verb*
drums
drumming
drummed
drummer *noun*
drummers
drumstick *noun*
drumsticks
drunk see **drink**
drunk *adjective* and *noun*
drunks
drunkard *noun*
drunkards
dry *adjective*
drier
driest
drily
dry *verb*
dries
drying
dried
dryness
★ **dual** *adjective*
dually
dub *verb*
dubs
dubbing
dubbed
duchess *noun*
duchesses
duck *noun*
ducks
duck *verb*
ducks
ducking
ducked
duckling *noun*
ducklings
duct *noun*
ducts
dud *noun*
duds
☆ **due**
✪ **duel** *noun*
duels
duet *noun*
duets
duff
duffel coat *noun*
duffel coats
dug see **dig**
dugout *noun*
dugouts
duke *noun*
dukes
dull *adjective*
duller
dullest
dully
dullness
duly
dumb *adjective*
dumber
dumbest
dumbfounded
dummy *noun*
dummies
dump *verb*
dumps
dumping
dumped
dump *noun*
dumps
dumpling *noun*
dumplings
dumpy *adjective*
dumpier
dumpiest
dune *noun*
dunes
dung
dungarees
dungeon *noun*
dungeons
duo *noun*
duos
duplicate *noun*
duplicates
duplicate *verb*
duplicates
duplicating
duplicated
duplication
durability
durable
duration
during

★ **Dual** means 'having two parts'. ! **duel**.
☆ **Due** means 'expected'. ! **dew**.
✪ A **duel** is a fight between two people. ! **dual**.

dusk
dust
dust *verb*
dusts
dusting
dusted
dustbin *noun*
dustbins
duster *noun*
dusters
dustman *noun*
dustmen
dustpan *noun*
dustpans
dusty *adjective*
dustier
dustiest
dutiful *adjective*
dutifully
duty *noun*
duties
duvet *noun*
duvets
dwarf *noun*
dwarfs *or* dwarves
dwarf *verb*
dwarfs
dwarfing
dwarfed
dwell *verb*
dwells
dwelling
dwelt
dwelling *noun*
dwellings
dwindle *verb*
dwindles
dwindling
dwindled
★ **dye** *verb*
dyes
dyeing
dyed
dye *noun*
dyes
dying see **die**
dyke *noun*
dykes
dynamic *adjective*
dynamically
dynamite
dynamo *noun*
dynamos
dynasty *noun*
dynasties
dyslexia
dyslexic
dystrophy *noun*

Ee

e-
e- stands for 'electronic' and makes words about computers and the Internet, e.g. **email** (spelt joined up), **e-commerce** and **e-shopping** (spelt with hyphens).

each
eager *adjective*
eagerly
eagerness
eagle *noun*
eagles
ear *noun*
ears
earache
eardrum *noun*
eardrums
earl *noun*
earls
early *adjective* and *adverb*
earlier
earliest
earmark *verb*
earmarks
earmarking
earmarked
earn *verb*
earns
earning
earned
earnest *adjective*
earnestly
earnings *plural noun*
earphones
earring *noun*
earrings
earth *noun*
earths
earthenware
earthly
earthquake *noun*
earthquakes
earthworm *noun*
earthworms
earthy *adjective*
earthier
earthiest
earwig *noun*
earwigs
ease *verb*
eases
easing
eased
ease *noun*

★ **Dye** means 'to change the colour of something'. ! **die**.

easel *noun*
easels
east *adjective*
and *adverb*
★ **east** *noun*
Easter
easterly *adjective*
and *noun*
easterlies
eastern
eastward *adjective*
and *adverb*
eastwards *adverb*
easy *adjective* and *adverb*
easier
easiest
easily
eat *verb*
eats
eating
ate
eaten
eatable
eaves
ebb *verb*
ebbs
ebbing
ebbed
ebb
ebony
eccentric
eccentricity *noun*
eccentricities
echo *verb*
echoes
echoing
echoed
echo *noun*
echoes
éclair *noun*
éclairs
eclipse *noun*
eclipses
ecological
ecology
economic
economical *adjective*
economically
economics
economist *noun*
economists
economize *verb*
economizes
economizing
economized
economy *noun*
economies
ecstasy *noun*
ecstasies
ecstatic *adjective*
ecstatically
eczema

-ed and -t
Some verbs ending in *l*, *m*, *n*, and *p* have past forms and past participles ending in *-ed* and *-t*, e.g. **burned/burnt**, **leaped/leapt**. Both forms are correct, and the *-t* form is especially common when it comes before a noun, e.g. *burnt cakes*.

edge *noun*
edges
edge *verb*
edges
edging
edged
edgeways
edgy *adjective*
edgier
edgiest
edible
edit *verb*
edits
editing
edited
edition *noun*
editions
editor *noun*
editors
editorial *noun*
editorials
educate *verb*
educates
educating
educated
education
educational
educator
eel *noun*
eels
eerie *adjective*
eerier
eeriest
eerily
eeriness
☆ **effect** *noun*
effects
effective *adjective*
effectively
effectiveness
effeminate
effervescence
effervescent
efficiency
efficient *adjective*
efficiently

★ You use a capital E in **the East**, meaning China, Japan, etc.
☆ An **effect** is something that is caused by something else. ! **affect**.

effort *noun*
efforts
effortless *adjective*
effortlessly
egg *noun*
eggs
egg *verb*
eggs
egging
egged

> **-ei- and -ie-**
> The rule 'i before e except after c' is true when it is pronounced -ee-, e.g. **thief**, **ceiling**. There are a few exceptions, of which the most important are **seize** and **protein**.

★ **Eid**
eiderdown *noun*
eiderdowns
☆ **eight**
eighteen
eighteenth
✪ **eighth** *adjective* and *noun*
eighthly
eightieth
eighty *noun*
eighties
either
eject *verb*
ejects
ejecting
ejected
ejection
elaborate *adjective*
elaborately
elaborate *verb*
elaborates
elaborating
elaborated
elaboration
elastic
elated
elation
elbow *noun*
elbows
elbow *verb*
elbows
elbowing
elbowed
elder *adjective* and *noun*
elders
elderberry *noun*
elderberries
elderly
eldest
elect *verb*
elects
electing
elected
election *noun*
elections
electorate
electric
electrical *adjective*
electrically
electrician *noun*
electricians
electricity
electrification
electrify *verb*
electrifies
electrifying
electrified
electrocute *verb*
electrocutes
electrocuting
electrocuted
electrocution
electromagnet *noun*
electromagnets
electron *noun*
electrons
electronic *adjective*
electronically
electronics
elegance
elegant *adjective*
elegantly
element *noun*
elements
elementary
elephant *noun*
elephants
elevate *verb*
elevates
elevating
elevated
elevation *noun*
elevations
eleven
eleventh
elf *noun*
elves
eligibility
eligible
eliminate *verb*
eliminates
eliminating
eliminated
elimination
élite *noun*
élites
elk *noun*
elk *or* elks

★ **Eid** is a Muslim festival.
☆ **Eight** is the number. ! **ate**.
✪ Note that there are two h's in **eighth**.

ellipse *noun*
ellipses
elliptical *adjective*
elliptically
elm *noun*
elms
elocution
eloquence
eloquent
else
elsewhere
elude *verb*
eludes
eluding
eluded
elusive *adjective*
elusively
elves see **elf**
★ **email** *noun*
emails
email *verb*
emails
emailing
emailed
emancipate *verb*
emancipates
emancipating
emancipated
emancipation
embankment *noun*
embankments
embark *verb*
embarks
embarking
embarked
embarkation
☆ **embarrass** *verb*
embarrasses
embarrassing
embarrassed
embarrassment
embassy *noun*
embassies
embedded
embers *plural noun*
emblem *noun*
emblems
embrace *verb*
embraces
embracing
embraced
embroider *verb*
embroiders
embroidering
embroidered
embroidery *noun*
embroideries
embryo *noun*
embryos
emerald *noun*
emeralds
emerge *verb*
emerges
emerging
emerged
emergence
emergency *noun*
emergencies
emery paper
emigrant *noun*
emigrants
emigrate *verb*
emigrates
emigrating
emigrated
emigration
eminence
eminent
✪ **emission** *noun*
emissions
emit *verb*
emits
emitting
emitted
emotion *noun*
emotions
emotional *adjective*
emotionally
emperor *noun*
emperors
emphasis *noun*
emphases
emphasize *verb*
emphasizes
emphasizing
emphasized
emphatic *adjective*
emphatically
empire *noun*
empires
employ *verb*
employs
employing
employed
employee *noun*
employees
employer *noun*
employers
employment
empress *noun*
empresses
empties *plural noun*
emptiness
empty *adjective*
emptier
emptiest
empty *verb*
empties
emptying
emptied
emu *noun*
emus

★ **Email** is short for **electronic mail**.
☆ Note that there are two rs in **embarrass** and **embarrassment**.
✪ An **emission** is something that escapes, like fumes. ! **omission**.

emulsion *noun*
emulsions
enable *verb*
enables
enabling
enabled
enamel *noun*
enamels
encampment *noun*
encampments

-ence
See the note at **-ance**.

enchant *verb*
enchants
enchanting
enchanted
enchantment
encircle *verb*
encircles
encircling
encircled
enclose *verb*
encloses
enclosing
enclosed
enclosure
encore *noun*
encores
encounter *verb*
encounters
encountering
encountered
encourage *verb*
encourages
encouraging
encouraged
encouragement
encyclopedia *noun*
encyclopedias
encyclopedic

end *verb*
ends
ending
ended
end *noun*
ends
endanger *verb*
endangers
endangering
endangered
endeavour *verb*
endeavours
endeavouring
endeavoured
ending *noun*
endings
endless *adjective*
endlessly
endurance
endure *verb*
endures
enduring
endured
enemy *noun*
enemies
energetic *adjective*
energetically
energy *noun*
energies
enforce *verb*
enforces
enforcing
enforced
enforceable
enforcement
engage *verb*
engages
engaging
engaged
engagement *noun*
engagements

engine *noun*
engines
engineer *noun*
engineers
engineering
engrave *verb*
engraves
engraving
engraved
engraver
engrossed
engulf *verb*
engulfs
engulfing
engulfed
enhance *verb*
enhances
enhancing
enhanced
enhancement
enjoy *verb*
enjoys
enjoying
enjoyed
enjoyable
enjoyment
enlarge *verb*
enlarges
enlarging
enlarged
enlargement *noun*
enlargements
enlist *verb*
enlists
enlisting
enlisted
enmity *noun*
enmities
★ **enormity** *noun*
enormities

★ An **enormity** is a wicked act. If you mean 'large size', use **enormousness**.

enormous *adjective*
enormously
enormousness
enough
enquire *verb*
enquires
enquiring
enquired
★ **enquiry** *noun*
enquiries
enrage *verb*
enrages
enraging
enraged
enrich *verb*
enriches
enriching
enriched
enrichment
enrol *verb*
enrols
enrolling
enrolled
enrolment
ensemble *noun*
ensembles
ensue *verb*
ensues
ensuing
ensued
ensure *verb*
ensures
ensuring
ensured

-ent
See the note at **-ant**.

entangle *verb*
entangles
entangling
entangled
entanglement
enter *verb*
enters
entering
entered
enterprise *noun*
enterprises
enterprising
entertain *verb*
entertains
entertaining
entertained
entertainer *noun*
entertainers
entertainment *noun*
entertainments
enthusiasm *noun*
enthusiasms
enthusiast *noun*
enthusiasts
enthusiastic *adjective*
enthusiastically
entire *adjective*
entirely
entirety
entitle *verb*
entitles
entitling
entitled
entrance *noun*
entrances
entrance *verb*
entrances
entrancing
entranced
entrant *noun*
entrants
entreat *verb*
entreats
entreating
entreated
entreaty *noun*
entreaties
entrust *verb*
entrusts
entrusting
entrusted
entry *noun*
entries
envelop *verb*
envelops
enveloping
enveloped
envelope *noun*
envelopes
envious *adjective*
enviously
environment *noun*
environments
environmental
environmentalist *noun*
environmentalists
envy *verb*
envies
envying
envied
envy *noun*
enzyme *noun*
enzymes
epic *noun*
epics
epidemic *noun*
epidemics
epilepsy
epileptic *adjective* and *noun*
epileptics
epilogue *noun*
epilogues

★ An **enquiry** is a question. ! **inquiry**.

episode *noun*
episodes
epistle *noun*
epistles
epitaph *noun*
epitaphs
epoch *noun*
epochs
equal *adjective*
equally
equal *verb*
equals
equalling
equalled
equal *noun*
equals
equality
equalize *verb*
equalizes
equalizing
equalized
equalizer *noun*
equalizers
equation *noun*
equations
equator
equatorial
equestrian
equilateral
equilibrium *noun*
equilibria
equinox *noun*
equinoxes
equip *verb*
equips
equipping
equipped
equipment
equivalence
equivalent

-er and -est
-er and *-est* make adjectives and adverbs meaning 'more' or 'most', e.g. **faster**, **slowest**. You can do this when the word has one syllable, and when a consonant comes at the end of the word after a single vowel you double it, e.g. **fatter**, **bigger**. You can use *-er* and *-est* with some two-syllable adjectives, e.g. **commoner**, **pleasantest**, and words ending in *y*, which change to *-ier* and *-iest*, e.g. **angrier**, **happiest**.

-er and -or
-er makes nouns meaning 'a person or thing that does something', e.g. a **helper** is a person who helps and an **opener** is a tool that opens things. You can make new words this way, e.g. **complainer**, **repairer**. Some words end in *-or*, e.g. **actor**, **visitor**, but you can't use *-or* to make new words.

era *noun*
eras
erase *verb*
erases
erasing
erased
eraser
erect *adjective*
erect *verb*
erects
erecting
erected
erection *noun*
erections
ermine *noun*
ermine
erode *verb*
erodes
eroding
eroded
erosion
errand *noun*
errands
erratic *adjective*
erratically
erroneous *adjective*
erroneously
error *noun*
errors
erupt *verb*
erupts
erupting
erupted
eruption
escalate *verb*
escalates
escalating
escalated
escalation
escalator *noun*
escalators
escape *verb*
escapes
escaping
escaped

escape *noun*
escapes
escort *verb*
escorts
escorting
escorted
escort *noun*
escorts
Eskimo *noun*
Eskimos *or* Eskimo
especially
espionage
esplanade *noun*
esplanades

-ess
makes nouns for female people and animals, e.g. **manageress**, **lioness**.

essay *noun*
essays
essence *noun*
essences
essential *adjective*
essentially
essential *noun*
essentials
establish *verb*
establishes
establishing
established
establishment *noun*
establishments
estate *noun*
estates
esteem *verb*
esteems
esteeming
esteemed
estimate *noun*
estimates
estimate *verb*
estimates
estimating
estimated
estuary *noun*
estuaries
etch *verb*
etches
etching
etched
etching *noun*
etchings
eternal *adjective*
eternally
eternity
ether
ethnic
etymology *noun*
etymologies
eucalyptus *noun*
eucalyptuses
euphemism *noun*
euphemisms
euphemistic *adjective*
euphemistically
Eurasian
European *adjective* and *noun*
Europeans
euthanasia
evacuate *verb*
evacuates
evacuating
evacuated
evacuation
evacuee
evade *verb*
evades
evading
evaded
evaluate *verb*
evaluates
evaluating
evaluated
evaluation
evangelical
evangelism
evangelist *noun*
evangelists
evaporate *verb*
evaporates
evaporating
evaporated
evaporation
evasion *noun*
evasions
evasive
eve *noun*
eves
even *adjective*
evenly
even *adverb*
even *verb*
evens
evening
evened
evening *noun*
evenings
evenness
event *noun*
events
eventful *adjective*
eventfully
eventual *adjective*
eventually
ever
evergreen *adjective* and *noun*
evergreens
everlasting

every
everybody
everyday
everyone
everything
everywhere
evict *verb*
evicts
evicting
evicted
eviction
evidence
evident *adjective*
evidently
evil *adjective*
evilly
evil *noun*
evils
evolution
evolutionary
evolve *verb*
evolves
evolving
evolved
★ **ewe** *noun*
ewes

ex-
ex- makes nouns with the meaning 'former' or 'who used to be', e.g. **ex-president**, **ex-wife**. You use a hyphen to make these words.

exact *adjective*
exactly
exactness
exaggerate *verb*
exaggerates
exaggerating
exaggerated
exaggeration
exalt *verb*
exalts
exalting
exalted
exam *noun*
exams
examination *noun*
examinations
examine *verb*
examines
examining
examined
examiner *noun*
examiners
example *noun*
examples
exasperate *verb*
exasperates
exasperating
exasperated
exasperation
excavate *verb*
excavates
excavating
excavated
excavation *noun*
excavations
excavator *noun*
excavators
exceed *verb*
exceeds
exceeding
exceeded
exceedingly
excel *verb*
excels
excelling
excelled
excellence
excellent *adjective*
excellently
☆ **except**
exception *noun*
exceptions
exceptional *adjective*
exceptionally
excerpt *noun*
excerpts
excess *noun*
excesses
excessive *adjective*
excessively
exchange *verb*
exchanges
exchanging
exchanged
exchange *noun*
exchanges
excitable *adjective*
excitably
excite *verb*
excites
exciting
excited
excitedly
excitement *noun*
excitements
exclaim *verb*
exclaims
exclaiming
exclaimed
exclamation *noun*
exclamations

★ A **ewe** is a female sheep. ! **yew, you.**
☆ You use **except** in e.g. *everyone except me*. ! **accept.**

exclude *verb*
excludes
excluding
excluded
exclusion
exclusive *adjective*
exclusively
excrement
excrete *verb*
excretes
excreting
excreted
excretion
excursion *noun*
excursions
excusable
excuse *verb*
excuses
excusing
excused
excuse *noun*
excuses
execute *verb*
executes
executing
executed
execution *noun*
executions
executioner *noun*
executioners
executive *noun*
executives
exempt *adjective*
exemption *noun*
exercise *noun*
exercises
★ **exercise** *verb*
exercises
exercising
exercised

exert *verb*
exerts
exerting
exerted
exertion *noun*
exertions
exhale *verb*
exhales
exhaling
exhaled
exhalation
exhaust *verb*
exhausts
exhausting
exhausted
exhaust *noun*
exhausts
exhaustion
exhibit *verb*
exhibits
exhibiting
exhibited
exhibit *noun*
exhibits
exhibition *noun*
exhibitions
exhibitor *noun*
exhibitors
exile *verb*
exiles
exiling
exiled
exile *noun*
exiles
exist *verb*
exists
existing
existed
existence *noun*
existences
exit *verb*
exits
exiting
exited
exit *noun*
exits
exorcism
exorcist
☆ **exorcize** *verb*
exorcizes
exorcizing
exorcized
exotic *adjective*
exotically
expand *verb*
expands
expanding
expanded
expanse *noun*
expanses
expansion
expect *verb*
expects
expecting
expected
expectant *adjective*
expectantly
expectation *noun*
expectations
expedition *noun*
expeditions
expel *verb*
expels
expelling
expelled
expenditure
expense *noun*
expenses
expensive
experience *verb*
experiences
experiencing
experienced

★ To **exercise** is to keep your body fit. ! **exorcise**.
☆ To **exorcise** is to get rid of evil spirits. ! **exercise**.

experience *noun*
experiences
experienced
experiment *verb*
experiments
experimenting
experimented
experiment *noun*
experiments
experimental *adjective*
experimentally
experimentation
expert *adjective* and *noun*
experts
expertise
expire *verb*
expires
expiring
expired
expiry
explain *verb*
explains
explaining
explained
explanation *noun*
explanations
explanatory
explode *verb*
explodes
exploding
exploded
exploit *noun*
exploits
exploit *verb*
exploits
exploiting
exploited
exploitation
exploration *noun*
explorations
exploratory
explore *verb*
explores
exploring
explored
explorer *noun*
explorers
explosion *noun*
explosions
explosive *adjective* and *noun*
explosives
export *verb*
exports
exporting
exported
export *noun*
exports
exporter *noun*
exporters
expose *verb*
exposes
exposing
exposed
exposure *noun*
exposures
express *adjective* and *noun*
expresses
express *verb*
expresses
expressing
expressed
expression *noun*
expressions
expressive *adjective*
expressively
expulsion *noun*
expulsions
exquisite *adjective*
exquisitely
extend *verb*
extends
extending
extended
extension *noun*
extensions
extensive *adjective*
extensively
extent *noun*
extents
exterior *noun*
exteriors
exterminate *verb*
exterminates
exterminating
exterminated
extermination
external *adjective*
externally
extinct
extinction
extinguish *verb*
extinguishes
extinguishing
extinguished
extinguisher *noun*
extinguishers
extra *adjective* and *noun*
extras
extract *verb*
extracts
extracting
extracted
extract *noun*
extracts
extraction *noun*
extractions
extraordinary *adjective*
extraordinarily

extrasensory
extraterrestrial
adjective and *noun*
extraterrestrials
extravagance
extravagant
adjective
extravagantly
extreme *adjective*
extremely
extreme *noun*
extremes
extremity *noun*
extremities
exuberance
exuberant *adjective*
exuberantly
exult *verb*
exults
exulting
exulted
exultant
exultation
eye *noun*
eyes
eye *verb*
eyes
eyeing
eyed
eyeball *noun*
eyeballs
eyebrow *noun*
eyebrows
eyelash *noun*
eyelashes
eyelid *noun*
eyelids
eyepiece *noun*
eyepieces
eyesight
eyesore *noun*
eyesores
eyewitness *noun*
eyewitnesses

Ff

-f
Most nouns ending in *-f* have plurals ending in *-ves*, e.g. **shelf - shelves**, but some have plurals ending in *-fs*, e.g. **chiefs**. Nouns ending in *-ff* have plurals ending in *-ffs*, e.g. **cuffs**.

fable *noun*
fables
fabric *noun*
fabrics
fabricate *verb*
fabricates
fabricating
fabricated
fabulous *adjective*
fabulously
face *noun*
faces
face *verb*
faces
facing
faced
facet *noun*
facets
facetious *adjective*
facetiously
facial *adjective*
facially
facilitate *verb*
facilitates
facilitating
facilitated
facility *noun*
facilities
fact *noun*
facts
factor *noun*
factors
factory *noun*
factories
factual *adjective*
factually
fad *noun*
fads
fade *verb*
fades
fading
faded
faeces
fag *noun*
fags
fagged
faggot *noun*
faggots
Fahrenheit
fail *verb*
fails
failing
failed
fail *noun*
fails
failing *noun*
failings
failure *noun*
failures

faint *adjective*
fainter
faintest
faintly
faint *verb*
faints
fainting
fainted
faint-hearted
faintness
fair *adjective*
fairer
fairest
★ **fair** *noun*
fairs
fairground *noun*
fairgrounds
fairly
fairness
fairy *noun*
fairies
fairyland
faith *noun*
faiths
faithful *adjective*
faithfully
faithfulness
fake *noun*
fakes
fake *verb*
fakes
faking
faked
faker
falcon *noun*
falcons
falconry
fall *verb*
falls
falling
fell
fallen
fall *noun*
falls
fallacious *adjective*
fallaciously
fallacy *noun*
fallacies
fallen see **fall**
fallout
fallow
falls *plural noun*
false *adjective*
falser
falsest
falsely
falsehood *noun*
falsehoods
falseness
falter *verb*
falters
faltering
faltered
fame
famed
familiar *adjective*
familiarly
familiarity
family *noun*
families
famine *noun*
famines
famished
famous *adjective*
famously
fan *verb*
fans
fanning
fanned
fan *noun*
fans
fanatic *noun*
fanatics
fanatical *adjective*
fanatically
fanciful *adjective*
fancifully
fancy *adjective*
fancier
fanciest
fancy *verb*
fancies
fancying
fancied
fancy *noun*
fancies
fanfare *noun*
fanfares
fang *noun*
fangs
fantastic *adjective*
fantastically
fantasy *noun*
fantasies
far *adjective* and *adverb*
farther
farthest
far-away
farce *noun*
farces
farcical *adjective*
farcically
fare *verb*
fares
faring
fared
☆ **fare** *noun*
fares
farewell
far-fetched

★ A **fair** is a group of outdoor entertainments or an exhibition. ! **fare**.
☆ A **fare** is money you pay, for example on a bus. ! **fair**.

farm *noun*
farms
farm *verb*
farms
farming
farmed
farmer *noun*
farmers
farmhouse *noun*
farmhouses
farmyard *noun*
farmyards
★ **farther**
☆ **farthest**
farthing *noun*
farthings
fascinate *verb*
fascinates
fascinating
fascinated
fascination
fascism
fascist *noun*
fascists
fashion *noun*
fashions
fashion *verb*
fashions
fashioning
fashioned
fashionable
fast *adjective* and *adverb*
faster
fastest
fast *verb*
fasts
fasting
fasted
fasten *verb*
fastens
fastening
fastened
fastener
fastening
fat *adjective*
fatter
fattest
fat *noun*
fats
fatal *adjective*
fatally
fatality *noun*
fatalities
✪ **fate** *noun*
fates
father *noun*
fathers
father-in-law *noun*
fathers-in-law
fathom *noun*
fathoms
fathom *verb*
fathoms
fathoming
fathomed
fatigue
fatigued
fatten *verb*
fattens
fattening
fattened
fattening
fatty *adjective*
fattier
fattiest
fault *noun*
faults
fault *verb*
faults
faulting
faulted
faultless *adjective*
faultlessly
faulty *adjective*
faultier
faultiest
fauna
favour *noun*
favours
favour *verb*
favours
favouring
favoured
favourable *adjective*
favourably
favourite *adjective* and *noun*
favourites
favouritism
fawn *noun*
fawns
fax *noun*
faxes
fax *verb*
faxes
faxing
faxed

-fe
Most nouns ending in *-fe* have plurals ending in *-ves*, e.g. **life - lives**.

fear *noun*
fears
fear *verb*
fears
fearing
feared
fearful *adjective*
fearfully

★ You can use **farther** or **further** in e.g. *farther up the road*. See **further**.
☆ You can use **farthest** or **furthest** in e.g. *the place farthest from here*. See **furthest**.
✪ **Fate** is a power that is thought to make things happen. ! **fête**.

fearless *adjective*
fearlessly
fearsome
feasible
feast *noun*
feasts
feast *verb*
feasts
feasting
feasted
★ **feat** *noun*
feats
feather *noun*
feathers
feathery
feature *noun*
features
feature *verb*
features
featuring
featured
☆ **February** *noun*
Februaries
fed see **feed**
federal
federation
fee *noun*
fees
feeble *adjective*
feebler
feeblest
feebly
feed *verb*
feeds
feeding
fed
feed *noun*
feeds
feedback
feel *verb*
feels
feeling
felt
feel *noun*
feeler *noun*
feelers
feeling *noun*
feelings
✪ **feet** see **foot**
feline
fell see **fall**
fell *verb*
fells
felling
felled
fell *noun*
fells
fellow *noun*
fellows
fellowship *noun*
fellowships
felt see **feel**
felt *noun*
felt-tip pen *or*
felt-tipped pen
noun
felt-tip pens *or*
felt-tipped pens
female *adjective* and
noun
females
feminine
femininity
feminism
feminist *noun*
feminists
fen *noun*
fens
fence *noun*
fences
fence *verb*
fences
fencing
fenced
fencer *adjective*
fencers
fencing
fend *verb*
fends
fending
fended
fender *noun*
fenders
ferment *verb*
ferments
fermenting
fermented
fermentation
ferment
fern *noun*
ferns
ferocious *adjective*
ferociously
ferocity
ferret *noun*
ferrets
ferret *verb*
ferrets
ferreting
ferreted
ferry *noun*
ferries
ferry *verb*
ferries
ferrying
ferried
fertile
fertility
fertilization

★ A **feat** is an achievement. ! **feet**.
☆ Note that **February** has two rs.
✪ **Feet** is the plural of foot. ! **feat**.

fertilize *verb*
fertilizes
fertilizing
fertilized
fertilizer *noun*
fertilizers
fervent *adjective*
fervently
fervour
festival *noun*
festivals
festive
festivity
festoon *verb*
festoons
festooning
festooned
fetal
fetch *verb*
fetches
fetching
fetched
★ **fête** *noun*
fêtes
fetlock *noun*
fetlocks
fetters *plural noun*
☆ **fetus** *noun*
fetuses
feud *noun*
feuds
feudal
feudalism
fever *noun*
fevers
fevered
feverish *adjective*
feverishly
few *adjective*
fewer
fewest
fez *noun*
fezzes
✪ **fiancé** *noun*
fiancés
✲ **fiancée** *noun*
fiancées
fiasco *noun*
fiascos
fib *noun*
fibs
fibber *noun*
fibbers
fibre *noun*
fibres
fibreglass
fibrous
fickle
fiction *noun*
fictions
fictional *adjective*
fictionally
fictitious *adjective*
fictitiously
fiddle *verb*
fiddles
fiddling
fiddled
fiddle *noun*
fiddles
fiddler *noun*
fiddlers
fiddling
fiddly
fidelity
fidget *verb*
fidgets
fidgeting
fidgeted
fidgety
field *noun*
fields
field *verb*
fields
fielding
fielded
fielder *noun*
fielders
field Marshal *noun*
field Marshals
fieldwork
fiend *noun*
fiends
fiendish *adjective*
fiendishly
fierce *adjective*
fiercer
fiercest
fiercely
fierceness
fiery *adjective*
fierier
fieriest
fife *noun*
fifes
fifteen
fifteenth
fifth
fifthly
fiftieth
fifty *noun*
fifties
fig *noun*
figs
fight *verb*
fights
fighting
fought
fight *noun*
fights

★ A **fête** is an outdoor entertainment with stalls. ! **fate**.
☆ You will also see this word spelt **foetus**.
✪ A woman's fi**ancé** is the man who is going to marry her.
✲ A man's fi**ancée** is the woman who is going to marry him.

fighter *noun*
fighters
figurative *adjective*
figuratively
figure *noun*
figures
figure *verb*
figures
figuring
figured
filament *noun*
filaments
file *verb*
files
filing
filed
file *noun*
files
filings *plural noun*
fill *verb*
fills
filling
filled
fill *noun*
fills
filler *noun*
fillers
fillet *noun*
fillets
filling *noun*
fillings
filly *noun*
fillies
film *noun*
films
film *verb*
films
filming
filmed
filter *noun*
filters
filter *verb*
filters
filtering
filtered
filth
filthy *adjective*
filthier
filthiest
fin *noun*
fins
final *adjective*
finally
final *noun*
finals
finale *noun*
finales
finalist *noun*
finalists
finality
finance
finance *verb*
finances
financing
financed
finances *plural noun*
financial *adjective*
financially
financier *noun*
financiers
finch *noun*
finches
find *verb*
finds
finding
found
finder *noun*
finders
findings *plural noun*
fine *adjective*
finer
finest
finely
fine *noun*
fines
fine *verb*
fines
fining
fined
finger *noun*
fingers
finger *verb*
fingers
fingering
fingered
fingernail *noun*
fingernails
fingerprint *noun*
fingerprints
finicky
finish *verb*
finishes
finishing
finished
finish *noun*
finishes
★ **fir** *noun*
firs
fire *noun*
fires
fire *verb*
fires
firing
fired
firearm *noun*
firearms
firefighter *noun*
firefighters
fireman *noun*
firemen
fireplace *noun*
fireplaces
fireproof

★ A fir is a tree. ! **fur**.

fireside *noun*
firesides
firewood
firework *noun*
fireworks
firm *adjective*
firmer
firmest
firmly
firm *noun*
firms
firmness
first *adjective* and *adverb*
firstly
first-class
first floor *noun*
first floors
first-hand *adjective*
first-rate
fish *noun*
fish *or* fishes
fish *verb*
fishes
fishing
fished
fisherman *noun*
fishermen
fishmonger *noun*
fishmongers
fishy *adjective*
fishier
fishiest
fission
fist *noun*
fists
fit *adjective*
fitter
fittest
fit *verb*
fits
fitting
fitted
fit *noun*
fits
fitness
fitter *noun*
fitters
fitting *adjective*
fitting *noun*
fittings
five
fiver *noun*
fivers
fix *verb*
fixes
fixing
fixed
fix *noun*
fixes
fixture *noun*
fixtures
fizz *verb*
fizzes
fizzing
fizzed
fizzy *adjective*
fizzier
fizziest
fizzle *verb*
fizzles
fizzling
fizzled
fjord *noun*
fjords
flabbergasted
flabby *adjective*
flabbier
flabbiest
flag *noun*
flags
flag *verb*
flags
flagging
flagged
flagpole *noun*
flagpoles
flagship *noun*
flagships
flagstaff *noun*
flagstaffs
flagstone *noun*
flagstones
★ **flair** *noun*
flake *noun*
flakes
flake *verb*
flakes
flaking
flaked
flaky *adjective*
flakier
flakiest
flame *noun*
flames
flame *verb*
flames
flaming
flamed
flamingo *noun*
flamingos
flan *noun*
flans
flank *noun*
flanks
flannel *noun*
flannels
flap *noun*
flaps

★ **Flair** is a special talent. ! **flare**.

flap *verb*
flaps
flapping
flapped
flapjack *noun*
flapjacks
★ **flare** *noun*
flares
flare *verb*
flares
flaring
flared
flash *noun*
flashes
flash *verb*
flashes
flashing
flashed
flashback *noun*
flashbacks
flashy *adjective*
flashier
flashiest
flask *noun*
flasks
flat *adjective*
flatter
flattest
flatly
flat *noun*
flats
flatness
flatten *verb*
flattens
flattening
flattened
flatter *verb*
flatters
flattering
flattered
flatterer *noun*
flatterers
flattery
flaunt *verb*
flaunts
flaunting
flaunted
flavour *noun*
flavours
flavour *verb*
flavours
flavouring
flavoured
flavouring
flaw *noun*
flaws
flawed
flawless *adjective*
flawlessly
flax
☆ **flea** *noun*
fleas
fleck *noun*
flecks
✪ **flee** *verb*
flees
fleeing
fled
fleece *noun*
fleeces
fleece *verb*
fleeces
fleecing
fleeced
fleecy *adjective*
fleecier
fleeciest
fleet *noun*
fleets
fleeting
flesh
fleshy *adjective*
fleshier
fleshiest
✲ **flew** see **fly**
flex *noun*
flexes
flex *verb*
flexes
flexing
flexed
flexibility
flexible *adjective*
flexibly
flick *verb*
flicks
flicking
flicked
flick *noun*
flicks
flicker *verb*
flickers
flickering
flickered
flight *noun*
flights
flimsy *adjective*
flimsier
flimsiest
flinch *verb*
flinches
flinching
flinched
fling *verb*
flings
flinging
flung
flint *noun*
flints
flinty *adjective*
flintier
flintiest

★ A **flare** is a bright light. ! **flair**.
☆ A **flea** is an insect. ! **flee**.
✪ To **flee** is to run away. ! **flea**.
✲ **Flew** is the past of **fly**. ! **flu**, **flue**.

flip *verb*
flips
flipping
flipped
flippancy
flippant *adjective*
flippantly
flipper *noun*
flippers
flirt *verb*
flirts
flirting
flirted
flirtation
flit *verb*
flits
flitting
flitted
float *verb*
floats
floating
floated
float *noun*
floats
flock *verb*
flocks
flocking
flocked
flock *noun*
flocks
flog *verb*
flogs
flogging
flogged
flood *verb*
floods
flooding
flooded
flood *noun*
floods
floodlight *noun*
floodlights
floodlit
floor *noun*
floors
floor *verb*
floors
flooring
floored
floorboard *noun*
floorboards
flop *verb*
flops
flopping
flopped
flop *noun*
flops
floppy *adjective*
floppier
floppiest
floppy disk *noun*
floppy disks
flora
floral
florist *noun*
florists
floss
flounder *verb*
flounders
floundering
floundered
★ **flour**
flourish *verb*
flourishes
flourishing
flourished
floury *adjective*
flourier
flouriest
flow *verb*
flows
flowing
flowed
flow *noun*
flows
☆ **flower** *noun*
flowers
flower *verb*
flowers
flowering
flowered
flowerpot *noun*
flowerpots
flowery
flown
✪ **flu**
fluctuate *verb*
fluctuates
fluctuating
fluctuated
fluctuation
✲ **flue** *noun*
flues
fluency
fluent *adjective*
fluently
fluff
fluffy *adjective*
fluffier
fluffiest
fluid *noun*
fluids
fluke *noun*
flukes
flung see **fling**
fluorescent
fluoridation
fluoride
flurry *noun*
flurries
flush *verb*
flushes
flushing
flushed

★ **Flour** is powder used in making bread. ! **flower**.
☆ A **flower** is a part of a plant. ! **flour**.
✪ **Flu** is an illness. ! **flew**, **flue**.
✲ A **flue** is a pipe for smoke and fumes. ! **flew**, **flu**.

flush *noun*
flushes
flush *adjective*
flustered
flute *noun*
flutes
flutter *verb*
flutters
fluttering
fluttered
flutter *noun*
flutters
fly *verb*
flies
flying
flew
flown
fly *noun*
flies
flyleaf *noun*
flyleaves
flyover *noun*
flyovers
flywheel *noun*
flywheels
foal *noun*
foals
foam *noun*
foam *verb*
foams
foaming
foamed
foamy *adjective*
foamier
foamiest
focal
focus *verb*
focuses
focusing
focused
focus *noun*
focuses *or* foci
fodder
foe *noun*
foes
foetus *noun* use **fetus**
fog *noun*
fogs
★ **foggy** *adjective*
foggier
foggiest
foghorn *noun*
foghorns
☆ **fogy** *noun*
fogies
foil *verb*
foils
foiling
foiled
foil *noun*
foils
fold *verb*
folds
folding
folded
fold *noun*
folds
folder *noun*
folders
foliage
folk
folklore
follow *verb*
follows
following
followed
follower *noun*
followers
fond *adjective*
fonder
fondest
fondly
fondness
font *noun*
fonts
food *noun*
foods
fool *noun*
fools
fool *verb*
fools
fooling
fooled
foolhardiness
foolhardy *adjective*
foolhardier
foolhardiest
foolish *adjective*
foolishly
foolishness
foolproof
✪ **foot** *noun*
feet
football *noun*
footballs
footballer *noun*
footballers
foothill *noun*
foothills
foothold *noun*
footholds
footing
footlights
footnote *noun*
footnotes
footpath *noun*
footpaths
footprint *noun*
footprints
footstep *noun*
footsteps

★ **Foggy** means 'covered in fog'. ! **fogy**.
☆ A **fogy** is someone with old-fashioned ideas. ! **foggy**.
✪ The plural is **foot** in e.g. *a six-foot pole*.

★ **for** *preposition* and *conjunction*
forbid *verb*
forbids
forbidding
forbade
forbidden
force *verb*
forces
forcing
forced
force *noun*
forces
forceful *adjective*
forcefully
forceps *plural noun*
forcible *adjective*
forcibly
ford *verb*
fords
fording
forded
ford *noun*
fords
☆ **fore** *adjective* and *noun*
forecast *verb*
forecasts
forecasting
forecast
forecasted
forecast *noun*
forecasts
forecourt *noun*
forecourts
forefathers *plural noun*
forefinger *noun*
forefingers
✪ **foregone** *adjective*
foreground *noun*
foregrounds
forehead *noun*
foreheads
foreign
foreigner *noun*
foreigners
foreman *noun*
foremen
foremost
forename *noun*
forenames
foresee *verb*
foresees
foreseeing
foresaw
foreseen
foreseeable
foresight
forest *noun*
forests
forester *noun*
foresters
forestry
foretell *verb*
foretells
foretelling
foretold
✲ **forever** *adverb*
forfeit *verb*
forfeits
forfeiting
forfeited
forfeit *noun*
forfeits
forgave see **forgive**
forge *verb*
forges
forging
forged
forge *noun*
forges
forgery *noun*
forgeries
forget *verb*
forgets
forgetting
forgot
forgotten
forgetful
forgetfulness
forget-me-not *noun*
forget-me-nots
forgive *verb*
forgives
forgiving
forgave
forgiven
forgiveness
fork *noun*
forks
fork *verb*
forks
forking
forked
fork-lift truck *noun*
fork-lift trucks
forlorn
form *verb*
forms
forming
formed
form *noun*
forms
formal *adjective*
formally
formality *noun*
formalities
format *noun*
formats
formation *noun*
formations

★ You use **for** in phrases like *a present for you*. ! **fore**.
☆ You use **fore** in phrases like *come to the fore*. ! **for**.
✪ You can use **foregone** in *a foregone conclusion*.
✲ You use **forever** in e.g. *They are forever complaining*. You can also use **for ever** in e.g. *The rain seemed to go on for ever*.

former *adjective*
formerly
formidable *adjective*
formidably
formula *noun*
formulas *or*
formulae
formulate *verb*
formulates
formulating
formulated
forsake *verb*
forsakes
forsaking
forsook
forsaken
fort *noun*
forts
★ **forth**
fortieth
fortification *noun*
fortifications
fortify *verb*
fortifies
fortifying
fortified
fortnight *noun*
fortnights
fortnightly
fortress *noun*
fortresses
fortunate *adjective*
fortunately
fortune *noun*
fortunes
fortune-teller *noun*
fortune-tellers
forty *noun*
forties
forward *adjective*
and *adverb*
forward *noun*
forwards
forwards *adverb*
fossil *noun*
fossils
fossilized
foster *verb*
fosters
fostering
fostered
foster child *noun*
foster children
foster parent *noun*
foster parents
fought see **fight**
☆ **foul** *adjective*
fouler
foulest
foully
✪ **foul** *verb*
fouls
fouling
fouled
✲ **foul** *noun*
fouls
foulness
found *verb*
founds
founding
founded
found see **find**
foundation *noun*
foundations
founder *noun*
founders
founder *verb*
founders
foundering
foundered
foundry *noun*
foundries
fountain *noun*
fountains
four *noun*
fours
fourteen *noun*
fourteens
fourteenth
✸ **fourth**
fourthly
❄ **fowl** *noun*
fowl *or* fowls
fox *noun*
foxes
fox *verb*
foxes
foxing
foxed
foxglove *noun*
foxgloves
foxy *adjective*
foxier
foxiest
foyer *noun*
foyers
fraction *noun*
fractions
fractionally
fracture *verb*
fractures
fracturing
fractured
fracture *noun*
fractures
fragile *adjective*
fragilely
fragility
fragment *noun*
fragments
fragmentary
fragmentation

★ You use **forth** in e.g. *to go forth*. ! **fourth**.
☆ **Foul** means 'dirty' or 'disgusting'. ! **fowl**.
✪ To **foul** is to break a rule in a game. ! **fowl**.
✲ A **foul** is breaking a rule in a game. ! **fowl**.
✸ You use **fourth** in e.g. *for the fourth time*. ! **forth**.
❄ A **fowl** is a kind of bird. ! **foul**.

fragrance *noun*
fragrances
fragrant
frail *adjective*
frailer
frailest
frailly
frailty *noun*
frailties
frame *verb*
frames
framing
framed
frame *noun*
frames
framework *noun*
frameworks
★ **franc** *noun*
francs
franchise *noun*
franchises
☆ **frank** *adjective*
franker
frankest
frankly
✪ **frank** *verb*
franks
franking
franked
frankness
frantic *adjective*
frantically
fraud *noun*
frauds
fraudulent *adjective*
fraudulently
fraught
frayed
freak *noun*
freaks
freakish
freckle *noun*
freckles
freckled
free *adjective*
freer
freest
freely
free *verb*
frees
freeing
freed
freedom *noun*
freedoms
freehand *adjective*
freewheel *verb*
freewheels
freewheeling
freewheeled
✲ **freeze** *verb*
freezes
freezing
froze
frozen
freezer *noun*
freezers
freight
freighter *noun*
freighters
frenzied
frenzy *noun*
frenzies
frequency *noun*
frequencies
frequent *adjective*
frequently
frequent *verb*
frequents
frequenting
frequented
fresh *adjective*
fresher
freshest
freshly
freshness
freshen *verb*
freshens
freshening
freshened
freshwater
fret *verb*
frets
fretting
fretted
fretful *adjective*
fretfully
fretsaw *noun*
fretsaws
fretwork
friar *noun*
friars
friary *noun*
friaries
friction
Friday *noun*
Fridays
fridge *noun*
fridges
friend *noun*
friends
friendless
friendliness
friendly *adjective*
friendlier
friendliest
friendship *noun*
friendships
✸ **frieze** *noun*
friezes
frigate *noun*
frigates

★ A **franc** is a French unit of money. ! **frank**.
☆ **Frank** means 'speaking honestly'. ! **franc**.
✪ To **frank** is to mark a letter with a postmark. ! **franc**.
✲ To **freeze** is to be very cold. ! **frieze**.
✸ A **frieze** is a strip of designs along a wall. ! **freeze**.

fright *noun*
frights
frighten *verb*
frightens
frightening
frightened
frightful *adjective*
frightfully
frill *noun*
frills
frilled
frilly *adjective*
frillier
frilliest
fringe *noun*
fringes
fringed
frisk *verb*
frisks
frisking
frisked
friskiness
frisky *adjective*
friskier
friskiest
friskily
fritter *verb*
fritters
frittering
frittered
fritter *noun*
fritters
frivolous *adjective*
frivolously
frivolity *noun*
frivolities
frizzy *adjective*
frizzier
frizziest
★ **fro**
frock *noun*
frocks
frog *noun*
frogs
frogman *noun*
frogmen
frolic *noun*
frolics
frolicsome
frolic *verb*
frolics
frolicking
frolicked
front *noun*
fronts
frontier *noun*
frontiers
frost
noun
frosts
frost *verb*
frosts
frosting
frosted
frostbite
frostbitten
frosty *adjective*
frostier
frostiest
froth *noun*
froth *verb*
froths
frothing
frothed
frothy *adjective*
frothier
frothiest
froth *verb*
froths
frothing
frothed
frown *verb*
frowns
frowning
frowned
frown *noun*
frowns
froze see **freeze**
frozen see **freeze**
frugal *adjective*
frugally
frugality
fruit *noun*
fruit *or* fruits
fruitful *adjective*
fruitfully
fruitless *adjective*
fruitlessly
fruity *adjective*
fruitier
fruitiest
frustrate *verb*
frustrates
frustrating
frustrated
frustration *noun*
frustrations
fry *verb*
fries
frying
fried
fudge
fuel *noun*
fuels
fuel *verb*
fuels
fuelling
fuelled
fug *noun*
fugs
fuggy *adjective*
fuggier
fuggiest

★ You use **fro** in *to and fro*.

fugitive *noun*
fugitives

-ful
-ful makes nouns for amounts, e.g. **handful**, **spoonful**. The plural of these words ends in *-fuls*, e.g. **handfuls**. *-ful* also makes adjectives, e.g. **graceful**, and when the adjective ends in *-y* following a consonant, you change the *y* to *i*, e.g. **beauty - beautiful**.

fulcrum *noun*
fulcra *or* fulcrums
fulfil *verb*
fulfils
fulfilling
fulfilled
fulfilment
full *adjective*
fully
fullness
fumble *verb*
fumbles
fumbling
fumbled
fume *verb*
fumes
fuming
fumed
fumes *plural noun*
fun
function *verb*
functions
functioning
functioned
function *noun*
functions
functional *adjective*
functionally
fund *noun*
funds
fundamental *adjective*
fundamentally
funeral *noun*
funerals
fungus *noun*
fungi
funk *verb*
funks
funking
funked
funnel *noun*
funnels
funny *adjective*
funnier
funniest
funnily
★ **fur** *noun*
furs
furious *adjective*
furiously
furl *verb*
furls
furling
furled
furlong *noun*
furlongs
furnace *noun*
furnaces
furnish *verb*
furnishes
furnishing
furnished
furniture
furrow *noun*
furrows
furry *adjective*
furrier
furriest
☆ **further** *adjective*
✪ **further** *verb*
furthers
furthering
furthered
furthermore
✲ **furthest**
furtive *adjective*
furtively
fury *noun*
furies
fuse *verb*
fuses
fusing
fused
fuse *noun*
fuses
fuselage *noun*
fuselages
fusion *noun*
fusions
fuss *verb*
fusses
fussing
fussed
fuss *noun*
fusses
fussiness
fussy *adjective*
fussier
fussiest
fussily
futile *adjective*
futilely
futility
futon *noun*
futons

★ **Fur** is the hair of animals. ! fir.
☆ You use **further** in e.g. *We need further information*. See **farther**.
✪ To **further** something is to make it progress.
✲ You use **furthest** in e.g. *Who has read the furthest?* See **farthest**.

future
fuzz
fuzziness *noun*
fuzzy *adjective*
fuzzier
fuzziest
fuzzily

Gg

gabardine *noun*
gabardines
gabble *verb*
gabbles
gabbling
gabbled
gable *noun*
gables
gabled
gadget *noun*
gadgets
Gaelic
gag *verb*
gags
gagging
gagged
gag *noun*
gags
gaiety
gaily
gain *verb*
gains
gaining
gained
gain *noun*
gains
gala *noun*
galas
galactic
galaxy *noun*
galaxies
gale *noun*
gales
gallant *adjective*
gallantly
gallantry
★ **galleon** *noun*
galleons
gallery *noun*
galleries
galley *noun*
galleys
☆ **gallon** *noun*
gallons
gallop *verb*
gallops
galloping
galloped
gallop *noun*
gallops
gallows
galore
galvanize *verb*
galvanizes
galvanizing
galvanized
gamble *verb*
gambles
gambling
gambled
gamble *noun*
gambles
gambler *noun*
gamblers
game *noun*
games
gamekeeper *noun*
gamekeepers
gammon
gander *noun*
ganders
gang *noun*
gangs
gang *verb*
gangs
ganging
ganged
gangplank *noun*
gangplanks
gangster *noun*
gangsters
gangway *noun*
gangways
gaol *noun* use **jail**
gaoler *noun* use **jailer**
gap *noun*
gaps
gape *verb*
gapes
gaping
gaped
garage *noun*
garages
garbage
garden *noun*
gardens
gardener *noun*
gardeners
gardening
gargle *verb*
gargles
gargling
gargled
gargoyle *noun*
gargoyles
garland *noun*
garlands
garlic

★ A **galleon** is a type of ship. ! **gallon**.
☆ A **gallon** is a measurement of liquid. ! **galleon**.

garment *noun*
garments
garnish *verb*
garnishes
garnishing
garnished
garrison *noun*
garrisons
garter *noun*
garters
gas *noun*
gases
gas *verb*
gasses
gassing
gassed
gaseous
gash *noun*
gashes
gasket *noun*
gaskets
gasoline
gasometer *noun*
gasometers
gasp *verb*
gasps
gasping
gasped
gasp *noun*
gasps
gastric
gate *noun*
gates
★ **gateau** *noun*
gateaux
gateway *noun*
gateways
gather *verb*
gathers
gathering
gathered
gathering *noun*
gatherings
gaudy *adjective*
gaudier
gaudiest
gauge *verb*
gauges
gauging
gauged
gauge *noun*
gauges
gaunt
gauntlet *noun*
gauntlets
gauze
gave see **give**
gay *adjective*
gayer
gayest
gaze *verb*
gazes
gazing
gazed
gaze *noun*
gazes
gazetteer *noun*
gazetteers
gear *noun*
gears
geese see **goose**
Geiger counter *noun*
Geiger counters
gel *noun*
gels
gelatine
gelding *noun*
geldings
gem *noun*
gems
gender *noun*
genders
gene *noun*
genes
genealogy *noun*
genealogies
general *adjective*
generally
general *noun*
generals
generalization *noun*
generalizations
generalize *verb*
generalizes
generalizing
generalized
generate *verb*
generates
generating
generated
generation *noun*
generations
generator *noun*
generators
generosity
generous *adjective*
generously
genetic *adjective*
genetically
genetics *plural noun*
genial *adjective*
genially
genie *noun*
genies
genitals *plural noun*
genius *noun*
geniuses
gent *noun*
gents

★ **Gateau** is a French word used in English. It means 'a rich cream cake'.

gentle *adjective*
gentler
gentlest
gently
gentleman *noun*
gentlemen
gentlemanly
gentleness
genuine *adjective*
genuinely
genus *noun*
genera

geo-
geo- means 'earth', e.g. **geography** (= the study of the earth).

geographer
geographical *adjective*
geographically
geography
geological *adjective*
geologically
geologist
geology
geometric *adjective*
geometrically
geometrical *adjective*
geometrically
geometry
geranium *noun*
geraniums
gerbil *noun*
gerbils
germ *noun*
germs
germinate *verb*
germinates
germinating
germinated
germination
gesticulate *verb*
gesticulates
gesticulating
gesticulated
gesture *noun*
gestures
get *verb*
gets
getting
got
getaway *noun*
getaways
geyser *noun*
geysers
ghastly *adjective*
ghastlier
ghastliest
ghetto *noun*
ghettos
ghost *noun*
ghosts
ghostly *adjective*
ghostlier
ghostliest
ghoulish *adjective*
ghoulishly
giant *noun*
giants
giddiness
giddy *adjective*
giddier
giddiest
giddily
gift *noun*
gifts
gifted
gigantic *adjective*
gigantically
giggle *verb*
giggles
giggling
giggled
giggle *noun*
giggles
★ **gild** *verb*
gilds
gilding
gilded
gills *plural noun*
gimmick *noun*
gimmicks
gin
ginger
gingerbread
gingerly
gingery
gipsy *noun* use **gypsy**
giraffe *noun*
giraffes
girder *noun*
girders
girdle *noun*
girdles
girl *noun*
girls
girlfriend *noun*
girlfriends
girlhood
girlish
☆ **giro** *noun*
giros
girth *noun*
girths
gist
give *verb*
gives
giving
gave
given

★ To **gild** something is to cover it with gold. ! **guild**.
☆ A **giro** is a system of paying money. ! **gyro**.

given see **give**
giver *noun*
givers
glacial
glacier *noun*
glaciers
glad *adjective*
gladder
gladdest
gladly
gladden *verb*
gladdens
gladdening
gladdened
gladiator *noun*
gladiators
gladness
glamorize *verb*
glamorizes
glamorizing
glamorized
glamorous *adjective*
glamorously
glamour
glance *verb*
glances
glancing
glanced
glance *noun*
glances
gland *noun*
glands
glandular
glare *verb*
glares
glaring
glared
glare *noun*
glares
glass *noun*
glasses
glassful *noun*
glassfuls
glassy *adjective*
glassier
glassiest
glaze *verb*
glazes
glazing
glazed
glaze *noun*
glazes
glazier *noun*
glaziers
gleam *noun*
gleams
gleam *verb*
gleams
gleaming
gleamed
glee
gleeful *adjective*
gleefully
glen *noun*
glens
glide *verb*
glides
gliding
glided
glider *noun*
gliders
glimmer *verb*
glimmers
glimmering
glimmered
glimmer *noun*
glimmers
glimpse *verb*
glimpses
glimpsing
glimpsed
glimpse *noun*
glimpses
glint *verb*
glints
glinting
glinted
glint *noun*
glints
glisten *verb*
glistens
glistening
glistened
glitter *verb*
glitters
glittering
glittered
gloat *verb*
gloats
gloating
gloated
global *adjective*
globally
globe *noun*
globes
gloom
gloominess
gloomy *adjective*
gloomier
gloomiest
gloomily
glorification
glorify *verb*
glorifies
glorifying
glorified
glorious *adjective*
gloriously
glory *noun*
glories
gloss *noun*
glosses

glossary *noun*
glossaries
glossy *adjective*
glossier
glossiest
glove *noun*
gloves
glow *verb*
glows
glowing
glowed
glow *noun*
glows
glower *verb*
glowers
glowering
glowered
glow-worm *noun*
glow-worms
glucose
glue *noun*
glues
glue *verb*
glues
gluing
glued
gluey *adjective*
gluier
gluiest
glum *adjective*
glummer
glummest
glumly
glutton *noun*
gluttons
gluttonous
gluttony
gnarled
★ **gnash** *verb*
gnashes
gnashing
gnashed
★ **gnat** *noun*
gnats
★ **gnaw** *verb*
gnaws
gnawing
gnawed
★ **gnome** *noun*
gnomes
go *verb*
goes
going
went
gone
go *noun*
goes
goal *noun*
goals
goalie *noun*
goalies
goalkeeper *noun*
goalkeepers
goalpost *noun*
goalposts
goat *noun*
goats
gobble *verb*
gobbles
gobbling
gobbled
gobbledegook
goblet *noun*
goblets
goblin *noun*
goblins
☆ **God**
✪ **god** *noun*
gods
godchild *noun*
godchildren
goddess *noun*
goddesses
godparent *noun*
godparents
goggles *plural noun*
gold
golden
goldfinch *noun*
goldfinches
goldfish *noun*
goldfish
golf
golfer *noun*
golfers
golfing
gondola *noun*
gondolas
gondolier *noun*
gondoliers
gone see **go**
gong *noun*
gongs
good *adjective*
better
best
goodbye *interjection*
Good Friday
good-looking
good-natured
goodness
goods *plural noun*
goodwill
gooey *adjective*
gooier
gooiest
goose *noun*
geese
gooseberry *noun*
gooseberries

★ In these words beginning with gn- the 'g' is silent.
☆ You use a capital G when you mean the Christian, Jewish, and Muslim creator.
✪ You use a small g when you mean any male divine being.

gore *verb*
gores
goring
gored
gorge *noun*
gorges
gorgeous *adjective*
gorgeously
★ **gorilla** *noun*
gorillas
gorse
gory *adjective*
gorier
goriest
gosling *noun*
goslings
gospel *noun*
gospels
gossip *verb*
gossips
gossiping
gossiped
gossip *noun*
gossips
got see **get**
gouge *verb*
gouges
gouging
gouged
gourd *noun*
gourds
govern *verb*
governs
governing
governed
government *noun*
governments
governor *noun*
governors
gown *noun*
gowns

grab *verb*
grabs
grabbing
grabbed
grace *noun*
graces
graceful *adjective*
gracefully
gracefulness
gracious *adjective*
graciously
grade *noun*
grades
grade *verb*
grades
grading
graded
gradient *noun*
gradients
gradual *adjective*
gradually
graduate *noun*
graduates
graduate *verb*
graduates
graduating
graduated
graduation
graffiti *plural noun*
grain *noun*
grains
grainy *adjective*
grainier
grainiest
gram *noun*
grams
grammar *noun*
grammars
grammatical *adjective*
grammatically

gramophone *noun*
gramophones
grand *adjective*
grander
grandest
grandly
grandad *noun*
grandads
grandchild *noun*
grandchildren
grandeur
grandfather *noun*
grandfathers
grandma *noun*
grandmas
grandmother *noun*
grandmothers
grandpa *noun*
grandpas
grandparent *noun*
grandparents
grandstand *noun*
grandstands
granite
granny *noun*
grannies
grant *verb*
grants
granting
granted
grant *noun*
grants
granulated
grape *noun*
grapes
grapefruit *noun*
grapefruit
grapevine *noun*
grapevines
graph *noun*
graphs

★ A **gorilla** is a large ape. ! **guerrilla**.

graphic *adjective*
graphically
graphics *plural noun*
graphite

-graphy
-graphy makes words for subjects of study, e.g. **geography** (= the study of the earth). A **bibliography** is a list of books on a subject, and the plural is **bibliographies**.

grapple *verb*
grapples
grappling
grappled
grasp *verb*
grasps
grasping
grasped
grasp *noun*
grasps
grass *noun*
grasses
grasshopper *noun*
grasshoppers
grassy *adjective*
grassier
grassiest
★ **grate** *verb*
grates
grating
grated
☆ **grate** *noun*
grates
grateful *adjective*
gratefully
grating *noun*
gratings
gratitude
grave *noun*
graves
grave *adjective*
graver
gravest
gravely
gravel
gravelled
gravestone *noun*
gravestones
graveyard *noun*
graveyards
gravitation
gravitational
gravity
gravy
graze *verb*
grazes
grazing
grazed
graze *noun*
grazes
grease
greasy *adjective*
greasier
greasiest
great *adjective*
greater
greatest
greatly
greatness
greed
greediness
greedy *adjective*
greedier
greediest
greedily
green *adjective* and *noun*
greener
greenest
greenery
greengage *noun*
greengages
greengrocer *noun*
greengrocers
greengrocery *noun*
greengroceries
greenhouse *noun*
greenhouses
greens *plural noun*
greet *verb*
greets
greeting
greeted
greeting *noun*
greetings
grenade *noun*
grenades
grew see **grow**
grey *adjective* and *noun*
greyer
greyest
greyhound *noun*
greyhounds
grid *noun*
grids
grief
grievance *noun*
grievances
grieve *verb*
grieves
grieving
grieved
✪ **grievous** *adjective*
grievously

★ To **grate** something is to shred it. ! **great**.
☆ A **grate** is a fireplace. ! **great**.
✪ Note that this word does not end *-ious*.

grill *verb*
grills
grilling
grilled
grill *noun*
grills
grim *adjective*
grimmer
grimmest
grimly
grimace *noun*
grimaces
grime
grimness
grimy *adjective*
grimier
grimiest
grin *noun*
grins
grin *verb*
grins
grinning
grinned
grind *verb*
grinds
grinding
ground
grinder *noun*
grinders
grindstone *noun*
grindstones
grip *verb*
grips
gripping
gripped
grip *noun*
grips
★ **grisly** *adjective*
grislier
grisliest
gristle
gristly *adjective*
gristlier
gristliest
grit *verb*
grits
gritting
gritted
grit *noun*
gritty *adjective*
grittlier
grittliest
☆ **grizzly** *adjective*
groan *verb*
groans
groaning
groaned
groan *noun*
groans
grocer *noun*
grocers
grocery *noun*
groceries
groggy *adjective*
groggier
groggiest
groin *noun*
groins
groom *verb*
grooms
grooming
groomed
groom *noun*
grooms
groove *noun*
grooves
grope *verb*
gropes
groping
groped
gross *adjective*
grosser
grossest
grossly
gross *noun*
gross
grossness
✪ **grotesque** *adjective*
grotesquely
grotty *adjective*
grottier
grottiest
ground *noun*
grounds
ground see **grind**
grounded
grounds *plural noun*
groundsheet *noun*
groundsheets
groundsman *noun*
groundsmen
group *noun*
groups
group *verb*
groups
grouping
grouped
grouse *verb*
grouses
grousing
groused
grouse *noun*
grouse
grove *noun*
groves
grovel *verb*
grovels
grovelling
grovelled
grow *verb*
grows
growing
grew
grown

★ **Grisly** means 'revolting' or 'horrible'. ! **grizzly**.
☆ You use **grizzly** in *grizzly bear*. ! **grisly**.
✪ **Grotesque** means 'strange' and 'ugly'. It sounds like 'grotesk'.

grower *noun*
growers
growl *verb*
growls
growling
growled
growl *noun*
growls
grown-up *noun*
grown-ups
growth *noun*
growths
grub *noun*
grubs
grubby *adjective*
grubbier
grubbiest
grudge *verb*
grudges
grudging
grudged
grudge *noun*
grudges
grudgingly
gruelling
gruesome
gruff *adjective*
gruffer
gruffest
gruffly
grumble *verb*
grumbles
grumbling
grumbled
grumbler *noun*
grumblers
grumpiness
grumpy *adjective*
grumpier
grumpiest
grumpily
grunt *verb*
grunts
grunting
grunted
grunt *noun*
grunts
guarantee *noun*
guarantees
guarantee *verb*
guarantees
guaranteeing
guaranteed
guard *verb*
guards
guarding
guarded
guard *noun*
guards
guardian *noun*
guardians
guardianship
★ **guerrilla** *noun*
guerrillas
guess *verb*
guesses
guessing
guessed
guess *noun*
guesses
guesswork
guest *noun*
guests
guidance
guide *verb*
guides
guiding
guided
guide *noun*
guides
guidelines *plural noun*
☆ **guild** *noun*
guilds
guillotine *noun*
guillotines
guilt
guilty *adjective*
guiltier
guiltiest
guinea *noun*
guineas
guinea pig *noun*
guinea pigs
guitar *noun*
guitars
guitarist
gulf *noun*
gulfs
gull *noun*
gulls
gullet *noun*
gullets
gullible
gully *noun*
gullies
gulp *verb*
gulps
gulping
gulped
gulp *noun*
gulps
gum *noun*
gums
gum *verb*
gums
gumming
gummed
gummy *adjective*
gummier
gummiest
gun *noun*
guns

★ A **guerrilla** is a member of a small army. ! **gorilla**.
☆ A **guild** is an organization of people. ! **gild**.

gun *verb*
guns
gunning
gunned
gunboat *noun*
gunboats
gunfire
gunman *noun*
gunmen
gunner *noun*
gunners
gunnery
gunpowder
gunshot *noun*
gunshots
★ **gurdwara** *noun*
gurdwaras
gurgle *verb*
gurgles
gurgling
gurgled
guru *noun*
gurus
☆ **Guru Granth Sahib**
gush *verb*
gushes
gushing
gushed
gust *noun*
gusts
gusty *adjective*
gustier
gustiest
gut *noun*
guts
gut *verb*
guts
gutting
gutted
gutter *noun*
gutters
guy *noun*
guys
guzzle *verb*
guzzles
guzzling
guzzled
gym *noun*
gyms
gymkhana *noun*
gymkhanas
gymnasium *noun*
gymnasiums
gymnast *noun*
gymnasts
gymnastics *plural noun*
gypsy *noun*
gypsies
✪ **gyro** *noun*
gyros
gyroscope *noun*
gyroscopes

Hh

habit *noun*
habits
habitat *noun*
habitats
habitual *adjective*
habitually
hack *verb*
hacks
hacking
hacked
hacker *noun*
hackers
hacksaw *noun*
hacksaws
had see **has**
haddock *noun*
haddock
hadn't *verb*
hag *noun*
hags
haggard
haggis *noun*
haggises
haggle *verb*
haggles
haggling
haggled
✲ **haiku** *noun*
haiku
hail *verb*
hails
hailing
hailed
hail
hailstone *noun*
hailstones
✸ **hair** *noun*
hairs
hairbrush *noun*
hairbrushes
haircut *noun*
haircuts
hairdresser *noun*
hairdressers
hairpin *noun*
hairpins
hair-raising
hairstyle *noun*
hairstyles

★ A Sikh place of worship.
☆ The holy book of Sikhs.
✪ A **gyro** is type of compass. ! **giro**.
✲ A Japanese poem.
✸ **Hair** is the covering on the head. ! **hare**.

hairy *adjective*
hairier
hairiest
hake *noun*
hake
halal
half *adjective* and *noun*
halves
half-baked
half-hearted *adjective*
half-heartedly
half-life *noun*
half-lives
half-mast
★ **halfpenny** *noun*
halfpennies *or* halfpence
half-term *noun*
half-terms
half-time *noun*
half-times
halfway
halibut *noun*
halibut
☆ **hall** *noun*
halls
hallo
✪ **Halloween**
hallucination *noun*
hallucinations
halo *noun*
haloes
halt *verb*
halts
halting
halted
halt *noun*
halts
halter *noun*
halters
halting *adjective*
haltingly
halve *verb*
halves
halving
halved
halves see **half**
ham *noun*
hams
hamburger *noun*
hamburgers
hammer *noun*
hammers
hammer *verb*
hammers
hammering
hammered
hammock *noun*
hammocks
hamper *verb*
hampers
hampering
hampered
hamper *noun*
hampers
hamster *noun*
hamsters
hand *noun*
hands
hand *verb*
hands
handing
handed
handbag *noun*
handbags
handbook *noun*
handbooks
handcuffs *plural noun*
handful *noun*
handfuls
handicap *noun*
handicaps
handicapped
handicraft *noun*
handicrafts
handiwork
handkerchief *noun*
handkerchiefs
handle *noun*
handles
handle *verb*
handles
handling
handled
handlebars *plural noun*
handrail *noun*
handrails
handsome *adjective*
handsomer
handsomest
handsomely
hands-on
handstand *noun*
handstands
handwriting
handwritten
handy *adjective*
handier
handiest
handyman *noun*
handymen
hang *verb*
hangs
hanging
hung

★ You use **halfpennies** when you mean several coins and **halfpence** for a sum of money.
☆ A **hall** is a large space in a building. **! haul.**
✪ You will also see this word spelt *Hallowe'en*.

★ **hangar** *noun*
hangars
☆ **hanger** *noun*
hangers
hang-glider *noun*
hang-gliders
hang-gliding
hangman *noun*
hangmen
hangover *noun*
hangovers
hank *noun*
hanks
hanker *verb*
hankers
hankering
hankered
hanky *noun*
hankies
✪ **Hanukkah**
haphazard *adjective*
haphazardly
happen *verb*
happens
happening
happened
happening *noun*
happenings
happiness
happy *adjective*
happier
happiest
happily
happy-go-lucky
✲ **harass** *verb*
harasses
harassing
harassed
harassment

harbour *noun*
harbours
harbour *verb*
harbours
harbouring
harboured
hard *adjective*
harder
hardest
hard *adverb*
harder
hardest
hardboard
hard-boiled
hard disk *noun*
hard disks
harden *verb*
hardens
hardening
hardened
hardly
hardness
hardship *noun*
hardships
hardware
hardwood *noun*
hardwoods
hardy *adjective*
hardier
hardiest
✹ **hare** *noun*
hares
hark *verb*
harks
harking
harked
harm *verb*
harms
harming
harmed
harm *noun*

harmful *adjective*
harmfully
harmless *adjective*
harmlessly
harmonic
harmonica *noun*
harmonicas
harmonious *adjective*
harmoniously
harmonization
harmonize *verb*
harmonizes
harmonizing
harmonized
harmony *noun*
harmonies
harness *verb*
harnesses
harnessing
harnessed
harness *noun*
harnesses
harp *noun*
harps
harp *verb*
harps
harping
harped
harpist *noun*
harpists
harpoon *noun*
harpoons
harpsichord *noun*
harpsichords
harrow *noun*
harrows
harsh *adjective*
harsher
harshest
harshly

★ A **hangar** is a shed for aircraft. ! **hanger**.
☆ A **hanger** is a thing for hanging clothes on. ! **hangar**.
✪ A Jewish festival.
✲ Note that there is only one r in **harass** and **harassment**.
✹ A **hare** is an animal like a large rabbit. ! **hair**.

harshness
harvest *noun*
harvests
harvest *verb*
harvests
harvesting
harvested
hash *noun*
hashes
hasn't *verb*
hassle *noun*
hassles
haste
hasten *verb*
hastens
hastening
hastened
hastiness
hasty *adjective*
hastier
hastiest
hastily
hatch *verb*
hatches
hatching
hatched
hatch *noun*
hatches
hatchback *noun*
hatchbacks
hatchet *noun*
hatchets
hate *verb*
hates
hating
hated
hate *noun*
hates
hateful *adjective*
hatefully
hatred
hat trick *noun*
hat tricks
haughtiness
haughty *adjective*
haughtier
haughtiest
haughtily
★ **haul** *verb*
hauls
hauling
hauled
haul *noun*
hauls
haunt *verb*
haunts
haunting
haunted
have *verb*
has
having
had
haven *noun*
havens
haven't *verb*
haversack *noun*
haversacks
hawk *noun*
hawks
hawk *verb*
hawks
hawking
hawked
hawker *noun*
hawkers
hawthorn *noun*
hawthorns
hay fever
haymaking
haystack *noun*
haystacks
hazard *noun*
hazards
hazardous
haze *noun*
hazes
hazel *noun*
hazels
haziness
hazy *adjective*
hazier
haziest
hazily
H-bomb *noun*
H-bombs
head *noun*
heads
head *verb*
heads
heading
headed
headache *noun*
headaches
headdress *noun*
headdresses
header *noun*
headers
heading *noun*
headings
headland *noun*
headlands
headlight *noun*
headlights
headline *noun*
headlines
headlong
headmaster *noun*
headmasters
headmistress *noun*
headmistresses
head-on
headphones

★ To **haul** is to pull something heavy. ! **hall**

headquarters *noun*
headquarters
headteacher *noun*
headteachers
headway
heal *verb*
heals
healing
healed
healer *noun*
healers
health
healthiness
healthy *adjective*
healthier
healthiest
healthily
heap *verb*
heaps
heaping
heaped
heap *noun*
heaps
★ **hear** *verb*
hears
hearing
heard
hearing *noun*
hearings
hearse *noun*
hearses
heart *noun*
hearts
hearth *noun*
hearths
heartiness
heartless
hearty *adjective*
heartier
heartiest
heartily
heat *verb*
heats
heating
heated
heat *noun*
heats
heater *noun*
heaters
heath *noun*
heaths
heathen *noun*
heathens
heather
heatwave *noun*
heatwaves
☆ **heave** *verb*
heaves
heaving
heaved *or* hove
heaven
heavenly
heaviness
heavy *adjective*
heavier
heaviest
heavily
heavyweight *noun*
heavyweights
Hebrew
hectare *noun*
hectares
hectic *adjective*
hectically
he'd *verb*
hedge *noun*
hedges
hedge *verb*
hedges
hedging
hedged
hedgehog *noun*
hedgehogs
hedgerow *noun*
hedgerows
heed *verb*
heeds
heeding
heeded
heed *noun*
heedless
heel *noun*
heels
heel *verb*
heels
heeling
heeled
hefty *adjective*
heftier
heftiest
heifer *noun*
heifers
height *noun*
heights
heighten *verb*
heightens
heightening
heightened
✪ **heir** *noun*
heirs
heiress *noun*
heiresses
held see **hold**
helicopter *noun*
helicopters
helium
helix *noun*
helices
hell
he'll *verb*
hellish *adjective*
hellishly

★ You use **hear** in e.g. *I can't hear you.* ! **here**.
☆ You use **hove** in e.g. *the ship hove to.*
✪ You do not pronounce the 'h' in **heir** (sounds like *air*).

hello
helm *noun*
helms
helmsman *noun*
helmsmen
helmet *noun*
helmets
helmeted
help *verb*
helps
helping
helped
help *noun*
helps
helper *noun*
helpers
helpful *adjective*
helpfully
helping *noun*
helpings
helpless *adjective*
helplessly
helter-skelter *noun*
helter-skelters
hem *noun*
hems
hem *verb*
hems
hemming
hemmed
hemisphere *noun*
hemispheres
hemp
hence
henceforth
herald *noun*
heralds
herald *verb*
heralds
heralding
heralded
heraldic
heraldry
herb *noun*
herbs
herbal
herbivore *noun*
herbivores
herd *noun*
herds
★ **herd** *verb*
herds
herding
herded
☆ **here**
hereditary
heredity
heritage *noun*
heritages
hermit *noun*
hermits
hermitage
hero *noun*
heroes
heroic *adjective*
heroically
✪ **heroin** *noun*
✲ **heroine** *noun*
heroines
heroism
heron *noun*
herons
herring *noun*
herring
herrings
✸ **hers**
herself
he's *verb*
hesitant *adjective*
hesitantly
hesitate *verb*
hesitates
hesitating
hesitated
hesitation
hexagon *noun*
hexagons
hexagonal
hibernate *verb*
hibernates
hibernating
hibernated
hibernation
hiccup *noun*
hiccups
hide *verb*
hides
hiding
hidden
hid
hidden
hide-and-seek
hideous *adjective*
hideously
hideout *noun*
hideouts
hiding *noun*
hidings
hieroglyphics *plural noun*
hi-fi *noun*
hi-fis
higgledy-piggledy
high *adjective*
higher
highest
highland *adjective*
highlands *plural noun*

★ A **herd** is a group of sheep. ! **heard**.
☆ You use **here** in e.g. *come here*. ! **hear**.
✪ **Heroin** is a drug. ! **heroine**.
✲ A **heroine** is a woman or girl in a story. ! **heroin**.
✸ You use **hers** in e.g. *the book is hers*. Note that there is no apostrophe in this word.

highlander *noun*
highlanders
highlight *noun*
highlights
highlighter *noun*
highlighters
highly
Highness *noun*
Highnesses
high-rise
highway *noun*
highways
highwayman *noun*
highwaymen
hijack *verb*
hijacks
hijacking
hijacked
hijacker *noun*
hijackers
hike *verb*
hikes
hiking
hiked
hike *noun*
hikes
hiker *noun*
hikers
hilarious *adjective*
hilariously
hilarity
hill *noun*
hills
hillside *noun*
hillsides
hilly *adjective*
hillier
hilliest
hilt *noun*
hilts
himself
hind *adjective*
hind *noun*
hinds
hinder *verb*
hinders
hindering
hindered
Hindi
hindrance *noun*
hindrances
Hindu *noun*
Hindus
hinge *noun*
hinges
hinge *verb*
hinges
hinging
hinged
hint *noun*
hints
hint *verb*
hints
hinting
hinted
hip *noun*
hips
hippo *noun*
hippos
hippopotamus *noun*
hippopotamuses
hire *verb*
hires
hiring
hired
hiss *verb*
hisses
hissing
hissed
histogram *noun*
histograms
historian *noun*
historians
historic
historical *adjective*
historically
history *noun*
histories
hit *verb*
hits
hitting
hit
hit *noun*
hits
hitch *verb*
hitches
hitching
hitched
hitch *noun*
hitches
hitch-hike *verb*
hitch-hikes
hitch-hiking
hitch-hiked
hitch-hiker *noun*
hitch-hikers
hi-tech
hither
hitherto
hive *noun*
hives
hoard *verb*
hoards
hoarding
hoarded
★ **hoard** *noun*
hoards
hoarder *noun*
hoarders
hoarding *noun*
hoardings
hoar frost

★ A **hoard** is a secret store. ! **horde**.

★ **hoarse** *adjective*
hoarser
hoarsest
hoax *verb*
hoaxes
hoaxing
hoaxed
hoax *noun*
hoaxes
hobble *verb*
hobbles
hobbling
hobbled
hobby *noun*
hobbies
hockey
hoe *noun*
hoes
hoe *verb*
hoes
hoeing
hoed
hog *noun*
hogs
hog *verb*
hogs
hogging
hogged
Hogmanay
hoist *verb*
hoists
hoisting
hoisted
hold *verb*
holds
holding
held
hold *noun*
holds
holdall *noun*
holdalls
holder *noun*
holders
hold-up *noun*
hold-ups
☆ **hole** *noun*
holes
✪ **holey** *adjective*
✲ **Holi**
holiday *noun*
holidays
holiness
hollow *adjective* and *adverb*
hollow *verb*
hollows
hollowing
hollowed
hollow *noun*
hollows
holly
holocaust *noun*
holocausts
hologram *noun*
holograms
holster *noun*
holsters
✸ **holy** *adjective*
holier
holiest
home *noun*
homes
home *verb*
homes
homing
homed
homeless
homely
home-made
homesick
homesickness
homestead *noun*
homesteads
homeward *adjective*
homewards *adjective* and *adverb*
homework
homing
homosexual *adjective* and *noun*
homosexuals
honest *adjective*
honestly
honesty
honey *noun*
honeys
honeycomb *noun*
honeycombs
honeymoon *noun*
honeymoons
honeysuckle
honk *verb*
honks
honking
honked
honk *noun*
honks
honour *verb*
honours
honouring
honoured
honour *noun*
honours
honourable *adjective*
honourably
hood *noun*
hoods

-hood
-hood makes nouns, e.g. **childhood**. Other noun suffixes are **-dom**, **-ment**, **-ness**, and **-ship**.

★ A **hoarse** voice is rough or croaking. ! **horse**.
☆ A **hole** is a gap or opening. ! **whole**.
✪ **Holey** means 'full of holes'. ! **holy**.
✲ A Hindu festival.
✸ You use **holy** in e.g. *a holy man*. ! **holey**.

hooded
hoof *noun*
hoofs
hook *noun*
hooks
hook *verb*
hooks
hooking
hooked
hooligan *noun*
hooligans
hoop *noun*
hoops
hoopla
hooray
hoot *verb*
hoots
hooting
hooted
hoot *noun*
hoots
hooter *noun*
hooters
hop *verb*
hops
hopping
hopped
hop *noun*
hops
hope *verb*
hopes
hoping
hoped
hope *noun*
hopes
hopeful *adjective*
hopefully
hopeless *adjective*
hopelessly
hopscotch
★ **horde** *noun*
hordes
horizon *noun*
horizons
horizontal *adjective*
horizontally
hormone *noun*
hormones
horn *noun*
horns
hornet *noun*
hornets
horoscope *noun*
horoscopes
horrible *adjective*
horribly
horrid
horrific *adjective*
horrifically
horrify *verb*
horrifies
horrifying
horrified
horror *noun*
horrors
horse *noun*
horses
horseback
horseman *noun*
horsemen
horsemanship
horsepower *noun*
horsepower
horseshoe *noun*
horseshoes
horsewoman *noun*
horsewomen
horticulture
hose *noun*
hoses
hospitable *adjective*
hospitably
hospital *noun*
hospitals
hospitality
host *noun*
hosts
hostage *noun*
hostages
hostel *noun*
hostels
hostess *noun*
hostesses
hostile
hostility *noun*
hostilities
hot *adjective*
hotter
hottest
hotly
hot *verb*
hots
hotting
hotted
hotel *noun*
hotels
hothouse *noun*
hothouses
hotpot *noun*
hotpots
hound *noun*
hounds
hound *verb*
hounds
hounding
hounded
☆ **hour** *noun*
hours
hourglass *noun*
hourglasses

★ A **horde** is a large crowd. ! **hoard**.
☆ An **hour** is a measure of time. ! **our**.

hourly *adjective* and *adverb*
house *noun*
houses
house *verb*
houses
housing
housed
houseboat *noun*
houseboats
household *noun*
households
householder *noun*
householders
housekeeper *noun*
housekeepers
housekeeping
housewife *noun*
housewives
housework
housing *noun*
housings
hove see **heave**
hover *verb*
hovers
hovering
hovered
hovercraft *noun*
hovercraft
however
howl *verb*
howls
howling
howled
howl *noun*
howls
howler *noun*
howlers
hub *noun*
hubs
huddle *verb*
huddles
huddling
huddled
hue *noun*
hues
huff
hug *verb*
hugs
hugging
hugged
hug *noun*
hugs
huge *adjective*
huger
hugest
hugely
hugeness
hulk *noun*
hulks
hulking
hull *noun*
hulls
hullabaloo *noun*
hullabaloos
hullo
hum *verb*
hums
humming
hummed
hum *noun*
hums
human *adjective* and *noun*
humans
humane *adjective*
humanely
humanitarian
humanity *noun*
humanities
humble *adjective*
humbler
humblest
humbly
humid
humidity
humiliate *verb*
humiliates
humiliating
humiliated
humiliation
humility
hummingbird *noun*
hummingbirds
humorous *adjective*
humorously
humour *noun*
humour *verb*
humours
humouring
humoured
hump *noun*
humps
hump *verb*
humps
humping
humped
humpback
humus
hunch *verb*
hunches
hunching
hunched
hunch *noun*
hunches
hunchback *noun*
hunchbacks
hunchbacked
hundred *noun*
hundreds
hundredth

hundredweight *noun*
hundredweights
hung see **hang**
hunger
hungry *adjective*
hungrier
hungriest
hungrily
hunk *noun*
hunks
hunt *verb*
hunts
hunting
hunted
hunt *noun*
hunts
hunter *noun*
hunters
hurdle *noun*
hurdles
hurdler *noun*
hurdlers
hurdling
hurl *verb*
hurls
hurling
hurled
hurrah *or* **hurray**
hurricane *noun*
hurricanes
hurriedly
hurry *verb*
hurries
hurrying
hurried
hurry *noun*
hurries
hurt *verb*
hurts
hurting
hurt
hurt *noun*
hurtle *verb*
hurtles
hurtling
hurtled
husband *noun*
husbands
hush *verb*
hushes
hushing
hushed
hush *noun*
husk *noun*
husks
huskiness
husky *adjective*
huskier
huskiest
huskily
husky *noun*
huskies
hustle *verb*
hustles
hustling
hustled
hutch *noun*
hutches
hyacinth *noun*
hyacinths
hybrid *noun*
hybrids
hydrangea *noun*
hydrangeas
hydrant *noun*
hydrants
hydraulic *adjective*
hydraulically
hydroelectric
hydrofoil *noun*
hydrofoils
hydrogen
hydrophobia
hyena *noun*
hyenas
hygiene
hygienic *adjective*
hygienically
hymn *noun*
hymns
hyperactive
hypermarket *noun*
hypermarkets
hyphen *noun*
hyphens
hyphenated
hypnosis
hypnotism
hypnotist
hypnotize *verb*
hypnotizes
hypnotizing
hypnotized
hypocrisy
hypocrite *noun*
hypocrites
hypocritical *adjective*
hypocritically
hypodermic
hypotenuse *noun*
hypotenuses
hypothermia
hypothesis *noun*
hypotheses
hypothetical *adjective*
hypothetically
hysteria
hysterical *adjective*
hysterically
hysterics *plural noun*

Ii

-i
Most nouns ending in -*i*, e.g. **ski**, **taxi**, have plurals ending in -*is*, e.g. **skis**, **taxis**.

-ible
See the note at **-able**.

-ic and **-ically**
Most adjectives ending in -*ic* have adverbs ending in -*ically*, e.g. **heroic** - **heroically**, **scientific** - **scientifically**. An exception is **public**, which has an adverb - **publicly**.

ice *noun*
ices
ice *verb*
ices
icing
iced
iceberg *noun*
icebergs
ice cream *noun*
ice creams
icicle *noun*
icicles
icing
icon *noun*
icons
icy *adjective*
icier
iciest
icily
I'd *verb*
idea *noun*
ideas
ideal *adjective*
ideally
ideal *noun*
ideals
identical *adjective*
identically
identification
identify *verb*
identifies
identifying
identified
identity *noun*
identities
idiocy *noun*
idiocies
idiom *noun*
idioms
idiomatic
idiot *noun*
idiots
idiotic *adjective*
idiotically
★ **idle** *adjective*
idler
idlest
idly
idle *verb*
idles
idling
idled
☆ **idol** *noun*
idols
idolatry
idolize *verb*
idolizes
idolizing
idolized

-ie-
See the note at **-ei-**.

igloo *noun*
igloos
igneous
ignite *verb*
ignites
igniting
ignited
ignition
ignorance
ignorant
ignore *verb*
ignores
ignoring
ignored
I'll *verb*
ill
illegal *adjective*
illegally
illegible *adjective*
illegibly
illegitimate
illiteracy
illiterate
illness *noun*
illnesses
illogical *adjective*
illogically
illuminate *verb*
illuminates
illuminating
illuminated
illumination *noun*
illuminations
illusion *noun*
illusions

★ **Idle** means 'lazy'. ! **idol**.
☆ An **idol** is someone people admire. ! **idle**.

illustrate *verb*
illustrates
illustrating
illustrated
illustration *noun*
illustrations
illustrious
I'm *verb*
image *noun*
images
imagery
imaginable
imaginary
imagination *noun*
imaginations
imaginative *adjective*
imaginatively
imagine *verb*
imagines
imagining
imagined
★ **imam** *noun*
imams
imbecile *noun*
imbeciles
imitate *verb*
imitates
imitating
imitated
imitation *noun*
imitations
imitator *noun*
imitators
immature
immaturity
immediate *adjective*
immediately
immense *adjective*
immensely
immensity
immerse *verb*
immerses
immersing
immersed
immersion
immigrant *noun*
immigrants
immigrate *verb*
immigrates
immigrating
immigrated
immigration
immobile
immobility
immobilize *verb*
immobilizes
immobilizing
immobilized
immoral *adjective*
immorally
immorality
immortal
immortality
immune
immunity *noun*
immunities
immunization
immunize *verb*
immunizes
immunizing
immunized
imp *noun*
imps
impish
impact *noun*
impacts
impair *verb*
impairs
impairing
impaired
impale *verb*
impales
impaling
impaled
impartial *adjective*
impartially
impartiality
impassable
impatience
impatient *adjective*
impatiently
impede *verb*
impedes
impeding
impeded
imperative
imperceptible *adjective*
imperceptibly
imperfect *adjective*
imperfectly
imperfection *noun*
imperfections
imperial
impersonal *adjective*
impersonally
impersonate *verb*
impersonates
impersonating
impersonated
impersonation *noun*
impersonations
impersonator *noun*
impersonators
impertinence
impertinent *adjective*
impertinently

★ A Muslim religious leader.

implement *verb*
implements
implementing
implemented
implement *noun*
implements
implication *noun*
implications
implore *verb*
implores
imploring
implored
imply *verb*
implies
implying
implied
impolite *adjective*
impolitely
import *verb*
imports
importing
imported
import *noun*
imports
importance
important *adjective*
importantly
importer *noun*
importers
impose *verb*
imposes
imposing
imposed
imposition *noun*
impositions
impossibility
impossible *adjective*
impossibly
impostor *noun*
impostors
impracticable
impractical
impress *verb*
impresses
impressing
impressed
impression *noun*
impressions
impressive *adjective*
impressively
imprison *verb*
imprisons
imprisoning
imprisoned
imprisonment
improbability
improbable *adjective*
improbably
impromptu
improper *adjective*
improperly
impropriety *noun*
improprieties
improve *verb*
improves
improving
improved
improvement *noun*
improvements
improvisation *noun*
improvisations
improvise *verb*
improvises
improvising
improvised
impudence
impudent *adjective*
impudently
impulse *noun*
impulses
impulsive *adjective*
impulsively
impure
impurity *adjective*
impurities

in-
in- makes words with the meaning 'not', e.g. **inedible**, **infertile**. There is a fixed number of these, and you cannot freely add *in-* as you can with *un-*. *in-* changes to *il-* or *im-* before certain sounds, e.g. **illogical**, **impossible**.

inability
inaccessible
inaccuracy *noun*
inaccuracies
inaccurate *adjective*
inaccurately
inaction
inactive
inactivity
inadequacy
inadequate *adjective*
inadequately
inanimate
inappropriate *adjective*
inappropriately
inattention
inattentive
inaudible *adjective*
inaudibly
incapable
incapacity
incendiary
incense *noun*

incense *verb*
incenses
incensing
incensed
incentive *noun*
incentives
incessant *adjective*
incessantly
inch *noun*
inches
incident *noun*
incidents
incidental *adjective*
incidentally
incinerator *noun*
incinerators
inclination *noun*
inclinations
incline *verb*
inclines
inclining
inclined
incline *noun*
inclines
include *verb*
includes
including
included
inclusion
inclusive
income *noun*
incomes
incompatible
incompetence
incompetent *adjective*
incompetently
incomplete *adjective*
incompletely
incomprehensible *adjective*
incomprehensibly
incongruity
incongruous *adjective*
incongruously
inconsiderate *adjective*
inconsiderately
inconsistency *noun*
inconsistencies
inconsistent *adjective*
inconsistently
inconspicuous *adjective*
inconspicuously
inconvenience
inconvenient *adjective*
inconveniently
incorporate *verb*
incorporates
incorporating
incorporated
incorporation
incorrect *adjective*
incorrectly
increase *verb*
increases
increasing
increased
increase *noun*
increases
increasingly
incredible *adjective*
incredibly
incredulity
incredulous
incubate *verb*
incubates
incubating
incubated
incubation
incubator *noun*
incubators
indebted
indecency
indecent *adjective*
indecently
indeed
indefinite *adjective*
indefinitely
indelible *adjective*
indelibly
indent *verb*
indents
indenting
indented
indentation
independence
independent *adjective*
independently
index *noun*
indexes
Indian *adjective* and *noun*
Indians
indicate *verb*
indicates
indicating
indicated
indication *noun*
indications
indicative
indicator *noun*
indicators
indifference
indifferent *adjective*
indifferently
indigestible
indigestion

indignant *adjective*
indignantly
indignation
indigo
indirect *adjective*
indirectly
indispensable *adjective*
indispensably
indistinct *adjective*
indistinctly
indistinguishable
individual *adjective*
individually
individual *noun*
individuals
individuality
indoctrinate *verb*
indoctrinates
indoctrinating
indoctrinated
indoctrination
indoor *adjective*
indoors *adverb*
induce *verb*
induces
inducing
induced
inducement *noun*
inducements
indulge *verb*
indulges
indulging
indulged
indulgence *noun*
indulgences
indulgent
industrial
industrialist *noun*
industrialists
industrialization
industrialize *verb*
industrializes
industrializing
industrialized
industrious *adjective*
industriously
industry *noun*
industries
ineffective *adjective*
ineffectively
ineffectual *adjective*
ineffectually
inefficiency *noun*
inefficiencies
inefficient *adjective*
inefficiently
inequality *noun*
inequalities
inert
inertia
inevitability
inevitable *adjective*
inevitably
inexhaustible
inexpensive *adjective*
inexpensively
inexperience
inexperienced
inexplicable *adjective*
inexplicably
infallibility
infallible *adjective*
infallibly
infamous *adjective*
infamously
infamy
infancy
infant *noun*
infants
infantile
infantry
infect *verb*
infects
infecting
infected
infection *noun*
infections
infectious *adjective*
infectiously
infer *verb*
infers
inferring
inferred
inference *noun*
inferences
inferior *adjective* and *noun*
inferiors
inferiority
infernal *adjective*
infernally
inferno *noun*
infernos
infested
infiltrate *verb*
infiltrates
infiltrating
infiltrated
infiltration
infinite *adjective*
infinitely
infinitive *noun*
infinitives
infinity
infirm
infirmary *noun*
infirmaries
infirmity

inflame *verb*
inflames
inflaming
inflamed
inflammable
inflammation *noun*
inflammations
inflammatory
inflatable
inflate *verb*
inflates
inflating
inflated
inflation
inflect *verb*
inflects
inflecting
inflected
inflection *noun*
inflections
inflexibility
inflexible *adjective*
inflexibly
inflict *verb*
inflicts
inflicting
inflicted
influence *verb*
influences
influencing
influenced
influence *noun*
influences
influential *adjective*
influentially
influenza
inform *verb*
informs
informing
informed
informal *adjective*
informally
informality
informant *noun*
informants
information
informative
informed
informer *noun*
informers
infrequency
infrequent *adjective*
infrequently
infuriate *verb*
infuriates
infuriating
infuriated

-ing
-ing makes present participles and nouns, e.g. **hunt - hunting**. You normally drop an e at the end, e.g. **change - changing**, **smoke - smoking**. An exception is **ageing**. Words ending in a consonant following a single vowel double the consonant, e.g. **run - running**.

ingenious *adjective*
ingeniously
ingenuity
ingot *noun*
ingots
ingrained
ingredient *noun*
ingredients
inhabit *verb*
inhabits
inhabiting
inhabited
inhabitant *noun*
inhabitants
inhale *verb*
inhales
inhaling
inhaled
inhaler *noun*
inhalers
inherent *adjective*
inherently
inherit *verb*
inherits
inheriting
inherited
inheritance
inhibited
inhospitable *adjective*
inhospitably
inhuman
inhumanity
initial *adjective*
initially
initial *noun*
initials
initiate *verb*
initiates
initiating
initiated
initiation
initiative *noun*
initiatives
inject *verb*
injects
injecting
injected
injection *noun*
injections
injure *verb*
injures
injuring
injured

injurious *adjective*
injuriously
injury *noun*
injuries
injustice *noun*
injustices
ink *noun*
inks
inkling *noun*
inklings
inky *adjective*
inkier
inkiest
inland
inlet *noun*
inlets
inn *noun*
inns
innkeeper *noun*
innkeepers
inner
innermost
innings *noun*
innings
innocence
innocent *adjective*
innocently
innocuous *adjective*
innocuously
innovation *noun*
innovations
innovative
innovator *noun*
innovators
innumerable
inoculate *verb*
inoculates
inoculating
inoculated
inoculation
input *verb*
inputs
inputting
input
input *noun*
inputs
inquest *noun*
inquests
inquire *verb*
inquires
inquiring
inquired
★ **inquiry** *noun*
inquiries
inquisitive *adjective*
inquisitively
insane *adjective*
insanely
insanitary
insanity
inscribe *verb*
inscribes
inscribing
inscribed
inscription *noun*
inscriptions
insect *noun*
insects
insecticide *noun*
insecticides
insecure *adjective*
insecurely
insecurity
insensitive *adjective*
insensitively
insensitivity
inseparable *adjective*
inseparably
insert *verb*
inserts
inserting
inserted
insertion *noun*
insertions
inshore *adjective* and *adverb*
inside *noun*
insides
inside *adverb, adjective,* and *preposition*
insight *noun*
insights
insignificance
insignificant *adjective*
insignificantly
insincere *adjective*
insincerely
insincerity
insist *verb*
insists
insisting
insisted
insistence
insistent *adjective*
insistently
insolence
insolent *adjective*
insolently
insolubility
insoluble *adjective*
insolubly
insomnia
inspect *verb*
inspects
inspecting
inspected

★ An **inquiry** is an official investigation. ! **enquiry**.

inspection *noun*
inspections
inspector *noun*
inspectors
inspiration
inspire *verb*
inspires
inspiring
inspired
install *verb*
installs
installing
installed
installation *noun*
installations
instalment *noun*
instalments
instance *noun*
instances
instant *adjective*
instantly
instant *noun*
instants
instantaneous *adjective*
instantaneously
instead
instep *noun*
insteps
instinct *noun*
instincts
instinctive *adjective*
instinctively
institute *verb*
institutes
instituting
instituted
institute *noun*
institutes
institution *noun*
institutions
instruct *verb*
instructs
instructing
instructed
instruction *noun*
instructions
instrument *noun*
instruments
instrumental
insufficient *adjective*
insufficiently
insulate *verb*
insulates
insulating
insulated
insulation
insulin
insult *verb*
insults
insulting
insulted
insult *noun*
insults
insurance
insure *verb*
insures
insuring
insured
intact
intake *noun*
intakes
integer *noun*
integers
integral *adjective*
integrally
integrate *verb*
integrates
integrating
integrated
integration
integrity
intellect *noun*
intellects
intellectual *adjective*
intellectually
intellectual *noun*
intellectuals
intelligence
intelligent *adjective*
intelligently
intelligibility
intelligible *adjective*
intelligibly
intend *verb*
intends
intending
intended
intense *adjective*
intensely
intensification
intensify *verb*
intensifies
intensifying
intensified
intensity *noun*
intensities
intensive *adjective*
intensively
intent *adjective*
intently
intent *noun*
intents
intention *noun*
intentions
intentional *adjective*
intentionally
interact *verb*
interacts
interacting
interacted
interaction

interactive
intercept *verb*
intercepts
intercepting
intercepted
interception
interchange *noun*
interchanges
interchangeable *adjective*
interchangeably
intercom *noun*
intercoms
intercourse
interest *verb*
interests
interesting
interested
interest *noun*
interests
interface *noun*
interfaces
interfere *verb*
interferes
interfering
interfered
interference
interior *noun*
interiors
interjection *noun*
interjections
interlock *verb*
interlocks
interlocking
interlocked
interlude *noun*
interludes
intermediate
interminable *adjective*
interminably
intermission *noun*
intermissions
intermittent *adjective*
intermittently
intern *verb*
interns
interning
interned
internal *adjective*
internally
international *adjective*
internationally
internee
internment
internet
interplanetary
interpret *verb*
interprets
interpreting
interpreted
interpretation *noun*
interpretations
interpreter *noun*
interpreters
interrogate *verb*
interrogates
interrogating
interrogated
interrogation
interrogative
interrogator *noun*
interrogators
interrupt *verb*
interrupts
interrupting
interrupted
interruption *noun*
interruptions
intersect *verb*
intersects
intersecting
intersected
intersection *noun*
intersections
interval *noun*
intervals
intervene *verb*
intervenes
intervening
intervened
intervention *noun*
interventions
interview *noun*
interviews
interview *verb*
interviews
interviewing
interviewed
interviewer *noun*
interviewers
intestinal
intestine
intimacy
intimate *adjective*
intimately
intimate *verb*
intimates
intimating
intimated
intimation *noun*
intimations
intimidate *verb*
intimidates
intimidating
intimidated
intimidation
into *preposition*
intolerable *adjective*
intolerably

intolerance
intolerant *adjective*
intolerantly
intonation *noun*
intonations
intoxicate *verb*
intoxicates
intoxicating
intoxicated
intoxication
intransitive
intrepid *adjective*
intrepidly
intricacy *noun*
intricacies
intricate *adjective*
intricately
intrigue *verb*
intrigues
intriguing
intrigued
introduce *verb*
introduces
introducing
introduced
introduction *noun*
introductions
introductory
intrude *verb*
intrudes
intruding
intruded
intruder *noun*
intruders
intrusion *noun*
intrusions
intrusive *adjective*
intrusively
intuition
intuitive *adjective*
intuitively
Inuit *noun*
Inuit *or* Inuits
inundate *verb*
inundates
inundating
inundated
inundation *noun*
inundations
invade *verb*
invades
invading
invaded
invader *noun*
invaders
invalid *noun*
invalids
invalid *adjective*
invalidly
invaluable
invariable *adjective*
invariably
invasion *noun*
invasions
invent *verb*
invents
inventing
invented
invention *noun*
inventions
inventive *adjective*
inventively
inventor *noun*
inventors
inverse *noun* and *adjective*
inversely
inversion *noun*
inversions
invert *verb*
inverts
inverting
inverted
invertebrate *noun*
invertebrates
invest *verb*
invests
investing
invested
investigate *verb*
investigates
investigating
investigated
investigation *noun*
investigations
investigator *noun*
investigators
investiture *noun*
investitures
investment *noun*
investments
investor *noun*
investors
invigilate *verb*
invigilates
invigilating
invigilated
invigilation
invigilator *noun*
invigilators
invigorate *verb*
invigorates
invigorating
invigorated
invincible
invisibility
invisible *adjective*
invisibly
invitation *noun*
invitations
invite *verb*
invites
inviting
invited

invoice *noun*
invoices
involuntary
involve *verb*
involves
involving
involved
involvement
inward *adjective*
inwardly
inwards *adverb*
iodine
ion *noun*
ions
iris *noun*
irises
iron *noun*
irons
iron *verb*
irons
ironing
ironed
ironic *adjective*
ironically
ironmonger *noun*
ironmongers
ironmongery
irony *noun*
ironies
irrational *adjective*
irrationally
irregular *adjective*
irregularly
irregularity *noun*
irregularities
irrelevance
irrelevant *adjective*
irrelevantly
irresistible *adjective*
irresistibly
irresponsible *adjective*
irresponsibly
irresponsibility
irreverence
irreverent *adjective*
irreverently
irrigate *verb*
irrigates
irrigating
irrigated
irrigation
irritability
irritable *adjective*
irritably
irritant
irritate *verb*
irritates
irritating
irritated
irritation *noun*
irritations

-ish
-ish makes words meaning 'rather' or 'fairly', e.g. **soft - softish.** You normally drop an e at the end, e.g. **blue - bluish.** Words ending in a consonant following a single vowel double the consonant, e.g. **fat - fattish.**

Islam
Islamic
island *noun*
islands
islander *noun*
islanders
★ **isle** *noun*
isles
isn't *verb*
isobar *noun*
isobars
isolate *verb*
isolates
isolating
isolated
isolation
isosceles *adjective*
isotope *noun*
isotopes
issue *verb*
issues
issuing
issued
issue *noun*
issues
isthmus *noun*
isthmuses
italics
itch *verb*
itches
itching
itched
itch *noun*
itches
itchy *adjective*
itchier
itchiest
item *noun*
items
itinerary *noun*
itineraries
it'll *verb*
☆ **its**
✪ **it's** *verb*
itself

★ An **isle** is a small island. ! **aisle**.
☆ You use **its** in e.g. *the cat licked its paw*. ! **it's**.
✪ You use **it's** in *it's* (= it is) *raining* and *it's* (= it has) *been raining*. ! **its**.

I've *verb*
ivory *adjective* and *noun*
ivories
ivy

-ize and -ise
You can use *-ize* or *-ise* at the end of many verbs, e.g. **realize** or **realise**, **privatize** or **privatise**. This book prefers *-ize*, but some words have to be spelt *-ise*, e.g. **advertise**, **exercise**, **supervise**. Check each spelling if you are not sure.

Jj

jab *verb*
jabs
jabbing
jabbed
jab *noun*
jabs
jabber *verb*
jabbers
jabbering
jabbered
jack *noun*
jacks
jack *verb*
jacks
jacking
jacked
jackal *noun*
jackals
jackass *noun*
jackasses
jackdaw *noun*
jackdaws
jacket *noun*
jackets
jack-in-the-box *noun*
jack-in-the-boxes
jackknife *verb*
jackknifes
jackknifing
jackknifed
jackpot *noun*
jackpots
jacuzzi *noun*
jacuzzis
jade
jaded
jagged
jaguar *noun*
jaguars
jail *noun*
jails
jail *verb*
jails
jailing
jailed
jailer *noun*
jailers
★ **Jain** *noun*
Jains
jam *noun*
jams
jam *verb*
jams
jamming
jammed
jamboree *noun*
jamborees
jammy *adjective*
jammier
jammiest
jangle *verb*
jangles
jangling
jangled
January *noun*
Januaries
jar *noun*
jars
jar *verb*
jars
jarring
jarred
jaundice
jaunt *noun*
jaunts
jauntiness
jaunty *adjective*
jauntier
jauntiest
jauntily
javelin *noun*
javelins
jaw *noun*
jaws
jay *noun*
jays
jazz
jazzy *adjective*
jazzier
jazziest
jealous *adjective*
jealously
jealousy
jeans
Jeep *noun*
Jeeps

★ A member of an Indian religion.

jeer *verb*
jeers
jeering
jeered
jellied
jelly *noun*
jellies
jellyfish *noun*
jellyfish
jerk *verb*
jerks
jerking
jerked
jerk *noun*
jerks
jerky *adjective*
jerkier
jerkiest
jerkily
jersey *noun*
jerseys
jest *verb*
jests
jesting
jested
jest *noun*
jests
jester *noun*
jesters
jet *noun*
jets
jet *verb*
jets
jetting
jetted
jet-propelled
jetty *noun*
jetties
Jew *noun*
Jews
jewel *noun*
jewels
jewelled
jeweller *noun*
jewellers
jewellery
Jewish
jib *noun*
jibs
jiffy *noun*
jiffies
jig *noun*
jigs
jig *verb*
jigs
jigging
jigged
jigsaw *noun*
jigsaws
jingle *verb*
jingles
jingling
jingled
jingle *noun*
jingles
job *noun*
jobs
jobcentre *noun*
jobcentres
jockey *noun*
jockeys
jodhpurs *plural noun*
jog *verb*
jogs
jogging
jogged
jogger *noun*
joggers
jogtrot *noun*
jogtrots
join *verb*
joins
joining
joined
join *noun*
joins
joiner *noun*
joiners
joinery
joint *noun*
joints
joint *adjective*
jointly
joist *noun*
joists
jojoba
joke *verb*
jokes
joking
joked
joke *noun*
jokes
joker *noun*
jokers
jollity
jolly *adjective*
jollier
jolliest
jolly *adverb*
jolly *verb*
jollies
jollying
jollied
jolt *verb*
jolts
jolting
jolted
jolt *noun*
jolts

jostle *verb*
jostles
jostling
jostled
jot *verb*
jots
jotting
jotted
jot *noun*
jots
jotter *noun*
jotters
joule *noun*
joules
journal *noun*
journals
journalism
journalist *noun*
journalists
journey *noun*
journeys
journey *verb*
journeys
journeying
journeyed
joust *verb*
jousts
jousting
jousted
jovial *adjective*
jovially
joviality
joy *noun*
joys
joyful *adjective*
joyfully
joyous *adjective*
joyously
joyride *noun*
joyrides
joystick *noun*
joysticks
jubilant *adjective*
jubilantly
jubilation
jubilee *noun*
jubilees
Judaism
judge *verb*
judges
judging
judged
judge *noun*
judges
judgement *noun*
judgements
judicial *adjective*
judicially
judicious *adjective*
judiciously
judo
jug *noun*
jugs
juggernaut *noun*
juggernauts
juggle *verb*
juggles
juggling
juggled
juggler *noun*
jugglers
★ **juice** *noun*
juices
juicy *adjective*
juicier
juiciest
jukebox *noun*
jukeboxes
July *noun*
Julys
jumble *verb*
jumbles
jumbling
jumbled
jumble *noun*
jumbo jet *noun*
jumbo jets
jump *verb*
jumps
jumping
jumped
jump *noun*
jumps
jumper *noun*
jumpers
jumpy *adjective*
jumpier
jumpiest
junction *noun*
junctions
June *noun*
Junes
jungle *noun*
jungles
jungly *adjective*
junglier
jungliest
junior *adjective* and *noun*
juniors
junk *noun*
junks
junket *noun*
junkets
juror *noun*
jurors
jury *noun*
juries
just *adjective*
justly

★ **Juice** is the liquid from fruit. ! **deuce**.

just *adverb*
justice *noun*
justices
justifiable *adjective*
justifiably
justification
justify *verb*
justifies
justifying
justified
jut *verb*
juts
jutting
jutted
juvenile

Kk

kaleidoscope *noun*
kaleidoscopes
kangaroo *noun*
kangaroos
karaoke
karate
kayak *noun*
kayaks
kebab *noun*
kebabs
keel *noun*
keels
keel *verb*
keels
keeling
keeled
keen *adjective*
keener
keenest
keenly
keenness
keep *verb*
keeps
keeping
kept
keep *noun*
keeps
keeper *noun*
keepers
keg *noun*
kegs
kennel *noun*
kennels
kept see **keep**
★ **kerb** *noun*
kerbs
kerbstone *noun*
kerbstones
☆ **kernel** *noun*
kernels
kestrel *noun*
kestrels
ketchup
kettle *noun*
kettles
kettledrum *noun*
kettledrums
✪ **key** *noun*
keys
keyboard *noun*
keyboards
keyhole *noun*
keyholes
keynote *noun*
keynotes
khaki
kibbutz *noun*
kibbutzim
kick *verb*
kicks
kicking
kicked
kick *noun*
kicks
kick-off *noun*
kick-offs
kid *noun*
kids
kid *verb*
kids
kidding
kidded
kidnap *verb*
kidnaps
kidnapping
kidnapped
kidnapper *noun*
kidnappers
kidney *noun*
kidneys
kill *verb*
kills
killing
killed
killer *noun*
killers
kiln *noun*
kilns
kilo *noun*
kilos
kilogram *noun*
kilograms
kilometre *noun*
kilometres
kilowatt *noun*
kilowatts
kilt *noun*
kilts
kin

★ A **kerb** is the edge of a pavement. ! **curb**.
☆ **Kernel** is part of a nut. ! **colonel**.
✪ A **key** is a device for opening a lock. ! **quay**.

kind *adjective*
kinder
kindest
kindly
kind *noun*
kinds
kindergarten *noun*
kindergartens
kind-hearted
kindle *verb*
kindles
kindling
kindled
kindliness
kindling
kindly *adjective*
kindlier
kindliest
kindness
kinetic
king *noun*
kings
kingdom *noun*
kingdoms
kingfisher *noun*
kingfishers
kingly
kink *noun*
kinks
kinky *adjective*
kinkier
kinkiest
kiosk *noun*
kiosks
kipper *noun*
kippers
kiss *verb*
kisses
kissing
kissed
kiss *noun*
kisses
kit *noun*
kits
kitchen *noun*
kitchens
kite *noun*
kites
kitten *noun*
kittens
kitty *noun*
kitties
kiwi *noun*
kiwis
knack
knapsack *noun*
knapsacks
knave *noun*
knaves
★ **knead** *verb*
kneads
kneading
kneaded
knee *noun*
knees
kneecap *noun*
kneecaps
kneel *verb*
kneels
kneeling
knelt
☆ **knew** see **know**
knickers *plural noun*
knife *noun*
knives
knife *verb*
knifes
knifing
knifed
✪ **knight** *noun*
knights
knight *verb*
knights
knighting
knighted
knighthood *noun*
knighthoods
knit *verb*
knits
knitting
knitted
knives see **knife**
knob *noun*
knobs
knobbly *adjective*
knobblier
knobbliest
knock *verb*
knocks
knocking
knocked
knock *noun*
knocks
knocker *noun*
knockers
knockout *noun*
knockouts
knot *noun*
knots
knot *verb*
knots
knotting
knotted
knotty *adjective*
knottier
knottiest
know *verb*
knows
knowing
knew
known

★ To **knead** is to work a mixture into a dough. ! **need**.
☆ **Knew** is the past tense of know. ! **new**.
✪ A **knight** is a soldier in old times. ! **night**.

know-all *noun*
know-alls
know-how
knowing *adjective*
knowingly
knowledge
knowledgeable *adjective*
knowledgeably
knuckle *noun*
knuckles
koala *noun*
koalas
kookaburra *noun*
kookaburras
Koran
kosher
kung fu

Ll

label *noun*
labels
label *verb*
labels
labelling
labelled
laboratory *noun*
laboratories
laborious *adjective*
laboriously
labour *noun*
labours
labourer *noun*
labourers
Labrador *noun*
Labradors
laburnum *noun*
laburnums
labyrinth *noun*
labyrinths
lace *noun*
laces
lace *verb*
laces
lacing
laced
lack *verb*
lacks
lacking
lacked
lack *noun*
lacquer
lacrosse
lad *noun*
lads
ladder *noun*
ladders
laden
ladle *noun*
ladles
lady *noun*
ladies
ladybird *noun*
ladybirds
ladylike
ladyship *noun*
ladyships
lag *verb*
lags
lagging
lagged
lager *noun*
lagers
lagoon *noun*
lagoons
laid see **lay**
lain see **lie**
lair *noun*
lairs
lake *noun*
lakes
lama *noun*
lamas
lamb *noun*
lambs
lame *adjective*
lamer
lamest
lamely
lameness
lament *verb*
laments
lamenting
lamented
lament *noun*
laments
lamentation *noun*
lamentations
laminated
lamp *noun*
lamps
lamp-post *noun*
lamp-posts
lampshade *noun*
lampshades
lance *noun*
lances
lance corporal *noun*
lance corporals
land *noun*
lands
land *verb*
lands
landing
landed

landing *noun*
landings
landlady *noun*
landladies
landlord *noun*
landlords
landmark *noun*
landmarks
landowner *noun*
landowners
landscape *noun*
landscapes
landslide *noun*
landslides
lane *noun*
lanes
language *noun*
languages
lankiness
lanky *adjective*
lankier
lankiest
lantern *noun*
lanterns
lap *verb*
laps
lapping
lapped
lap *noun*
laps
lapel *noun*
lapels
lapse *verb*
lapses
lapsing
lapsed
lapse *noun*
lapses
laptop *noun*
laptops
lapwing *noun*
lapwings
larch *noun*
larches
lard
larder *noun*
larders
large *adjective*
larger
largest
largely
largeness
lark *noun*
larks
lark *verb*
larks
larking
larked
larva *noun*
larvae
lasagne *noun*
lasagnes
laser *noun*
lasers
lash *verb*
lashes
lashing
lashed
lash *noun*
lashes
lass *noun*
lasses
lasso *noun*
lassos
lasso *verb*
lassoes
lassoing
lassoed
last *adjective* and *adverb*
lastly
last *verb*
lasts
lasting
lasted
last *noun*
latch *noun*
latches
late *adjective* and *adverb*
later
latest
lately
lateness
latent
lateral *adjective*
laterally
lathe *noun*
lathes
lather *noun*
lathers
Latin
latitude *noun*
latitudes
latter *adjective*
latterly
lattice *noun*
lattices
laugh *verb*
laughs
laughing
laughed
laugh *noun*
laughs
laughable *adjective*
laughably
laughter
launch *verb*
launches
launching
launched

launch *noun*
launches
launder *verb*
launders
laundering
laundered
launderette *noun*
launderettes
laundry *noun*
laundries
laurel *noun*
laurels
lava
lavatory *noun*
lavatories
lavender
lavish *adjective*
lavishly
law *noun*
laws
lawcourt *noun*
lawcourts
lawful *adjective*
lawfully
lawless *adjective*
lawlessly
lawn *noun*
lawns
lawnmower *noun*
lawnmowers
lawsuit *noun*
lawsuits
lawyer *noun*
lawyers
lax *adjective*
laxly
laxative *noun*
laxatives
lay *verb*
lays
laying
laid
lay see **lie**
layabout *noun*
layabouts
layer *noun*
layers
layman *noun*
laymen
layout *noun*
layouts
laze *verb*
lazes
lazing
lazed
laziness
lazy *adjective*
lazier
laziest
lazily
lead *verb*
leads
leading
led
★ **lead** *noun*
leads
leader *noun*
leaders
leadership
leaf *noun*
leaves
leaflet *noun*
leaflets
leafy *adjective*
leafier
leafiest
league *noun*
leagues
leak *verb*
leaks
leaking
leaked
☆ **leak** *noun*
leaks
leakage *noun*
leakages
leaky *adjective*
leakier
leakiest
lean *verb*
leans
leaning
leaned *or* leant
lean *adjective*
leaner
leanest
leap *verb*
leaps
leaping
leapt
leaped
leap *noun*
leaps
leapfrog
leap year *noun*
leap years
learn *verb*
learns
learning
learnt *or* learned
✪ **learned** *adjective*
learner *noun*
learners
lease *noun*
leases
leash *noun*
leashes
least *adjective* and *noun*
leather *noun*
leathers

★ A **lead** (pronounced *leed*) is a cord for leading a dog. **Lead** (pronounced *led*) is a metal.
☆ A **leak** is a hole or crack that liquid or gas can get through. ! **leek**
✪ Pronounced *ler-nid*.

leathery
leave *verb*
leaves
leaving
left
leave *noun*
leaves see **leaf**
lectern *noun*
lecterns
lecture *verb*
lectures
lecturing
lectured
lecture *noun*
lectures
lecturer *noun*
lecturers
led see **lead**
ledge *noun*
ledges
lee
★ **leek** *noun*
leeks
leer *verb*
leers
leering
leered
leeward
left *adjective* and *noun*
left see **leave**
left-handed
leftovers *plural noun*
leg *noun*
legs
legacy *noun*
legacies
legal *adjective*
legally
legality
legalize *verb*
legalizes
legalizing
legalized
legend *noun*
legends
legendary
legibility
legible *adjective*
legibly
legion *noun*
legions
legislate *verb*
legislates
legislating
legislated
legislation
legislator *noun*
legislators
legitimacy
legitimate *adjective*
legitimately
leisure
leisurely
lemon *noun*
lemons
lemonade *noun*
lemonades
lend *verb*
lends
lending
lent
length *noun*
lengths
lengthen *verb*
lengthens
lengthening
lengthened
lengthways *adverb*
lengthwise *adverb*
lengthy *adjective*
lengthier
lengthiest
lengthily
lenience
lenient *adjective*
leniently
lens *noun*
lenses
☆ **Lent**
lent see **lend**
lentil *noun*
lentils
leopard *noun*
leopards
leotard *noun*
leotards
leper *noun*
lepers
leprosy
less
✪ **lessen** *verb*
lessens
lessening
lessened
lesser
✲ **lesson** *noun*
lessons
lest *conjunction*
let *verb*
lets
letting
let

★ A **leek** is a vegetable. ! **leak**.
☆ **Lent** is the Christian time of fasting. ! **lent**.
✪ To **lessen** something is to make it less. **lesson**.
✲ A **lesson** is a period of learning. ! **lessen**.

-let
-let makes nouns meaning 'a small version of', e.g. **booklet**, **piglet**. It also makes words for pieces of jewellery, e.g. **anklet** (worn on the ankle), **bracelet** (from a French word *bras* meaning 'arm')

lethal *adjective*
lethally
let's *verb*
letter *noun*
letters
letter box *noun*
letter boxes
lettering
lettuce *noun*
lettuces
leukaemia
level *verb*
levels
levelling
levelled
level *adjective* and *noun*
levels
lever *noun*
levers
leverage
liability *noun*
liabilities
liable
liar *noun*
liars
liberal *adjective*
liberally
liberate *verb*
liberates
liberating
liberated
liberation
liberty *noun*
liberties
librarian *noun*
librarians
librarianship
library *noun*
libraries
licence *noun*
licences
license *verb*
licenses
licensing
licensed
lichen *noun*
lichens
lick *verb*
licks
licking
licked
lick *noun*
licks
lid *noun*
lids
★ **lie** *verb*
lies
lying
lay
lain
☆ **lie** *verb*
lies
lying
lied
lie *noun*
lies
lieutenant *noun*
lieutenants
life *noun*
lives
lifebelt *noun*
lifebelts
lifeboat *noun*
lifeboats
life cycle *noun*
life cycles
lifeguard *noun*
lifeguards
lifeless *adjective*
lifelessly
lifelike
lifelong
lifestyle *noun*
lifestyles
lifetime *noun*
lifetimes
lift *verb*
lifts
lifting
lifted
lift *noun*
lifts
lift-off *noun*
lift-offs
light *adjective*
lighter
lightest
lightly
light *verb*
lights
lighting
lit *or* lighted
light *noun*
lights
lighten *verb*
lightens
lightening
lightened

★ As in *to lie on the bed.*
☆ Meaning 'to say something untrue'.

lighter *noun*
lighters
lighthouse *noun*
lighthouses
lighting
lightning
lightweight
like *verb*
likes
liking
liked
like *preposition*
likeable
likely *adjective*
likelier
likeliest
liken *verb*
likens
likening
likened
likeness *noun*
likenesses
likewise
liking *noun*
likings
lilac *noun*
lilacs
lily *noun*
lilies
limb *noun*
limbs
limber *verb*
limbers
limbering
limbered
lime *noun*
limes
limelight
limerick *noun*
limericks
limestone
limit *noun*
limits
limit *verb*
limits
limiting
limited
limitation *noun*
limitations
limited
limitless
limp *adjective*
limper
limpest
limply
limp *verb*
limps
limping
limped
limp *noun*
limps
limpet *noun*
limpets
line *noun*
lines
line *verb*
lines
lining
lined
linen
liner *noun*
liners
linesman *noun*
linesmen

-ling
-ling makes words for small things, e.g. **duckling**.

linger *verb*
lingers
lingering
lingered
lingerie
linguist *noun*
linguists
linguistic
linguistics
lining *noun*
linings
link *verb*
links
linking
linked
link *noun*
links
lino
linoleum
lint
lion *noun*
lions
lioness *noun*
lionesses
lip *noun*
lips
lip-read *verb*
lip-reads
lip-reading
lip-read
lipstick *noun*
lipsticks
liquid *adjective* and *noun*
liquids
liquidizer *noun*
liquidizers
liquor *noun*
liquors

liquorice
lisp *noun*
lisps
lisp *verb*
lisps
lisping
lisped
list *noun*
lists
list *verb*
lists
listing
listed
listen *verb*
listens
listening
listened
listener *noun*
listeners
listless *adjective*
listlessly
lit see **light**
literacy
literal *adjective*
literally
literary
literate
literature
litmus
litre *noun*
litres
litter *noun*
litters
litter *verb*
litters
littering
littered
★ **little** *adjective* and *adverb*
less
least
live *verb*
lives
living
lived
live *adjective*
livelihood *noun*
livelihoods
liveliness
lively *adjective*
livelier
liveliest
liver *noun*
livers
livery *noun*
liveries
lives see **life**
livestock
livid
living *noun*
livings
lizard *noun*
lizards
llama *noun*
llamas
load *verb*
loads
loading
loaded
load *noun*
loads
loaf *noun*
loaves
loaf *verb*
loafs
loafing
loafed
loafer *noun*
loafers
loam
loamy *adjective*
loamier
loamiest
☆ **loan** *noun*
loans
loan *verb*
loans
loaning
loaned
✪ **loath** *adjective*
✲ **loathe** *verb*
loathes
loathing
loathed
loathsome
loaves see **loaf**
lob *verb*
lobs
lobbing
lobbed
lobby *noun*
lobbies
lobby *verb*
lobbies
lobbying
lobbied
lobe *noun*
lobes
lobster *noun*
lobsters
local *adjective*
locally
local *noun*
locals
locality *noun*
localities
locate *verb*
locates
locating
located

★ You can also use **littler** and **littlest** when you are talking about size.
☆ A **loan** is a thing that is lent to someone. ! **lone**.
✪ **Loath** means 'unwilling'. ! **loathe**.
✲ To **loathe** is to dislike very much. ! **loath**.

location *noun*
locations
★ **loch** *noun*
lochs
☆ **lock** *noun*
locks
lock *verb*
locks
locking
locked
locker *noun*
lockers
locket *noun*
lockets
locomotive *noun*
locomotives
locust *noun*
locusts
lodge *noun*
lodges
lodge *verb*
lodges
lodging
lodged
lodger *noun*
lodgers
lodgings *plural noun*
loft *noun*
lofts
lofty *adjective*
loftier
loftiest
loftily
log *noun*
logs
log *verb*
logs
logging
logged
logarithm *noun*
logarithms
logbook *noun*
logbooks
logic
logical *adjective*
logically
logo *noun*
logos

-logy
-logy makes words for subjects of study, e.g. **archaeology** (= the study of ancient remains). Most of these words end in *-ology*, but an important exception is **genealogy**. Some words have plurals, e.g. **genealogies**.

loiter *verb*
loiters
loitering
loitered
loiterer *noun*
loiterers
loll *verb*
lolls
lolling
lolled
lollipop *noun*
lollipops
lolly *noun*
lollies
✪ **lone**
loneliness
lonely *adjective*
lonelier
loneliest
long *adjective* and *adverb*
longer
longest
long *verb*
longs
longing
longed
longitude *noun*
longitudes
longitudinal *adjective*
longitudinally
loo *noun*
loos
look *verb*
looks
looking
looked
look *noun*
looks
lookout *noun*
lookouts
loom *noun*
looms
loom *verb*
looms
looming
loomed
loop *noun*
loops
loop *verb*
loops
looping
looped
loophole *noun*
loopholes
loose *adjective*
looser
loosest
loosely
loose *verb*
looses
loosing
loosed

★ A **loch** is a lake in Scotland. ! **lock**.
☆ A **lock** is a mechanism for keeping something closed. ! **loch**.
✪ **Lone** means 'alone'. ! **loan**.

loosen *verb*
loosens
loosening
loosened
looseness
loot *verb*
loots
looting
looted
loot *noun*
looter *noun*
looters
lopsided
lord *noun*
lords
lordly
lordship
lorry *noun*
lorries
lose *verb*
loses
losing
lost
loser *noun*
losers
loss *noun*
losses
lot *noun*
lots
lotion *noun*
lotions
lottery *noun*
lotteries
lotto
loud *adjective*
louder
loudest
loudly
loudness
loudspeaker *noun*
loudspeakers
lounge *noun*
lounges
lounge *verb*
lounges
lounging
lounged
louse *noun*
lice
lousy *adjective*
lousier
lousiest
lousily
lout *noun*
louts
lovable *adjective*
lovably
love *verb*
loves
loving
loved
love *noun*
loves
loveliness
lovely *adjective*
lovelier
loveliest
lover *noun*
lovers
loving *adjective*
lovingly
low *adjective*
lower
lowest
low *verb*
lows
lowing
lowed
lower *verb*
lowers
lowering
lowered
lowland *adjective*
lowlands *plural nouns*
lowlander *noun*
lowlanders
lowliness
lowly *adjective*
lowlier
lowliest
lowness
loyal *adjective*
loyally
loyalty *noun*
loyalties
lozenge *noun*
lozenges
lubricant *noun*
lubricants
lubricate *verb*
lubricates
lubricating
lubricated
lubrication
lucid *adjective*
lucidly
lucidity
luck
lucky *adjective*
luckier
luckiest
luckily
ludicrous *adjective*
ludicrously
ludo

lug *verb*
lugs
lugging
lugged
luggage
lukewarm
lull *verb*
lulls
lulling
lulled
lull *noun*
lulls
lullaby *noun*
lullabies
lumber *verb*
lumbers
lumbering
lumbered
lumber *noun*
lumberjack *noun*
lumberjacks
luminosity
luminous
lump *noun*
lumps
lump *verb*
lumps
lumping
lumped
lumpy *adjective*
lumpier
lumpiest
lunacy *noun*
lunacies
lunar
lunatic *noun*
lunatics
lunch *noun*
lunches
lung *noun*
lungs
lunge *verb*
lunges
lunging *or* lungeing
lunged
lupin *noun*
lupins
lurch *verb*
lurches
lurching
lurched
lurch *noun*
lurches
lure *verb*
lures
luring
lured
lurk *verb*
lurks
lurking
lurked
luscious *adjective*
lusciously
lush *adjective*
lusher
lushest
lushly
lushness
lust *noun*
lusts
lustful *adjective*
lustfully
lustre *noun*
lustres
lustrous
lute *noun*
lutes
luxury *noun*
luxuries
luxurious *adjective*
luxuriously
Lycra

-ly
-ly makes adverbs from adjectives, e.g. **slow - slowly**. When the adjective ends in *-y* following a consonant, you change the *y* to *i*, e.g. **happy - happily**. *-ly* is also used to make some adjectives, e.g. **lovely**, and some words that are adjectives and adverbs, e.g. **kindly**, **hourly**.

lying see **lie**
lynch *verb*
lynches
lynching
lynched
lyre *noun*
lyres
lyric *noun*
lyrics
lyrical *adjective*
lyrically
lyrics *plural noun*

Mm

ma *noun*
mas
mac *noun*
macs
macabre
macaroni
machine *noun*
machines

machinery
mackerel *noun*
mackerel
mackintosh *noun*
mackintoshes
mad *adjective*
madder
maddest
madly
madam
madden *verb*
maddens
maddening
maddened
★ **made** see **make**
madman *noun*
madmen
madness
magazine *noun*
magazines
maggot *noun*
maggots
magic *noun*
and *adjective*
magical *adjective*
magically
magician *noun*
magicians
magistrate *noun*
magistrates
magma
magnesium
magnet *noun*
magnets
magnetism
magnetic *adjective*
magnetically
magnetize *verb*
magnetizes
magnetizing
magnetized
magnificent *adjective*
magnificently
magnificence
magnification
magnifier
magnify *verb*
magnifies
magnifying
magnified
magnitude *noun*
magnitudes
magnolia *noun*
magnolias
magpie *noun*
magpies
mahogany
☆ **maid** *noun*
maids
maiden *noun*
maidens
✪ **mail** *noun*
mail *verb*
mails
mailing
mailed
maim *verb*
maims
maiming
maimed
✲ **main** *adjective*
mainly
mainland
mainly
mains *plural noun*
maintain *verb*
maintains
maintaining
maintained
maintenance
maisonette *noun*
maisonettes
maize
majestic *adjective*
majestically
majesty *noun*
majesties
major *adjective*
major *noun*
majors
majority *noun*
majorities
make *verb*
makes
making
made
make *noun*
makes
make-believe
maker *noun*
makers
make-up
maladjusted
malaria
✹ **male** *adjective* and *noun*
males
malevolence
malevolent *adjective*
malevolently
malice
malicious *adjective*
maliciously
mallet *noun*
mallets
malnourished
malnutrition
malt
malted

★ You use **made** in e.g. *I made a cake*. ! **maid**.
☆ A **maid** is a female servant. ! **made**.
✪ **Mail** is letters and parcels sent by post. ! **male**.
✲ **Main** means 'most important'. ! **mane**.
✹ A **male** is a man or an animal of the same gender as a man. ! **mail**.

mammal *noun*
mammals
mammoth *adjective* and *noun*
mammoths
man *noun*
men
man *verb*
mans
manning
manned
manage *verb*
manages
managing
managed
manageable
management
manager *noun*
managers
manageress *noun*
manageresses
★ **mane** *noun*
manes
manger *noun*
mangers
mangle *verb*
mangles
mangling
mangled
mango *noun*
mangoes
manhandle *verb*
manhandles
manhandling
manhandled
manhole *noun*
manholes
mania *noun*
manias
maniac *noun*
maniacs
manic *adjective*
manically
manifesto *noun*
manifestos
manipulate *verb*
manipulates
manipulating
manipulated
manipulation
manipulator
mankind
manliness
manly *adjective*
manlier
manliest
☆ **manner** *noun*
manners
manoeuvrable
manoeuvre *verb*
manoeuvres
manoeuvring
manoeuvred
manoeuvre *noun*
manoeuvres
man-of-war *noun*
men-of-war
✪ **manor** *noun*
manors
mansion *noun*
mansions
manslaughter
mantelpiece *noun*
mantelpieces
mantle *noun*
mantles
manual *adjective*
manually
manual *noun*
manuals
manufacture *verb*
manufactures
manufacturing
manufactured
manufacture *noun*
manufacturer *noun*
manufacturers
manure
manuscript *noun*
manuscripts
Manx
many *adjective* and *noun*
more
most
Maori *noun*
Maoris
map *noun*
maps
map *verb*
maps
mapping
mapped
maple *noun*
maples
mar *verb*
mars
marring
marred
marathon *noun*
marathons
marauder *noun*
marauders
marauding
marble *noun*
marbles
March *noun*
Marches

★ A **mane** is the long piece of hair on a horse or lion. ! **main**.
☆ You use **manner** in e.g. *a friendly manner*. ! **manor**.
✪ A **manor** is a big house in the country. ! **manner**.

march *verb*
marches
marching
marched
march *noun*
marches
marcher *noun*
marchers
★ **mare** *noun*
mares
margarine
margin *noun*
margins
marginal *adjective*
marginally
marigold *noun*
marigolds
marijuana
marina *noun*
marinas
marine *adjective* and *noun*
marines
mariner *noun*
mariners
marionette *noun*
marionettes
mark *verb*
marks
marking
marked
mark *noun*
marks
market *noun*
markets
market *verb*
markets
marketing
marketed
marksman *noun*
marksmen
marksmanship
marmalade
maroon *verb*
maroons
marooning
marooned
maroon *adjective* and *noun*
marquee *noun*
marquees
marriage *noun*
marriages
marrow *noun*
marrows
marry *verb*
marries
marrying
married
marsh *noun*
marshes
marshal *noun*
marshals
marshmallow *noun*
marshmallows
marshy *adjective*
marshier
marshiest
marsupial *noun*
marsupials
martial
Martian *noun*
Martians
martin *noun*
martins
martyr *noun*
martyrs
martyrdom
marvel *verb*
marvels
marvelling
marvelled
marvel *noun*
marvels
marvellous *adjective*
marvellously
Marxism
Marxist
marzipan
mascot *noun*
mascots
masculine
masculinity
mash *verb*
mashes
mashing
mashed
mash *noun*
mask *noun*
masks
mask *verb*
masks
masking
masked
☆ **Mason** *noun*
Masons
✪ **mason** *noun*
masons
masonry
✲ **Mass** *noun*
Masses
mass *noun*
masses
mass *verb*
masses
massing
massed
massacre *verb*
massacres
massacring
massacred

★ A **mare** is a female horse. ! **mayor**.
☆ You use a capital M when you mean a member of the Freemasons.
✪ Use a small m when you mean someone who builds with stone.
✲ Use a capital M when you mean the Roman Catholic service.

massacre *noun*
massacres
massage *verb*
massages
massaging
massaged
massage *noun*
massive *adjective*
massively
mast *noun*
masts
master *noun*
masters
master *verb*
masters
mastering
mastered
masterly
mastermind *noun*
masterminds
masterpiece *noun*
masterpieces
mastery
★ **mat** *noun*
mats
matador *noun*
matadors
match *verb*
matches
matching
matched
match *noun*
matches
mate *noun*
mates
mate *verb*
mates
mating
mated
material *noun*
materials
materialistic
maternal *adjective*
maternally
maternity
mathematical *adjective*
mathematically
mathematician *noun*
mathematicians
mathematics
maths
matinée *noun*
matinées
matrimonial
matrimony
matrix *noun*
matrices
matron *noun*
matrons
☆ **matt**
matted
matter *verb*
matters
mattering
mattered
matter *noun*
matters
matting
mattress *noun*
mattresses
mature
maturity
mauve
maximum *adjective* and *noun*
maxima *or* maximums
May *noun*
Mays
may *verb*
might
may
maybe
May Day
✪ **mayday** *noun*
maydays
mayonnaise
✲ **mayor** *noun*
mayors
mayoress *noun*
mayoresses
maypole *noun*
maypoles
maze *noun*
mazes
meadow *noun*
meadows
meagre
meal *noun*
meals
mean *adjective*
meaner
meanest
meanly
mean *verb*
means
meaning
meant
meander *verb*
meanders
meandering
meandered
meaning *noun*
meanings
meaningful *adjective*
meaningfully
meaningless *adjective*
meaninglessly

★ A **mat** is a covering for a floor. ! **matt**.
☆ **Matt** means 'not shiny'. ! **mat**.
✪ An international radio signal.
✲ You use **mayor** in e.g. *the Mayor of London*. ! **mare**.

meanness
means *plural noun*
meantime
meanwhile
measles *plural noun*
measly *adjective*
measlier
measliest
measure *verb*
measures
measuring
measured
measure *noun*
measures
measurement *noun*
measurements
★ **meat** *noun*
meats
meaty *adjective*
meatier
meatiest
mechanic *noun*
mechanics
mechanical *adjective*
mechanically
mechanics
mechanism *noun*
mechanisms
medal *noun*
medals
medallist *noun*
medallists
meddle *verb*
meddles
meddling
meddled
meddler *noun*
meddlers
meddlesome
media *plural noun*
median *noun*
medians
medical *adjective*
medically
medicine *noun*
medicines
medicinal
medieval
mediocre
mediocrity
meditate *verb*
meditates
meditating
meditated
meditation
Mediterranean
medium *adjective*
medium *noun*
media *or* mediums
meek *adjective*
meeker
meekest
meekly
meekness
☆ **meet** *verb*
meets
meeting
met
meeting *noun*
meetings
megaphone *noun*
megaphones
melancholy
mellow *adjective*
mellower
mellowest
melodious *adjective*
melodiously
melodrama *noun*
melodramas
melodramatic *adjective*
melodramatically
melody *noun*
melodies
melodic
melon *noun*
melons
melt *verb*
melts
melting
melted
member *noun*
members
membership
Member of Parliament *noun*
Members of Parliament
membrane *noun*
membranes
memoirs *plural noun*
memorable *adjective*
memorably
memorial *noun*
memorials
memorize *verb*
memorizes
memorizing
memorized
memory *noun*
memories
men see **man**
menace *verb*
menaces
menacing
menaced

★ **Meat** is the flesh of an animal. ! **meet**.
☆ People **meet** when they come together. ! **meat**.

menace *noun*
menaces
menagerie *noun*
menageries
mend *verb*
mends
mending
mended
mender *noun*
menders
menstrual
menstruation

-ment
-ment makes nouns from adjectives e.g. **contentment**. There is a fixed number of these, and you cannot freely add *-ment* as you can with *-ness*. When the adjective ends in *-y* following a consonant, you change the *y* to *i*, e.g. **merry - merriment**.

mental *adjective*
mentally
mention *verb*
mentions
mentioning
mentioned
mention *noun*
mentions
menu *noun*
menus
mercenary *adjective* and *noun*
mercenaries
merchandise
merchant *noun*
merchants
merciful *adjective*
mercifully
merciless *adjective*
mercilessly
mercury
mercy *noun*
mercies
mere *adjective*
mere *noun*
meres
merely *adverb*
merge *verb*
merges
merging
merged
merger *noun*
mergers
meridian *noun*
meridians
meringue *noun*
meringues
merit *noun*
merits
merit *verb*
merits
meriting
merited
mermaid *noun*
mermaids
merriment
merry *adjective*
merrier
merriest
merrily
merry-go-round *noun*
merry-go-rounds
mesh *noun*
meshes
mess *noun*
messes
mess *verb*
messes
messing
messed
message *noun*
messages
messenger *noun*
messengers
Messiah
messiness
messy *adjective*
messier
messiest
messily
met see **meet**
★ **metal** *noun*
metals
metallic
metallurgical
metallurgist
metallurgy
metamorphosis *noun*
metamorphoses
metaphor *noun*
metaphors
metaphorical *adjective*
metaphorically
meteor *noun*
meteors
meteoric
meteorite *noun*
meteorites
meteorological
meteorologist
meteorology
☆ **meter** *noun*
meters
methane

★ **Metal** is a hard substance used to make things. ! **mettle**.
☆ A **meter** is a device that shows how much of something has been used. ! **metre**.

method *noun*
methods
methodical *adjective*
methodically
Methodist *noun*
Methodists
meths
methylated spirit
meticulous *adjective*
meticulously
★ **metre** *noun*
metres
metric *adjective*
metrical *adjective*
metrically
metronome *noun*
metronomes
☆ **mettle**
mew *verb*
mews
mewing
mewed
miaow *verb*
miaows
miaowing
miaowed
mice see **mouse**

micro-
micro- makes words meaning 'small', e.g. **microwave**. When the word begins with a vowel you add a hyphen, e.g. **micro-organism**.

microbe *noun*
microbes
microchip *noun*
microchips
microcomputer *noun*
microcomputers
microfilm *noun*
microfilms
microphone *noun*
microphones
microprocessor *noun*
microprocessors
microscope *noun*
microscopes
microscopic *adjective*
microscopically
microwave *noun*
microwaves
microwave *verb*
microwaves
microwaving
microwaved
✪ **mid**
midday
middle *noun*
middles
Middle Ages
Middle East
midge *noun*
midges
midget *noun*
midgets
midland *adjective*
midnight
midst
midsummer
midway
midwife *noun*
midwives
midwifery
✲ **might** *noun*
might see **may**
mightiness
mighty *adjective*
mightier
mightiest
mightily
migraine *noun*
migraines
migrant *noun*
migrants
migrate *verb*
migrates
migrating
migrated
migration *noun*
migrations
migratory
mike *noun*
mikes
mild *adjective*
milder
mildest
mildly
mildness
mile *noun*
miles
mileage *noun*
mileages
milestone *noun*
milestones
militancy
militant
militarism
militaristic
military
milk *noun*
milk *verb*
milks
milking
milked

★ A **metre** is a unit of length. ! **meter**.
☆ As in *to be on your mettle*. ! **metal**.
✪ You use a hyphen, e.g. *mid-August*.
✲ **Might** means 'force' or 'strength'. ! **mite**.

milkman *noun*
milkmen
milky *adjective*
milkier
milkiest
Milky Way
mill *noun*
mills
mill *verb*
mills
milling
milled
millennium *noun*
millenniums
miller *noun*
millers
millet
milligram *noun*
milligrams
millilitre *noun*
millilitres
millimetre *noun*
millimetres
million *noun*
millions
millionth
millionaire *noun*
millionaires
millstone *noun*
millstones
milometer *noun*
milometers
mime *verb*
mimes
miming
mimed
mime *noun*
mimes
mimic *verb*
mimics
mimicking
mimicked
mimic *noun*
mimics
mimicry
minaret *noun*
minarets
mince *verb*
minces
mincing
minced
mince *noun*
mincemeat
mincer *noun*
mincers
mind *noun*
minds
mind *verb*
minds
minding
minded
mindless *adjective*
mindlessly
mine *adjective*
mine *verb*
mines
mining
mined
mine *noun*
mines
minefield *noun*
minefields
miner *noun*
miners
mineral *noun*
minerals
mingle *verb*
mingles
mingling
mingled

mini-
mini- makes words meaning 'small', e.g. **miniskirt**. You do not normally need a hyphen.

mingy *adjective*
mingier
mingiest
miniature *adjective* and *noun*
miniatures
minibus *noun*
minibuses
minim *noun*
minims
minimal *adjective*
minimally
minimize *verb*
minimizes
minimizing
minimized
minimum *adjective* and *noun*
minima *or* minimums
minister *noun*
ministers
ministry *noun*
ministries
mink *noun*
minks
minnow *noun*
minnows
minor *adjective* and *noun*
minors
minority *noun*
minorities
minstrel *noun*
minstrels

mint *noun*
mints
mint *verb*
mints
minting
minted
minus *preposition*
minute *adjective*
minutely
minute *noun*
minutes
miracle *noun*
miracles
miraculous *adjective*
miraculously
mirage *noun*
mirages
mirror *noun*
mirrors
mirth
misbehave *verb*
misbehaves
misbehaving
misbehaved
misbehaviour
miscarriage *noun*
miscarriages
miscellaneous
miscellany *noun*
miscellanies
mischief
mischievous *adjective*
mischievously
miser *noun*
misers
miserable *adjective*
miserably
miserly
misery *noun*
miseries
misfire *verb*
misfires
misfiring
misfired
misfit *noun*
misfits
misfortune *noun*
misfortunes
mishap *noun*
mishaps
misjudge *verb*
misjudges
misjudging
misjudged
mislay *verb*
mislays
mislaying
mislaid
mislead *verb*
misleads
misleading
misled
misprint *noun*
misprints
miss *verb*
misses
missing
missed
miss *noun*
misses
missile *noun*
missiles
missing
mission *noun*
missions
missionary *noun*
missionaries
misspell *verb*
misspells
misspelling
misspelt *or*
misspelled
★ **mist** *noun*
mists
mistake *noun*
mistakes
mistake *verb*
mistakes
mistaking
mistook
mistaken
mister
mistiness
mistletoe
mistreat *verb*
mistreats
mistreating
mistreated
mistreatment
mistress *noun*
mistresses
mistrust *verb*
mistrusts
mistrusting
mistrusted
misty *adjective*
mistier
mistiest
mistily
misunderstand *verb*
misunderstands
misunderstanding
misunderstood
misunderstanding *noun*
misunderstandings
misuse *verb*
misuses
misusing
misused
misuse *noun*
misuses

★ **Mist** is damp air that is difficult to see through. ! **missed**.

★ **mite** *noun*
mites
mitre *noun*
mitres
mitten *noun*
mittens
mix *verb*
mixes
mixing
mixed
mixer *noun*
mixers
mixture *noun*
mixtures
mix-up *noun*
mix-ups
moan *verb*
moans
moaning
moaned
moan *noun*
moans
moat *noun*
moats
mob *noun*
mobs
mob *verb*
mobs
mobbing
mobbed
mobile *adjective* and *noun*
mobiles
mobility
mobilization
mobilize *verb*
mobilizes
mobilizing
mobilized
moccasin *noun*
moccasins
mock *adjective*
mock *verb*
mocks
mocking
mocked
mockery *noun*
mockeries
mock-up *noun*
mock-ups
mode *noun*
modes
model *noun*
models
model *verb*
models
modelling
modelled
modem *noun*
modems
moderate *adjective*
moderately
moderate *verb*
moderates
moderating
moderated
moderation
modern
modernity
modernization
modernize *verb*
modernizes
modernizing
modernized
modest *adjective*
modestly
modesty
modification *noun*
modifications
modify *verb*
modifies
modifying
modified
module *noun*
modules
moist *adjective*
moister
moistest
moisture
moisten *verb*
moistens
moistening
moistened
molar *noun*
molars
mole *noun*
moles
molecular
molecule *noun*
molecules
molehill *noun*
molehills
molest *verb*
molests
molesting
molested
mollusc *noun*
molluscs
molten
moment *noun*
moments
momentary *adjective*
momentarily
momentous *adjective*
momentously
momentum
monarch *noun*
monarchs
monarchy *noun*
monarchies

★ A **mite** is a tiny insect. ! **might**.

monastery *noun*
monasteries
monastic
Monday *noun*
Mondays
money
mongoose *noun*
mongooses
mongrel *noun*
mongrels
monitor *verb*
monitors
monitoring
monitored
monitor *noun*
monitors
monk *noun*
monks
monkey *noun*
monkeys
monogram *noun*
monograms
monologue *noun*
monologues
monopolize *verb*
monopolizes
monopolizing
monopolized
monopoly *noun*
monopolies
monorail *noun*
monorails
monotonous *adjective*
monotonously
monotony
monsoon *noun*
monsoons
monster *noun*
monsters
monstrosity *noun*
monstrosities
monstrous *adjective*
monstrously
month *noun*
months
monthly *adjective* and *adverb*
monument *noun*
monuments
monumental *adjective*
monumentally
moo *verb*
moos
mooing
mooed
mood *noun*
moods
moodiness
moody *adjective*
moodier
moodiest
moodily
moon *noun*
moons
moonlight
moonlit
★ **moor** *verb*
moors
mooring
moored
☆ **moor** *noun*
moors
moorhen *noun*
moorhens
mooring *noun*
moorings
✪ **moose** *noun*
moose
mop *noun*
mops
mop *verb*
mops
mopping
mopped
mope *verb*
mopes
moping
moped
moped *noun*
mopeds
moraine *noun*
moraines
moral *adjective*
morally
moral *noun*
morals
morale
morality
morals *plural noun*
morbid *adjective*
morbidly
✲ **more** *adjective, adverb,* and *noun*
moreover
Mormon *noun*
Mormons
morning *noun*
mornings
moron *noun*
morons
moronic *adjective*
moronically
morose *adjective*
morosely
morphine
morris dance *noun*
morris dances
Morse code

★ To **moor** a boat is to tie it up. ! **more**.
☆ A **moor** is an area of rough land. ! **more**.
✪ A **moose** is an American elk. ! **mouse**, **mousse**.
✲ You use **more** in e.g. *I'd like more to eat.* ! **moor**.

morsel *noun*
morsels
mortal *adjective*
mortally
mortality
mortar
mortgage *noun*
mortgages
mortuary *noun*
mortuaries
mosaic *noun*
mosaics
mosque *noun*
mosques
mosquito *noun*
mosquitoes
moss *noun*
mosses
mossy *adjective*
mossier
mossiest
most *adjective, adverb,* and *noun*
mostly *adverb*
motel *noun*
motels
moth *noun*
moths
mother *noun*
mothers
motherhood
mother-in-law *noun*
mothers-in-law
motherly
motion *noun*
motions
motionless
motivate *verb*
motivates
motivating
motivated
motive *noun*
motives
motor *noun*
motors
motorbike *noun*
motorbikes
motor boat *noun*
motor boats
motor car *noun*
motor cars
motorcycle *noun*
motorcycles
motorcyclist *noun*
motorcyclists
motorist *noun*
motorists
motorway *noun*
motorways
mottled
motto *noun*
mottoes
mould *verb*
moulds
moulding
moulded
mould *noun*
moulds
mouldy *adjective*
mouldier
mouldiest
moult *verb*
moults
moulting
moulted
mound *noun*
mounds
mount *verb*
mounts
mounting
mounted
mount *noun*
mounts
mountain *noun*
mountains
mountaineer *noun*
mountaineers
mountaineering
mountainous
mourn *verb*
mourns
mourning
mourned
mourner *noun*
mourners
mournful *adjective*
mournfully
★ **mouse** *noun*
mice
mousetrap *noun*
mousetraps
☆ **mousse** *noun*
mousses
moustache *noun*
moustaches
mousy *adjective*
mousier
mousiest
mouth *noun*
mouths
mouthful *noun*
mouthfuls
mouthpiece *noun*
mouthpieces
movable
move *verb*
moves
moving
moved
move *noun*
moves

★ A **mouse** is a small animal. ! **moose, mousse.**
☆ A **mousse** is a creamy pudding. ! **moose, mouse.**

movement *noun*
movements
movie *noun*
movies
mow *verb*
mows
mowing
mowed
mown
mower *noun*
mowers
much *adjective, adverb,* and *noun*
muck *noun*
muck *verb*
mucks
mucking
mucked
mucky *adjective*
muckier
muckiest
mud
muddle *verb*
muddles
muddling
muddled
muddle *noun*
muddles
muddler *noun*
muddlers
muddy *adjective*
muddier
muddiest
mudguard *noun*
mudguards
muesli
★ **muezzin** *noun*
muezzins
muffle *verb*
muffles
muffling
muffled
mug *noun*
mugs
mug *verb*
mugs
mugging
mugged
mugger *noun*
muggers
muggy *adjective*
muggier
muggiest
mule *noun*
mules

multi-
multi- makes words with the meaning 'many', e.g. **multicultural**. You do not normally need a hyphen.

multiple *adjective* and *noun*
multiples
multiplication
multiply *verb*
multiplies
multiplying
multiplied
multiracial
multitude *noun*
multitudes
mumble *verb*
mumbles
mumbling
mumbled
mummify *verb*
mummifies
mummifying
mummified
mummy *noun*
mummies
mumps
munch *verb*
munches
munching
munched
mundane
municipal
mural *noun*
murals
murder *verb*
murders
murdering
murdered
murder *noun*
murders
murderer *noun*
murderers
murderous *adjective*
murderously
murky *adjective*
murkier
murkiest
murmur *verb*
murmurs
murmuring
murmured
murmur *noun*
murmurs
☆ **muscle** *noun*
muscles
muscle *verb*
muscles
muscling
muscled
muscular
museum *noun*
museums
mushroom *noun*
mushrooms

★ A man who calls Muslims to prayer.
☆ A **muscle** is a part of the body. ! **mussel**.

mushroom *verb*
mushrooms
mushrooming
mushroomed
music
musical *adjective*
musically
musical *noun*
musicals
musician *noun*
musicians
musket *noun*
muskets
musketeer *noun*
musketeers
Muslim *noun*
Muslims
muslin
★ **mussel** *noun*
mussels
must
mustard
muster *verb*
musters
mustering
mustered
mustiness
musty *adjective*
mustier
mustiest
mutation *noun*
mutations
mute *adjective*
mutely
mute *noun*
mutes
muted
mutilate *verb*
mutilates
mutilating
mutilated
mutilation
mutineer *noun*
mutineers
mutiny *noun*
mutinies
mutinous *adjective*
mutinously
mutiny *verb*
mutinies
mutinying
mutinied
mutter *verb*
mutters
muttering
muttered
mutton
mutual *adjective*
mutually
muzzle *verb*
muzzles
muzzling
muzzled
muzzle *noun*
muzzles
myself
mysterious *adjective*
mysteriously
mystery *noun*
mysteries
mystification
mystify *verb*
mystifies
mystifying
mystified
myth *noun*
myths
mythical
mythological *adjective*
mythology

Nn

nab *verb*
nabs
nabbing
nabbed
nag *verb*
nags
nagging
nagged
nag *noun*
nags
nail *noun*
nails
nail *verb*
nails
nailing
nailed
naive *adjective*
naively
naivety
naked
nakedness
name *noun*
names
name *verb*
names
naming
named
nameless
namely
nanny *noun*
nannies
nap *noun*
naps
napkin *noun*
napkins

★ A **mussel** is a shellfish. ! **muscle**.

nappy *noun*
nappies
narcissus *noun*
narcissi
narcotic *noun*
narcotics
narrate *verb*
narrates
narrating
narrated
narration *noun*
narrations
narrative *noun*
narratives
narrator *noun*
narrators
narrow *adjective*
narrower
narrowest
narrowly
nasal *adjective*
nasally
nastiness
nasturtium *noun*
nasturtiums
nasty *adjective*
nastier
nastiest
nastily
nation *noun*
nations
national *adjective*
nationally
nationalism
nationalist
nationality *noun*
nationalities
nationalization
nationalize *verb*
nationalizes
nationalizing
nationalized
nationwide *adjective*
native *adjective* and *noun*
natives
Native American *noun*
Native Americans
nativity *noun*
nativities
natural *adjective*
naturally
natural *noun*
naturals
naturalist *noun*
naturalists
naturalization
naturalize *verb*
naturalizes
naturalizing
naturalized
nature *noun*
natures
naughtiness
naughty *adjective*
naughtier
naughtiest
naughtily
nausea
nautical
★ **naval** *adjective*
nave *noun*
naves
☆ **navel** *noun*
navels
navigable
navigate *verb*
navigates
navigating
navigated
navigation
navigator *noun*
navigators
navy *noun*
navies
Nazi *noun*
Nazis
Nazism
near *adjective* and *adverb*
nearer
nearest
near *preposition*
near *verb*
nears
nearing
neared
nearby
nearly
neat *adjective*
neater
neatest
neatly
neatness
necessarily
necessary
necessity *noun*
necessities
neck *noun*
necks
neckerchief *noun*
neckerchiefs
necklace *noun*
necklaces
nectar
nectarine *noun*
nectarines
need *verb*
needs
needing
needed

★ **Naval** means 'to do with a navy'. ! **navel**.
☆ A **navel** is a small hollow in your stomach. ! **naval**.

★ **need** *noun*
needs
needle *noun*
needles
needless *adjective*
needlessly
needlework
needy *adjective*
needier
neediest
negative *adjective*
negatively
negative *noun*
negatives
neglect *verb*
neglects
neglecting
neglected
neglect *noun*
neglectful *adjective*
neglectfully
negligence
negligent *adjective*
negligently
negligible *adjective*
negligibly
negotiate *verb*
negotiates
negotiating
negotiated
negotiation *noun*
negotiations
negotiator *noun*
negotiators
neigh *verb*
neighs
neighing
neighed
neigh *noun*
neighs
neighbour *noun*
neighbours
neighbouring
neighbourhood *noun*
neighbourhoods
neighbourly
neither *adjective* and *conjunction*
neon
nephew *noun*
nephews
nerve *noun*
nerves
nerve-racking
nervous *adjective*
nervously
nervousness

-ness
-ness makes nouns from adjectives, e.g. **soft - softness**. When the adjective ends in *-y* following a consonant, you change the *y* to *i*, e.g. **lively - liveliness**.

nest *noun*
nests
nest *verb*
nests
nesting
nested
nestle *verb*
nestles
nestling
nestled
nestling *noun*
nestlings
net *noun*
nets
net *adjective*
netball
nettle *noun*
nettles
network *noun*
networks
neuter *adjective*
neuter *verb*
neuters
neutering
neutered
neutral *adjective*
neutrally
neutrality
neutralize *verb*
neutralizes
neutralizing
neutralized
neutron *noun*
neutrons
never
nevertheless *conjunction*
☆ **new** *adjective*
newer
newest
newly
newcomer *noun*
newcomers
newness
news
newsagent *noun*
newsagents
newsletter *noun*
newsletters
newspaper *noun*
newspapers

★ To **need** is to require something. ! **knead**.
☆ You use **new** in e.g *She has a new bike*. ! **knew**.

newt *noun*
newts
New Testament
newton *noun*
newtons
next *adjective* and *adverb*
next door
nib *noun*
nibs
nibble *verb*
nibbles
nibbling
nibbled
nice *adjective*
nicer
nicest
nicely
niceness
nicety *noun*
niceties
nick *verb*
nicks
nicking
nicked
nick *noun*
nicks
nickel *noun*
nickels
nickname *noun*
nicknames
nicotine
niece *noun*
nieces
★ **night** *noun*
nights
nightclub *noun*
nightclubs
nightdress *noun*
nightdresses
nightfall
nightingale *noun*
nightingales
nightly
nightmare *noun*
nightmares
nightmarish
nil
nimble *adjective*
nimbler
nimblest
nimbly
nine *noun*
nines
nineteen *noun*
nineteens
nineteenth
ninetieth
ninety *noun*
nineties
ninth *adjective*
ninthly
nip *verb*
nips
nipping
nipped
nip *noun*
nips
nipple *noun*
nipples
nippy *adjective*
nippier
nippiest
nit *noun*
nits
nitrate *noun*
nitrates
nitric acid
nitrogen
nitty-gritty
nitwit *noun*
nitwits
nobility
noble *adjective*
nobler
noblest
nobly
noble *noun*
nobles
nobleman *noun*
noblemen
noblewoman *noun*
noblewomen
nobody *noun*
nobodies
nocturnal *adjective*
nocturnally
nod *verb*
nods
nodding
nodded
noise *noun*
noises
noiseless *adjective*
noiselessly
noisiness
noisy *adjective*
noisier
noisiest
noisily
nomad *noun*
nomads
nomadic
no man's land
nominate *verb*
nominates
nominating
nominated
nomination *noun*
nominations

★ **Night** is the opposite of day. ! **knight**.

-nomy
-nomy makes words for subjects of study, e.g. **astronomy** (= the study of the stars). Most of these words end in *-onomy*.

★ **none**

non-
non- makes words meaning 'not', e.g. **non-existent**, **non-smoker**. You use a hyphen to make these words. When an *un-* word has a special meaning, e.g. **unprofessional**, you can use *non-* to make a word without the special meaning, e.g. **non-professional**.

non-existent
non-fiction
non-flammable
nonsense
nonsensical *adjective*
nonsensically
non-stop
noodle
noon
no one
noose *noun*
nooses
normal *adjective*
normally
normality
north *adjective* and *adverb*
☆ **north** *noun*
north-east *noun* and *adjective*
northerly *adjective* and *noun*
northerlies
northern
northerner *noun*
northerners
northward *adjective* and *adverb*
northwards *adverb*
north-west
nose *noun*
noses
nose *verb*
noses
nosing
nosed
nosedive *verb*
nosedives
nosediving
nosedived
nosedive *noun*
nosedives
nosiness
nostalgia
nostalgic *adjective*
nostalgically
nostril *noun*
nostrils
nosy *adjective*
nosier
nosiest
nosily
notable *adjective*
notably
notch *noun*
notches
note *noun*
notes
note *verb*
notes
noting
noted
notebook *noun*
notebooks
notepaper
nothing
notice *verb*
notices
noticing
noticed
notice *noun*
notices
noticeable *adjective*
noticeably
noticeboard *noun*
noticeboards
notion *noun*
notions
notoriety
notorious *adjective*
notoriously
nougat
nought *noun*
noughts
noun *noun*
nouns
nourish *verb*
nourishes
nourishing
nourished
nourishment
novel *adjective*
novel *noun*
novels
novelist *noun*
novelists
novelty *noun*
novelties

★ You use **none** in e.g. *none of us went.* **! nun.**
☆ You use a capital N in **the North**, when you mean a particular region.

November *noun*
Novembers
novice *noun*
novices
nowadays
nowhere
nozzle *noun*
nozzles
nuclear
nucleus *noun*
nuclei
nude *adjective* and *noun*
nudes
nudge *verb*
nudges
nudging
nudged
nudist *noun*
nudists
nudity
nugget *noun*
nuggets
nuisance *noun*
nuisances
numb *adjective*
numbly
number *noun*
numbers
number *verb*
numbers
numbering
numbered
numbness
numeracy
numeral *noun*
numerals
numerate
numerator *noun*
numerators
numerical *adjective*
numerically
numerous
★ **nun** *noun*
nuns
nunnery *noun*
nunneries
nurse *noun*
nurses
nurse *verb*
nurses
nursing
nursed
nursery *noun*
nurseries
nurture *verb*
nurtures
nurturing
nurtured
nut *noun*
nuts
nutcrackers *plural noun*
nutmeg *noun*
nutmegs
nutrient *noun*
nutrients
nutrition
nutritional *adjective*
nutritionally
nutritious
nutshell *noun*
nutshells
nutty *adjective*
nuttier
nuttiest
nuzzle *verb*
nuzzles
nuzzling
nuzzled
nylon *adjective* and *noun*
nylons
nymph *noun*
nymphs

Oo

-o
Most nouns ending in *-o*, e.g. **hero**, **potato**, have plurals ending in *-oes*, e.g. **heroes**, **potatoes**, but a few end in *-os*. The most important are **kilos**, **photos**, **pianos**, **radios**, **ratios**, **solos**, **videos**, **zeros**. Verbs ending in *-o* usually have the forms *-oes* and *-oed*, e.g. **video** - **videoes** - **videoed**.

oak *noun*
oaks
☆ **oar** *noun*
oars
oarsman *noun*
oarsmen
oarswoman *noun*
oarswomen
oasis *noun*
oases
oath *noun*
oaths
oatmeal
oats *plural noun*

★ A **nun** is a member of a convent. ! **none**.
☆ An **oar** is used for rowing a boat. ! **or**, **ore**.

obedience
obedient *adjective*
obediently
obey *verb*
obeys
obeying
obeyed
obituary *noun*
obituaries
object *noun*
objects
object *verb*
objects
objecting
objected
objection *noun*
objections
objectionable
objective *adjective*
objectively
objective *noun*
objectives
objector *noun*
objectors
obligation *noun*
obligations
obligatory
oblige *verb*
obliges
obliging
obliged
oblique *adjective*
obliquely
oblong *adjective* and *noun*
oblongs
oboe *noun*
oboes
oboist *noun*
oboists
obscene *adjective*
obscenely
obscenity *noun*
obscenities
obscure *adjective*
obscurer
obscurest
obscurely
obscurity
observance *noun*
observances
observant *adjective*
observantly
observation *noun*
observations
observatory *noun*
observatories
observe *verb*
observes
observing
observed
observer *noun*
observers
obsessed
obsession *noun*
obsessions
obsolete
obstacle *noun*
obstacles
obstinacy
obstinate *adjective*
obstinately
obstruct *verb*
obstructs
obstructing
obstructed
obstruction *noun*
obstructions
obstructive *adjective*
obstructively
obtain *verb*
obtains
obtaining
obtained
obtainable
obtuse *adjective*
obtuser
obtusest
obtusely
obvious *adjective*
obviously
occasion *noun*
occasions
occasional *adjective*
occasionally
occupant *noun*
occupants
occupation *noun*
occupations
occupy *verb*
occupies
occupying
occupied
occur *verb*
occurs
occurring
occurred
occurrence *noun*
occurrences
ocean *noun*
oceans
o'clock
octagon *noun*
octagons
octagonal *adjective*
octagonally
octave *noun*
octaves
October *noun*
Octobers

octopus *noun*
octopuses
odd *adjective*
odder
oddest
oddly
oddity *noun*
oddities
oddments *plural noun*
oddness
odds *plural noun*
odour *noun*
odours
odorous
oesophagus *noun*
oesophagi *or* oesophaguses
★ **of**
☆ **off**
offence *noun*
offences
offend *verb*
offends
offending
offended
offender *noun*
offenders
offensive *adjective*
offensively
offer *verb*
offers
offering
offered
offer *noun*
offers
offhand
office *noun*
offices
officer *noun*
officers
official *adjective*
officially
official *noun*
officials
officious *adjective*
officiously
off-licence *noun*
off-licences
offset *verb*
offsets
offsetting
offset
offshore *adjective* and *adverb*
offside
offspring *noun*
offspring
often
ogre *noun*
ogres
ohm *noun*
ohms
oil *noun*
oils
oil *verb*
oils
oiling
oiled
oilfield *noun*
oilfields
oilskin *noun*
oilskins
oil well *noun*
oil wells
oily *adjective*
oilier
oiliest
ointment *noun*
ointments
old *adjective*
older
oldest
Old Testament
olive *noun*
olives
Olympic Games *plural noun*
Olympics *plural noun*
ombudsman *noun*
ombudsmen
omelette *noun*
omelettes
omen *noun*
omens
ominous *adjective*
ominously
✪ **omission** *noun*
omissions
omit *verb*
omits
omitting
omitted
omnivorous
once
✲ **one** *adjective* and *noun*
ones
oneself
one-sided
one-way
ongoing
onion *noun*
onions
onlooker *noun*
onlookers
only
onshore *adjective* and *adverb*

★ You use **of** in e.g. *a box of matches*. ! **off**.
☆ You use **off** in e.g. *turn off the light*. ! **of**.
✪ An **omission** is something left out. ! **emission**.
✲ You use **one** in e.g. *one more time*. ! **won**.

onto *preposition*
onward *adjective* and *adverb*
onwards *adverb*
ooze *verb*
oozes
oozing
oozed
opaque
open *adjective*
openly
open *verb*
opens
opening
opened
opener *noun*
openers
opening *noun*
openings
opera *noun*
operas
operate *verb*
operates
operating
operated
operatic
operation *noun*
operations
operator *noun*
operators
opinion *noun*
opinions
opium
opponent *noun*
opponents
opportunity *noun*
opportunities
oppose *verb*
opposes
opposing
opposed
opposite *adjective*
opposite *noun*
opposites
opposition
oppress *verb*
oppresses
oppressing
oppressed
oppression
oppressive *adjective*
oppressively
oppressor *noun*
oppressors
opt *verb*
opts
opting
opted
optical *adjective*
optically
optician *noun*
opticians
optimism
optimist *noun*
optimists
optimistic *adjective*
optimistically
option *noun*
options
optional *adjective*
optionally
opulence
opulent *adjective*
opulently
★ **or** *conjunction*
☆ **oral** *adjective*
orally
orange *adjective* and *noun*
oranges
orangeade *noun*
orangeades
orang-utan *noun*
orang-utans
oration *noun*
orations
orator *noun*
orators
oratorical
oratorio *noun*
oratorios
oratory
orbit *noun*
orbits
orbit *verb*
orbits
orbiting
orbited
orbital
orchard *noun*
orchards
orchestra *noun*
orchestras
orchestral
orchid *noun*
orchids
ordeal *noun*
ordeals
order *noun*
orders
order *verb*
orders
ordering
ordered
orderliness
orderly
ordinal number *noun*
ordinal numbers
ordinary *adjective*
ordinarily
✪ **ore** *noun*
ores

★ You use **or** in e.g. *Do you want a cake or a biscuit?* ! **oar, ore.**
☆ **Oral** means spoken aloud. ! **aural.**
✪ **Ore** is rock with metal in it. ! **oar, or.**

organ *noun*
organs
organic *adjective*
organically
organism *noun*
organisms
organist *noun*
organists
organization *noun*
organizations
organize *verb*
organizes
organizing
organized
organizer *noun*
organizers
oriental
orienteering
origami
origin *noun*
origins
original *adjective*
originally
originality
originate *verb*
originates
originating
originated
origination
originator *noun*
originators
ornament *noun*
ornaments
ornamental *adjective*
ornamentally
ornamentation
ornithological
ornithologist
ornithology
orphan *noun*
orphans
orphanage *noun*
orphanages
orthodox
Orthodox Church
orthodoxy
oscillate *verb*
oscillates
oscillating
oscillated
oscillation *noun*
oscillations
ostrich *noun*
ostriches
other *adjective* and *noun*
others
otherwise
otter *noun*
otters
ought
ounce *noun*
ounces
ours
ourselves
outback
outboard motor *noun*
outboard motors
outbreak *noun*
outbreaks
outburst *noun*
outbursts
outcast *noun*
outcasts
outcome *noun*
outcomes
outcry *noun*
outcries
outdated
outdo *verb*
outdoes
outdoing
outdid
outdone
outdoor *adjective*
outdoors *adverb*
outer
outfit *noun*
outfits
outgrow *verb*
outgrows
outgrowing
outgrew
outgrown
outhouse *noun*
outhouses
outing *noun*
outings
outlast *verb*
outlasts
outlasting
outlasted
outlaw *noun*
outlaws
outlaw *verb*
outlaws
outlawing
outlawed
outlet *noun*
outlets
outline *noun*
outlines
outline *verb*
outlines
outlining
outlined
outlook *noun*
outlooks
outlying

outnumber *verb*
outnumbers
outnumbering
outnumbered
outpatient *noun*
outpatients
outpost *noun*
outposts
output *verb*
outputs
outputting
output
output *noun*
outputs
outrage *noun*
outrages
outrage *verb*
outrages
outraging
outraged
outrageous *adjective*
outrageously
outright
outset
outside *adverb* and *preposition*
outside *noun*
outsides
outsider *noun*
outsiders
outskirts *plural noun*
outspoken
outstanding *adjective*
outstandingly
outward *adjective*
outwardly
outwards *adverb*
outweigh *verb*
outweighs
outweighing
outweighed

outwit *verb*
outwits
outwitting
outwitted
oval *adjective* and *noun*
ovals
ovary *noun*
ovaries
oven *noun*
ovens
over *adverb* and *preposition*
over *noun*
overs

over-
over- makes words meaning 'too' or 'too much', e.g. **overactive** and **overcook**. You do not need a hyphen, except in some words beginning with e, e.g. **over-eager**.

overall *adjective*
overalls *plural noun*
overarm *adjective*
overboard
overcast
overcoat *noun*
overcoats
overcome *verb*
overcomes
overcoming
overcame
overcome
overdo *verb*
overdoes
overdoing
overdid
overdone

overdose *noun*
overdoses
overdue
overflow *verb*
overflows
overflowing
overflowed
overgrown
overhang *verb*
overhangs
overhanging
overhung
overhaul *verb*
overhauls
overhauling
overhauled
overhead *adjective*
overheads *plural noun*
overhear *verb*
overhears
overhearing
overheard
overland *adjective*
overlap *verb*
overlaps
overlapping
overlapped
overlook *verb*
overlooks
overlooking
overlooked
overnight
overpower *verb*
overpowers
overpowering
overpowered
overrun *verb*
overruns
overrunning
overran
overrun

overseas *adjective* and *adverb*
oversight *noun*
oversights
oversleep *verb*
oversleeps
oversleeping
overslept
overtake *verb*
overtakes
overtaking
overtook
overtaken
overthrow *verb*
overthrows
overthrowing
overthrew
overthrown
overthrow *noun*
overthrows
overtime
overture *noun*
overtures
overturn *verb*
overturns
overturning
overturned
overwhelm *verb*
overwhelms
overwhelming
overwhelmed
overwork *verb*
overworks
overworking
overworked
overwork *noun*
ovum *noun*
ova
owe *verb*
owes
owing
owed
owl *noun*
owls
own *adjective*
own *verb*
owns
owning
owned
owner *noun*
owners
ownership
ox *noun*
oxen
oxidation
oxide *noun*
oxides
oxidize *verb*
oxidizes
oxidizing
oxidized
oxygen
oyster *noun*
oysters
oz. *abbreviation*
ozone

Pp

pa *noun*
pas
pace *noun*
paces
pace *verb*
paces
pacing
paced
pacemaker *noun*
pacemakers
pacification
pacifism
pacifist *noun*
pacifists
pacify *verb*
pacifies
pacifying
pacified
pack *verb*
packs
packing
packed
pack *noun*
packs
package *noun*
packages
packet *noun*
packets
pad *noun*
pads
pad *verb*
pads
padding
padded
padding
paddle *verb*
paddles
paddling
paddled
paddle *noun*
paddles
paddock *noun*
paddocks
paddy *noun*
paddies
padlock *noun*
padlocks
pagan *adjective* and *noun*
pagans

page *noun*
pages
pageant *noun*
pageants
pageantry
pagoda *noun*
pagodas
paid see **pay**
★ **pail** *noun*
pails
☆ **pain** *noun*
pains
pain *verb*
pains
paining
pained
painful *adjective*
painfully
painkiller *noun*
painkillers
painless *adjective*
painlessly
painstaking
paint *noun*
paints
paint *verb*
paints
painting
painted
paintbox *noun*
paintboxes
paintbrush *noun*
paintbrushes
painter *noun*
painters
painting *noun*
paintings
✪ **pair** *noun*
pairs
pair *verb*
pairs
pairing
paired
pal *noun*
pals
palace *noun*
palaces
palate *noun*
palates
✲ **pale** *adjective*
paler
palest
paleness
palette *noun*
palettes
paling *noun*
palings
palisade *noun*
palisades
pall *verb*
palls
palling
palled
pallid
pallor
palm *noun*
palms
palm *verb*
palms
palming
palmed
palmistry
Palm Sunday
paltry *adjective*
paltrier
paltriest
pampas *plural noun*
pamper *verb*
pampers
pampering
pampered
pamphlet *noun*
pamphlets
pan *noun*
pans
pancake *noun*
pancakes
panda *noun*
pandas
pandemonium
pander *verb*
panders
pandering
pandered
✹ **pane** *noun*
panes
panel *noun*
panels
pang *noun*
pangs
panic
panic *verb*
panics
panicking
panicked
panicky
pannier *noun*
panniers
panorama *noun*
panoramas
panoramic *adjective*
panoramically
pansy *noun*
pansies
pant *verb*
pants
panting
panted

★ A **pail** is a bucket. ! **pale**.
☆ A **pain** is an unpleasant feeling caused by injury or disease. ! **pane**.
✪ A **pair** is a set of two. ! **pear**.
✲ **Pale** means 'almost white'. ! **pail**.
✹ A **pane** is a piece of glass in a window. ! **pain**.

panther *noun*
panthers
panties *plural noun*
pantomime *noun*
pantomimes
pantry *noun*
pantries
pants *plural noun*
paper *noun*
papers
paper *verb*
papers
papering
papered
paperback *noun*
paperbacks
papier mâché
papyrus *noun*
papyri
parable *noun*
parables
parachute *noun*
parachutes
parachutist
parade *noun*
parades
parade *verb*
parades
parading
paraded
paradise
paradox *noun*
paradoxes
paradoxical *adjective*
paradoxically
paraffin
paragraph *noun*
paragraphs
parallel
parallelogram *noun*
parallelograms
paralyse *verb*
paralyses
paralysing
paralysed
paralysis *noun*
paralyses
paralytic *adjective*
paralytically
parapet *noun*
parapets
paraphernalia
paraphrase *verb*
paraphrases
paraphrasing
paraphrased
parasite *noun*
parasites
parasitic *adjective*
parasitically
parasol *noun*
parasols
paratrooper
paratroops *plural noun*
parcel *noun*
parcels
parched
parchment
pardon *verb*
pardons
pardoning
pardoned
pardon *noun*
pardons
pardonable
parent *noun*
parents
parentage
parental
parenthood
parenthesis *noun*
parentheses
parish *noun*
parishes
parishioner *noun*
parishioners
park *noun*
parks
park *verb*
parks
parking
parked
parka *noun*
parkas
parliament *noun*
parliaments
parliamentary
parody *noun*
parodies
parole
parrot *noun*
parrots
parsley
parsnip *noun*
parsnips
parson *noun*
parsons
parsonage *noun*
parsonages
part *noun*
parts
part *verb*
parts
parting
parted
partial *adjective*
partially
partiality

participant *noun*
participants
participate *verb*
participates
participating
participated
participation
participle *noun*
participles
particle *noun*
particles
particular *adjective*
particularly
particulars *plural noun*
parting *noun*
partings
partition *noun*
partitions
partly
partner *noun*
partners
partnership
partridge *noun*
partridges
part-time *adjective*
party *noun*
parties
pass *verb*
passes
passing
passed
pass *noun*
passes
passable
passage *noun*
passages
passageway *noun*
passageways
★ **passed** see **pass**
passenger *noun*
passengers
passer-by *noun*
passers-by
passion *noun*
passions
passionate *adjective*
passionately
passive *adjective*
passively
Passover
passport *noun*
passports
password *noun*
passwords
☆ **past** *noun, adjective, and preposition*
pasta *noun*
pastas
paste *noun*
pastes
paste *verb*
pastes
pasting
pasted
pastel *noun*
pastels
pasteurization
pasteurize *verb*
pasteurizes
pasteurizing
pasteurized
pastille *noun*
pastilles
pastime *noun*
pastimes
pastoral
pastry *noun*
pastries
pasture *noun*
pastures
pasty *noun*
pasties
pasty *adjective*
pastier
pastiest
pat *verb*
pats
patting
patted
pat *noun*
pats
patch *noun*
patches
patch *verb*
patches
patching
patched
patchwork
patchy *adjective*
patchier
patchiest
patent *adjective*
patently
patent *verb*
patents
patenting
patented
patent *noun*
patents
paternal *adjective*
paternally
path *noun*
paths
pathetic *adjective*
pathetically
patience
patient *adjective*
patiently

★ You use **passed** in e.g. *We passed the house.* ! **past**.
☆ You use **past** in e.g. *We went past the house.* ! **passed**.

patient *noun*
patients
patio *noun*
patios
patriot *noun*
patriots
patriotic *adjective*
patriotically
patriotism
patrol *verb*
patrols
patrolling
patrolled
patrol *noun*
patrols
patron *noun*
patrons
patronage
patronize *verb*
patronizes
patronizing
patronized
patter *verb*
patters
pattering
pattered
patter *noun*
patters
pattern *noun*
patterns
pause *verb*
pauses
pausing
paused
pause *noun*
pauses
pave *verb*
paves
paving
paved
pavement *noun*
pavements
pavilion *noun*
pavilions
paw *noun*
paws
paw *verb*
paws
pawing
pawed
pawn *noun*
pawns
pawn *verb*
pawns
pawning
pawned
pawnbroker *noun*
pawnbrokers
pay *verb*
pays
paying
paid
pay *noun*
payment *noun*
payments
pea *noun*
peas
★ **peace**
peaceful *adjective*
peacefully
peach *noun*
peaches
peacock *noun*
peacocks
☆ **peak** *noun*
peaks
✪ **peak** *verb*
peaks
peaking
peaked
peaked
✲ **peal** *verb*
peals
pealing
pealed
✸ **peal** *noun*
peals
peanut *noun*
peanuts
❄ **pear** *noun*
pears
pearl *noun*
pearls
pearly *adjective*
pearlier
pearliest
peasant *noun*
peasants
peasantry
peat
pebble *noun*
pebbles
pebbly *adjective*
pebblier
pebbliest
peck *verb*
pecks
pecking
pecked
peck *noun*
pecks
peckish
peculiar *adjective*
peculiarly
peculiarity *noun*
peculiarities
pedal *noun*
pedals
pedal *verb*
pedals
pedalling
pedalled

★ **Peace** is a time when there is no war. ! **piece**
☆ A **peak** is the top of something. ! **peek**
✪ To **peak** is to reach the highest point. ! **peek**
✲ To **peal** is to make a ringing sound of bells. ! **peel**
✸ A **peal** is a ringing of bells. ! **peel**
❄ A **pear** is a fruit. ! **pair**

★ **peddle** *verb*
peddles
peddling
peddled
pedestal *noun*
pedestals
pedestrian *noun*
pedestrians
pedestrian *adjective*
pedigree *noun*
pedigrees
pedlar *noun*
pedlars
☆ **peek** *verb*
peeks
peeking
peeked
✪ **peel** *noun*
peels
✲ **peel** *verb*
peels
peeling
peeled
peep *verb*
peeps
peeping
peeped
peep *noun*
peeps
✸ **peer** *verb*
peers
peering
peered
peer *noun*
peers
peerless
peewit *noun*
peewits
peg *noun*
pegs
peg *verb*
pegs
pegging
pegged
Pekinese *noun*
Pekinese
pelican *noun*
pelicans
pellet *noun*
pellets
pelt *verb*
pelts
pelting
pelted
pelt *noun*
pelts
pen *noun*
pens
penalize *verb*
penalizes
penalizing
penalized
penalty *noun*
penalties
pence see **penny**
pencil *noun*
pencils
pencil *verb*
pencils
pencilling
pencilled
pendant *noun*
pendants
pendulum *noun*
pendulums
penetrate *verb*
penetrates
penetrating
penetrated
penetration
penfriend *noun*
penfriends
penguin *noun*
penguins
penicillin
peninsula *noun*
peninsulas
peninsular
penis *noun*
penises
penitence
penitent
penknife *noun*
penknives
pennant *noun*
pennants
penniless
penny *noun*
pennies *or* pence
pension *noun*
pensions
pensioner *noun*
pensioners
pentagon *noun*
pentagons
pentathlon *noun*
pentathlons
peony *noun*
peonies
people *plural noun*
people *noun*
peoples
pepper *noun*
peppers
peppermint *noun*
peppermints
peppery
perceive *verb*
perceives
perceiving
perceived
per cent

★ To **peddle** is to sell things on the street. ! **pedal**
☆ To **peek** is to look secretly at something. ! **peak**
✪ **Peel** is the skin of fruit and vegetables. ! **peal**
✲ To **peel** something is to take the skin off it. ! **peal**
✸ To **peer** is to look closely at something. ! **pier**.

percentage *noun*
percentages
perceptible *adjective*
perceptibly
perception *noun*
perceptions
perceptive *adjective*
perceptively
perch *verb*
perches
perching
perched
perch *noun*
perch
percolator *noun*
percolators
percussion
percussive
perennial *adjective*
perennially
perennial *noun*
perennials
perfect *adjective*
perfectly
perfect *verb*
perfects
perfecting
perfected
perfection
perforate *verb*
perforates
perforating
perforated
perforation *noun*
perforations
perform *verb*
performs
performing
performed
performance *noun*
performances
performer *noun*
performers
perfume *noun*
perfumes
perhaps
peril *noun*
perils
perilous *adjective*
perilously
perimeter *noun*
perimeters
period *noun*
periods
periodic *adjective*
periodically
periodical *noun*
periodicals
periscope *noun*
periscopes
perish *verb*
perishes
perishing
perished
perishable
perm *noun*
perms
perm *verb*
perms
perming
permed
permanence
permanent *adjective*
permanently
permissible
permission
permissive *adjective*
permissively
permissiveness
permit *verb*
permits
permitting
permitted
permit *noun*
permits
perpendicular
perpetual *adjective*
perpetually
perpetuate *verb*
perpetuates
perpetuating
perpetuated
perplex *verb*
perplexes
perplexing
perplexed
perplexity
persecute *verb*
persecutes
persecuting
persecuted
persecution *noun*
persecutions
persecutor *noun*
persecutors
perseverance
persevere *verb*
perseveres
persevering
persevered
persist *verb*
persists
persisting
persisted
persistence
persistent *adjective*
persistently
★ **person** *noun*
persons *or* people
personal *adjective*
personally
personality *noun*
personalities

★ The normal plural is **people**: *three people came*. **Persons** is formal, e.g. in official reports.

personnel *plural noun*
perspective *noun*
perspectives
perspiration
perspire *verb*
perspires
perspiring
perspired
persuade *verb*
persuades
persuading
persuaded
persuasion
persuasive *adjective*
persuasively
perverse *adjective*
perversely
perversion *noun*
perversions
perversity
pervert *verb*
perverts
perverting
perverted
pervert *noun*
perverts
★ **Pesach**
pessimism
pessimist *noun*
pessimists
pessimistic *adjective*
pessimistically
pest *noun*
pests
pester *verb*
pesters
pestering
pestered
pesticide *noun*
pesticides
pestle *noun*
pestles
pet *noun*
pets
petal *noun*
petals
petition *noun*
petitions
petrify *verb*
petrifies
petrifying
petrified
petrochemical *noun*
petrochemicals
petrol
petroleum
petticoat *noun*
petticoats
pettiness
petty *adjective*
pettier
pettiest
pettily
pew *noun*
pews
pewter
pharmacy *noun*
pharmacies
phase *noun*
phases
phase *verb*
phases
phasing
phased
pheasant *noun*
pheasants
phenomenal *adjective*
phenomenally
phenomenon *noun*
phenomena
philatelist *noun*
philatelists
philately
philosopher *noun*
philosophers
philosophical *adjective*
philosophically
philosophy *noun*
philosophies
phobia *noun*
phobias

-phobia
-phobia makes words meaning 'a strong fear or dislike', e.g. **xenophobia** (= a dislike of strangers'). It comes from a Greek word and is only used with other Greek or Latin words.

phoenix *noun*
phoenixes
phone *noun*
phones
phone *verb*
phones
phoning
phoned

-phone
-phone makes words to do with sound, e.g. **telephone**, **saxophone**. You can sometimes make adjectives by using *-phonic*, e.g. **telephonic**, and nouns by using *-phony*, e.g. **telephony**.

★ The Hebrew name for Passover.

phonecard *noun*
phonecards
phone-in *noun*
phone-ins
phosphorescence
phosphorescent
phosphoric
phosphorus
photo *noun*
photos

photo-
photo- makes words to do with light, e.g. **photograph, photocopy**. It is also used in more technical words such as **photochemistry** (= the chemistry of light) and as a separate word in **photo** (= photograph) and **photo finish** (= close finish to a race).

photocopier *noun*
photocopiers
photocopy *noun*
photocopies
photocopy *verb*
photocopies
photocopying
photocopied
photoelectric
photograph *noun*
photographs
photograph *verb*
photographs
photographing
photographed
photographer *noun*
photographers
photographic *adjective*
photographically
photography
phrase *noun*
phrases
phrase *verb*
phrases
phrasing
phrased
physical *adjective*
physically
physician *noun*
physicians
physicist *noun*
physicists
physics
physiological *adjective*
physiologically
physiologist *noun*
physiologists
physiology
★ **pi**
pianist *noun*
pianists
piano *noun*
pianos
piccolo *noun*
piccolos
pick *verb*
picks
picking
picked
pick *noun*
picks
pickaxe *noun*
pickaxes
picket *noun*
pickets
picket *verb*
pickets
picketing
picketed
pickle *noun*
pickles
pickle *verb*
pickles
pickling
pickled
pickpocket *noun*
pickpockets
pick-up *noun*
pick-ups
picnic *noun*
picnics
picnic *verb*
picnics
picnicking
picnicked
picnicker *noun*
picnickers
pictogram *noun*
pictograms
pictorial *adjective*
pictorially
picture *noun*
pictures
picture *verb*
pictures
picturing
pictured
picturesque
☆ **pie** *noun*
pies
✪ **piece** *noun*
pieces
piece *verb*
pieces
piecing
pieced

★ **Pi** is a Greek letter, used in mathematics. ! **pie**.
☆ A **pie** is a food with pastry. ! **pi**.
✪ You use **piece** in e.g. *a piece of cake*. ! **peace**.

piecemeal
pie chart *noun*
pie charts
★ **pier** *noun*
piers
pierce *verb*
pierces
piercing
pierced
pig *noun*
pigs
pigeon *noun*
pigeons
pigeon-hole *noun*
pigeon-holes
piggy *noun*
piggies
piggyback *noun*
piggybacks
piglet *noun*
piglets
pigment *noun*
pigments
pigmy *noun*
use **pygmy**
pigsty *noun*
pigsties
pigtail *noun*
pigtails
pike *noun*
pikes
pilchard *noun*
pilchards
pile *noun*
piles
pile *verb*
piles
piling
piled
pilfer *verb*
pilfers
pilfering
pilfered
pilgrim *noun*
pilgrims
pilgrimage *noun*
pilgrimages
pill *noun*
pills
pillage *verb*
pillages
pillaging
pillaged
pillar *noun*
pillars
pillion *noun*
pillions
pillow *noun*
pillows
pillowcase *noun*
pillowcases
pilot *noun*
pilots
pilot *verb*
pilots
piloting
piloted
pimple *noun*
pimples
pimply *adjective*
pimplier
pimpliest
pin *noun*
pins
pin *verb*
pins
pinning
pinned
pinafore *noun*
pinafores
pincer *noun*
pincers
pinch *verb*
pinches
pinching
pinched
pinch *noun*
pinches
pincushion *noun*
pincushions
pine *noun*
pines
pine *verb*
pines
pining
pined
pineapple *noun*
pineapples
ping-pong
pink *adjective*
pinker
pinkest
pink *noun*
pinks
pint *noun*
pints
pioneer *noun*
pioneers
pious *adjective*
piously
pip *noun*
pips
pipe *noun*
pipes
pipe *verb*
pipes
piping
piped
pipeline *noun*
pipelines

★ A **pier** is a long building on stilts going into the sea. ! **peer**.

piper *noun*
pipers
piracy
pirate *noun*
pirates
★ **pistil** *noun*
pistils
★ **pistol** *noun*
pistols
piston *noun*
pistons
pit *noun*
pits
pit *verb*
pits
pitting
pitted
pitch *noun*
pitches
pitch *verb*
pitches
pitching
pitched
pitch-black
pitcher *noun*
pitchers
pitchfork *noun*
pitchforks
pitfall *noun*
pitfalls
pitiful *adjective*
pitifully
pitiless *adjective*
pitilessly
pity *verb*
pities
pitying
pitied
pity *noun*
pivot *noun*
pivots
pivot *verb*
pivots
pivoting
pivoted
pixie *noun*
pixies
pizza *noun*
pizzas
pizzicato
placard *noun*
placards
☆ **place** *noun*
places
place *verb*
places
placing
placed
placid *adjective*
placidly
plague *noun*
plagues
plague *verb*
plagues
plaguing
plagued
✪ **plaice** *noun*
plaice
plaid *noun*
plaids
✲ **plain** *adjective*
plainer
plainest
plainly
plain *noun*
plains
plain clothes
plainness
plaintiff *noun*
plaintiffs
plaintive
plaintively
plait *noun*
plaits
plait *verb*
plaits
plaiting
plaited
plan *noun*
plans
plan *verb*
plans
planning
planned
✹ **plane** *noun*
planes
❄ **plane** *verb*
planes
planing
planed
planet *noun*
planets
planetary
plank *noun*
planks
plankton
planner *noun*
planners
plant *noun*
plants
plant *verb*
plants
planting
planted
plantation *noun*
plantations
planter *noun*
planters

★ A **pistil** is a part of a flower and a **pistol** is a gun.
☆ You use **place** in e.g. *a place in the country*. ! **plaice**.
✪ A **plaice** is a fish. ! **place**.
✲ **Plain** means 'not pretty or decorated'. ! **plane**.
✹ A **plane** is an aeroplane, a level surface, a tool, or a tree. ! **plain**.
❄ To **plane** wood is to make it smooth with a tool. ! **plain**.

plaque *noun*
plaques
plasma
plaster *noun*
plasters
plaster *verb*
plasters
plastering
plastered
plasterer *noun*
plasterers
plaster of Paris
plastic *adjective* and *noun*
plastics
Plasticine
plate *noun*
plates
plate *verb*
plates
plating
plated
plateau *noun*
plateaux
plateful *noun*
platefuls
platform *noun*
platforms
platinum
platoon *noun*
platoons
platypus *noun*
platypuses
play *verb*
plays
playing
played
play *noun*
plays
playback *noun*
playbacks
player *noun*
players
playful *adjective*
playfully
playfulness
playground *noun*
playgrounds
playgroup *noun*
playgroups
playmate *noun*
playmates
play-off *noun*
play-offs
playtime *noun*
playtimes
playwright *noun*
playwrights
plea *noun*
pleas
plead *verb*
pleads
pleading
pleaded
pleasant *adjective*
pleasanter
pleasantest
pleasantly
please *verb*
pleases
pleasing
pleased
pleasurable *adjective*
pleasurably
pleasure *noun*
pleasures
pleat *noun*
pleats
pleated
pledge *verb*
pledges
pledging
pledged
pledge *noun*
pledges
plentiful *adjective*
plentifully
plenty
pliable
pliers *plural noun*
plight *noun*
plights
plod *verb*
plods
plodding
plodded
plodder *noun*
plodders
plop *verb*
plops
plopping
plopped
plop *noun*
plops
plot *noun*
plots
plot *verb*
plots
plotting
plotted
plotter *noun*
plotters
plough *noun*
ploughs
plough *verb*
ploughs
ploughing
ploughed
ploughman *noun*
ploughmen

plover *noun*
plovers
pluck *verb*
plucks
plucking
plucked
pluck *noun*
plucky *adjective*
pluckier
pluckiest
pluckily
plug *noun*
plugs
plug *verb*
plugs
plugging
plugged
★ **plum** *noun*
plums
plumage
☆ **plumb** *verb*
plumbs
plumbing
plumbed
plumber *noun*
plumbers
plumbing
plume *noun*
plumes
plumed
plump *adjective*
plumper
plumpest
plump *verb*
plumps
plumping
plumped
plunder *verb*
plunders
plundering
plundered
plunder *noun*
plunderer *noun*
plunderers
plunge *verb*
plunges
plunging
plunged
plunge *noun*
plunges
plural *adjective* and *noun*
plurals
plus *preposition*
plus *noun*
pluses
plutonium
plywood
pneumatic
pneumonia
poach *verb*
poaches
poaching
poached
poacher *noun*
poachers
pocket *noun*
pockets
pocket *verb*
pockets
pocketing
pocketed
pocketful *noun*
pocketfuls
pod *noun*
pods
podgy *adjective*
podgier
podgiest
poem *noun*
poems
poet *noun*
poets
poetic *adjective*
poetically
poetry
point *noun*
points
point *verb*
points
pointing
pointed
point-blank *adjective*
pointed *adjective*
pointedly
pointer *noun*
pointers
pointless *adjective*
pointlessly
poise *noun*
poise *verb*
poises
poising
poised
poison *noun*
poisons
poison *verb*
poisons
poisoning
poisoned
poisoner *noun*
poisoners
poisonous *adjective*
poisonously
poke *verb*
pokes
poking
poked
poke *noun*
pokes
poker *noun*
pokers

★ A **plum** is a fruit. ! **plumb**.
☆ To **plumb** water is to see how deep it is. ! **plum**.

★ **polar**
Polaroid
★ **pole** *noun*
poles
police *plural noun*
policeman *noun*
policemen
police officer *noun*
police officers
policewoman *noun*
policewomen
policy *noun*
policies
polio
poliomyelitis
polish *verb*
polishes
polishing
polished
polish *noun*
polishes
polished
polite *adjective*
politer
politest
politely
politeness
political *adjective*
politically
politician *noun*
politicians
politics
polka *noun*
polkas
☆ **poll** *noun*
polls
pollen
pollute *verb*
pollutes
polluting
polluted
pollution
polo
polo neck *noun*
polo necks
poltergeist *noun*
poltergeists
polygon *noun*
polygons
polystyrene
polythene
pomp
pomposity
pompous *adjective*
pompously
pond *noun*
ponds
ponder *verb*
ponders
pondering
pondered
ponderous *adjective*
ponderously
pony *noun*
ponies
ponytail *noun*
ponytails
pony-trekking
poodle *noun*
poodles
pool *noun*
pools
pool *verb*
pools
pooling
pooled
poor *adjective*
poorer
poorest
poorly
poorly *adjective* and *adverb*
pop *verb*
pops
popping
popped
pop *noun*
pops
popcorn
Pope *noun*
Popes
poplar *noun*
poplars
poppadom *noun*
poppadoms
poppy *noun*
poppies
popular *adjective*
popularly
popularity
popularize *verb*
popularizes
popularizing
popularized
populated
population *noun*
populations
populous
porcelain
porch *noun*
porches
porcupine *noun*
porcupines
pore *noun*
pores
✪ **pore** *verb*
pores
poring
pored
pork

★ A **pole** is a long thin stick. ! **poll**.
☆ A **poll** is a vote in an election. ! **pole**.
✪ To **pore** over something is to study it closely. ! **pour**.

pornographic
pornography
porosity
porous
porpoise *noun*
porpoises
porridge
port *noun*
ports
portable
portcullis *noun*
portcullises
porter *noun*
porters
porthole *noun*
portholes
portion *noun*
portions
portliness
portly *adjective*
portlier
portliest
portrait *noun*
portraits
portray *verb*
portrays
portraying
portrayed
portrayal *noun*
portrayals
pose *verb*
poses
posing
posed
pose *noun*
poses
poser *noun*
posers
posh *adjective*
posher
poshest
position *noun*
positions
positive *adjective*
positively
positive *noun*
positives
posse *noun*
posses
possess *verb*
possesses
possessing
possessed
possession *noun*
possessions
possessive *adjective*
possessively
possessor *noun*
possessors
possibility *noun*
possibilities
possible *adjective*
possibly
post *verb*
posts
posting
posted
post *noun*
posts
postage
postal
postbox *noun*
postboxes
postcard *noun*
postcards
postcode *noun*
postcodes
poster *noun*
posters
postman *noun*
postmen
postmark *noun*
postmarks
post-mortem *noun*
post-mortems
postpone *verb*
postpones
postponing
postponed
postponement *noun*
postponements
postscript *noun*
postscripts
posture *noun*
postures
posy *noun*
posies
pot *noun*
pots
pot *verb*
pots
potting
potted
potassium
potato *noun*
potatoes
potency
potent *adjective*
potently
potential *adjective*
potentially
potential *noun*
potentials
pothole *noun*
potholes
potholer *noun*
potholer
potholing
potion *noun*
potions
potter *noun*
potters

potter *verb*
potters
pottering
pottered
pottery *noun*
potteries
potty *adjective*
pottier
pottiest
pottily
potty *noun*
potties
pouch *noun*
pouches
poultry
pounce *verb*
pounces
pouncing
pounced
pound *noun*
pounds
pound *verb*
pounds
pounding
pounded
★ **pour** *verb*
pours
pouring
poured
pout *verb*
pouts
pouting
pouted
poverty
powder *noun*
powders
powder *verb*
powders
powdering
powdered
powdery
power *noun*
powers
powered
powerful *adjective*
powerfully
powerhouse *noun*
powerhouses
powerless
practicable
practical *adjective*
practically
practice *noun*
practices
practise *verb*
practises
practising
practised
prairie *noun*
prairies
praise *verb*
praises
praising
praised
praise *noun*
praises
pram *noun*
prams
prance *verb*
prances
prancing
pranced
prank *noun*
pranks
prawn *noun*
prawns
☆ **pray** *verb*
prays
praying
prayed
prayer *noun*
prayers

pre-
pre- makes words meaning 'before', e.g. **pre-date** (= to exist before something else), **prefabricated** (= made in advance). Many are spelt joined up, but not all.

preach *verb*
preaches
preaching
preached
preacher *noun*
preachers
precarious *adjective*
precariously
precaution *noun*
precautions
precede *verb*
precedes
preceding
preceded
precedence
precedent *noun*
precedents
precinct *noun*
precincts
precious *adjective*
preciously
precipice *noun*
precipices
précis *noun*
précis
precise *adjective*
precisely
precision
predator *noun*
predators
predatory

★ To **pour** a liquid is to tip it from a jug etc. ! **pore**.
☆ To **pray** is to say prayers. ! **prey**.

predecessor *noun*
predecessors
predict *verb*
predicts
predicting
predicted
predictable *adjective*
predictably
prediction *noun*
predictions
predominance
predominant *adjective*
predominantly
predominate *verb*
predominates
predominating
predominated
preface *noun*
prefaces
prefect *noun*
prefects
prefer *verb*
prefers
preferring
preferred
preferable *adjective*
preferably
preference *noun*
preferences
prefix *noun*
prefixes
pregnancy *noun*
pregnancies
pregnant
prehistoric
prehistory
prejudice *noun*
prejudices
prejudiced
preliminary *adjective* and *noun*
preliminaries
prelude *noun*
preludes
premier *noun*
premiers
première *noun*
premières
premises *plural noun*
premium *noun*
premiums
Premium Bond *noun*
Premium Bonds
preoccupation *noun*
preoccupations
preoccupied
prep
preparation *noun*
preparations
preparatory
prepare *verb*
prepares
preparing
prepared
preposition *noun*
prepositions
prescribe *verb*
prescribes
prescribing
prescribed
prescription *noun*
prescriptions
presence
present *adjective*
presently
present *noun*
presents
present *verb*
presents
presenting
presented
presentation *noun*
presentations
presenter *noun*
presenters
preservation
preservative *noun*
preservatives
preserve *verb*
preserves
preserving
preserved
preside *verb*
presides
presiding
presided
presidency *noun*
presidencies
president *noun*
presidents
presidential *adjective*
presidentially
press *verb*
presses
pressing
pressed
press *noun*
presses
press-up *noun*
press-ups
pressure *noun*
pressures
pressurize *verb*
pressurizes
pressurizing
pressurized
prestige
prestigious *adjective*
prestigiously
presumably

presume *verb*
presumes
presuming
presumed
presumption *noun*
presumptions
presumptuous *adjective*
presumptuously
pretence *noun*
pretences
pretend *verb*
pretends
pretending
pretended
pretender *noun*
pretenders
prettiness
pretty *adjective* and *adverb*
prettier
prettiest
prettily
prevail *verb*
prevails
prevailing
prevailed
prevalent
prevent *verb*
prevents
preventing
prevented
prevention
preventive
preview *noun*
previews
previous *adjective*
previously
★ **prey** *verb*
preys
preying
preyed
prey *noun*
price *noun*
prices
price *verb*
prices
pricing
priced
priceless
prick *verb*
pricks
pricking
pricked
prick *noun*
pricks
prickle *noun*
prickles
prickly *adjective*
pricklier
prickliest
pride *noun*
prides
priest *noun*
priests
priestess *noun*
priestesses
priesthood
prig *noun*
prigs
priggish *adjective*
priggishly
prim *adjective*
primmer
primmest
primly
primness
primary *adjective*
primarily
primate *noun*
primates
prime *adjective*
prime *verb*
primes
priming
primed
prime *noun*
primes
prime minister *noun*
prime ministers
primer *noun*
primers
primeval
primitive *adjective*
primitively
primrose *noun*
primroses
prince *noun*
princes
princely
princess *noun*
princesses
☆ **principal** *adjective*
principally
✪ **principal** *noun*
principals
✲ **principle** *noun*
principles
print *verb*
prints
printing
printed
print *noun*
prints
printer *noun*
printers
printout *noun*
printouts
priority *noun*
priorities

★ To **prey** on animals is to hunt and kill them. ! **pray**.
☆ **Principal** means 'chief' or 'main'. ! **principle**.
✪ A **principal** is a head of a college. ! **principle**.
✲ A **principle** is a rule or belief. ! **principal**.

★ **prise** *verb*
prises
prising
prised
prism *noun*
prisms
prison *noun*
prisons
prisoner *noun*
prisoners
privacy
private *adjective*
privately
private *noun*
privates
privatization
privatize *verb*
privatizes
privatizing
privatized
privet
privilege *noun*
privileges
privileged
prize *noun*
prizes
☆ **prize** *verb*
prizes
prizing
prized
pro *noun*
pros

pro-
pro- makes words meaning 'in favour of', e.g. **pro-choice**. In this type of word you use a hyphen.

probability *noun*
probabilities
probable *adjective*
probably
probation
probationary
probe *verb*
probes
probing
probed
probe *noun*
probes
problem *noun*
problems
procedure *noun*
procedures
proceed *verb*
proceeds
proceeding
proceeded
proceedings *plural noun*
proceeds *plural noun*
process *noun*
processes
process *verb*
processes
processing
processed
procession *noun*
processions
proclaim *verb*
proclaims
proclaiming
proclaimed
proclamation *noun*
proclamations
prod *verb*
prods
prodding
prodded
prodigal *adjective*
prodigally
produce *verb*
produces
producing
produced
produce *noun*
producer *noun*
producers
product *noun*
products
production *noun*
productions
productive *adjective*
productively
productivity
profession *noun*
professions
professional *adjective*
professionally
professional *noun*
professionals
professor *noun*
professors
proficiency
proficient *adjective*
proficiently
profile *noun*
profiles
✪ **profit** *noun*
profits
profit *verb*
profits
profiting
profited
profitable *adjective*
profitably
profound *adjective*
profoundly
profundity
profuse *adjective*
profusely

★ To **prise** something is to open it. ! **prize**.
☆ To **prize** something is to value it highly. ! **prise**.
✪ A **profit** is extra money made by selling something. ! **prophet**.

profusion
★ **program** *noun*
programs
program *verb*
programs
programming
programmed
★ **programme** *noun*
programmes
progress *noun*
progress *verb*
progresses
progressing
progressed
progression
progressive *adjective*
progressively
prohibit *verb*
prohibits
prohibiting
prohibited
prohibition *noun*
prohibitions
project *noun*
projects
project *verb*
projects
projecting
projected
projection *noun*
projections
projectionist *noun*
projectionists
projector *noun*
projectors
prologue *noun*
prologues
prolong *verb*
prolongs
prolonging
prolonged
promenade *noun*
promenades
prominence
prominent *adjective*
prominently
promise *verb*
promises
promising
promised
promise *noun*
promises
promontory *noun*
promontories
promote *verb*
promotes
promoting
promoted
promoter *noun*
promoter
promotion *noun*
promotions
prompt *adjective*
prompter
promptest
promptly
prompt *verb*
prompts
prompting
prompted
prompter *noun*
prompters
promptness
prone
prong *noun*
prongs
pronoun *noun*
pronouns
pronounce *verb*
pronounces
pronouncing
pronounced
pronouncement *noun*
pronouncements
pronunciation *noun*
pronunciations
proof *adjective* and *noun*
proofs
prop *verb*
props
propping
propped
prop *noun*
props
propaganda
propel *verb*
propels
propelling
propelled
propellant *noun*
propellants
propeller *noun*
propellers
proper *adjective*
properly
property *noun*
properties
prophecy *noun*
prophecies
prophesy *verb*
prophesies
prophesying
prophesied
☆ **prophet** *noun*
prophets
prophetic *adjective*
prophetically
proportion *noun*
proportions

★ You use **program** when you are talking about computers. In other meanings you use **programme**.
☆ A **prophet** is someone who makes predictions about the future. ! **profit**.

proportional *adjective*
proportionally
proportionate *adjective*
proportionately
propose *verb*
proposes
proposing
proposed
proposal *noun*
proposals
proprietor *noun*
proprietors
propulsion
prose
prosecute *verb*
prosecutes
prosecuting
prosecuted
prosecution *noun*
prosecutions
prosecutor *noun*
prosecutors
prospect *noun*
prospects
prospect *verb*
prospects
prospecting
prospected
prospector *noun*
prospectors
prosper *verb*
prospers
prospering
prospered
prosperity
prosperous *adjective*
prosperously
prostitute *noun*
prostitutes
protect *verb*
protects
protecting
protected
protection
protective *adjective*
protectively
protector *noun*
protectors
protein *noun*
proteins
protest *verb*
protests
protesting
protested
protest *noun*
protests
protester *noun*
protesters
Protestant *noun*
Protestants
proton *noun*
protons
protoplasm
prototype *noun*
prototypes
protractor *noun*
protractors
protrude *verb*
protrudes
protruding
protruded
protrusion *noun*
protrusions
proud *adjective*
prouder
proudest
proudly
prove *verb*
proves
proving
proved
proverb *noun*
proverbs
proverbial *adjective*
proverbially
provide *verb*
provides
providing
provided
province *noun*
provinces
provincial
provision *noun*
provisions
provisional *adjective*
provisionally
provocative *adjective*
provocatively
provoke *verb*
provokes
provoking
provoked
provocation *noun*
provocations
prow *noun*
prows
prowl *verb*
prowls
prowling
prowled
prowler *noun*
prowlers
prudence
prudent *adjective*
prudently
prune *noun*
prunes
prune *verb*
prunes
pruning
pruned

pry *verb*
pries
prying
pried
psalm *noun*
psalms
pseudonym *noun*
pseudonyms
psychiatric
psychiatrist *noun*
psychiatrists
psychiatry
psychic
psychological *adjective*
psychologically
psychologist *noun*
psychologists
psychology
pub *noun*
pubs
puberty
public *adjective* and *noun*
publicly
publication *noun*
publications
publicity
publicize *verb*
publicizes
publicizing
publicized
publish *verb*
publishes
publishing
published
publisher *noun*
publishers
puck *noun*
pucks
pucker *verb*
puckers
puckering
puckered
pudding *noun*
puddings
puddle *noun*
puddles
puff *verb*
puffs
puffing
puffed
puff *noun*
puffs
puffin *noun*
puffins
pull *verb*
pulls
pulling
pulled
pull *noun*
pulls
pulley *noun*
pulleys
pullover *noun*
pullovers
pulp *noun*
pulps
pulp *verb*
pulps
pulping
pulped
pulpit *noun*
pulpits
pulse *noun*
pulses
pulverize *verb*
pulverizes
pulverizing
pulverized
puma *noun*
pumas
pumice
pump *verb*
pumps
pumping
pumped
pump *noun*
pumps
pumpkin *noun*
pumpkins
pun *noun*
puns
pun *verb*
puns
punning
punned
punch *verb*
punches
punching
punched
punch *noun*
punches
punch *noun*
punches
punchline *noun*
punchlines
punch-up *noun*
punch-ups
punctual *adjective*
punctually
punctuality
punctuate *verb*
punctuates
punctuating
punctuated
punctuation
puncture *noun*
punctures
punish *verb*
punishes
punishing
punished

punishment *noun*
punishments
punk *noun*
punks
punt *noun*
punts
punt *verb*
punts
punting
punted
puny *adjective*
punier
puniest
pup *noun*
pups
pupa *noun*
pupae
pupil *noun*
pupils
puppet *noun*
puppets
puppy *noun*
puppies
purchase *verb*
purchases
purchasing
purchased
purchase *noun*
purchases
purchaser *noun*
purchasers
purdah
pure *adjective*
purer
purest
purely
purge *verb*
purges
purging
purged
purge *noun*
purges
purification
purifier *noun*
purifiers
purify *verb*
purifies
purifying
purified
★ **Puritan** *noun*
Puritans
puritan *noun*
puritans
puritanical *adjective*
puritanically
purity
purple *noun*
purpose *noun*
purposes
purposely
purr *verb*
purrs
purring
purred
purse *noun*
purses
pursue *verb*
pursues
pursuing
pursued
pursuer *noun*
pursuers
pursuit *noun*
pursuits
☆ **pus** *noun*
push *verb*
pushes
pushing
pushed
push *noun*
pushes
pushchair *noun*
pushchairs
✪ **puss** *or* **pussy** *noun*
pusses *or* pussies
✲ **put** *verb*
puts
putting
put
✸ **putt** *verb*
putts
putting
putted
putter *noun*
putters
putty
puzzle *verb*
puzzles
puzzling
puzzled
puzzle *noun*
puzzles
pygmy *noun*
pygmies
pyjamas
pylon *noun*
pylons
pyramid *noun*
pyramids
pyramidal
python *noun*
pythons

Qq

quack *verb*
quacks
quacking
quacked
quack *noun*
quacks

★ You use a capital P when you are talking about people in history, and a small p when you mean anyone who is morally strict.
☆ **Pus** is yellow stuff produced in sore places on the body. ! **puss**.
✪ **Puss** is a word for a cat. ! **pus**.
✲ To **put** something somewhere is to place it there. ! **putt**.
✸ To **putt** a ball is to tap it gently. ! **put**.

quad *noun*
quads
quadrangle *noun*
quadrangles
quadrant *noun*
quadrants
quadrilateral *noun*
quadrilaterals
quadruple *adjective* and *noun*
quadruple *verb*
quadruples
quadrupling
quadrupled
quadruplet *noun*
quadruplets
quail *verb*
quails
quailing
quailed
quail *noun*
quail *or* quails
quaint *adjective*
quainter
quaintest
quaintly
quaintness *noun*
quake *verb*
quakes
quaking
quaked
Quaker *noun*
Quakers
qualification *noun*
qualifications
qualify *verb*
qualifies
qualifying
qualified
quality *noun*
qualities
quantity *noun*
quantities
quarantine
quarrel *noun*
quarrels
quarrel *verb*
quarrels
quarrelling
quarrelled
quarrelsome
quarry *noun*
quarries
quart *noun*
quarts
quarter *noun*
quarters
quartet *noun*
quartets
quartz
quaver *verb*
quavers
quavering
quavered
quaver *noun*
quavers
★ **quay** *noun*
quays
queasy *adjective*
queasier
queasiest
queen *noun*
queens
queer *adjective*
queerer
queerest
quench *verb*
quenches
quenching
quenched
query *verb*
queries
querying
queried
query *noun*
queries
quest *noun*
quests
question *noun*
questions
question *verb*
questions
questioning
questioned
questionable *adjective*
questionably
questioner *noun*
questioner
questionnaire *noun*
questionnaires
☆ **queue** *noun*
queues
queue *verb*
queues
queueing
queued
quibble *verb*
quibbles
quibbling
quibbled
quibble *noun*
quibbles
quiche *noun*
quiches
quick *adjective*
quicker
quickest
quickly
quicken *verb*
quickens
quickening
quickened

★ A **quay** is a place where ships tie up. ! **key**.
☆ A **queue** is a line of people waiting for something. ! **cue**.

quicksand *noun*
quicksands
quid *noun*
quid
quiet *adjective*
quieter
quietest
quietly
quieten *verb*
quietens
quietening
quietened
quill *noun*
quills
quilt *noun*
quilts
quintet *noun*
quintets
quit *verb*
quits
quitting
quitted
quit
quitter *noun*
quitters
quite
quiver *verb*
quivers
quivering
quivered
quiver *noun*
quivers
quiz *noun*
quizzes
quiz *verb*
quizzes
quizzing
quizzed
quoit *noun*
quoits
quota *noun*
quotas
quotation *noun*
quotations
quote *verb*
quotes
quoting
quoted
quotient *noun*
quotients

Rr

rabbi *noun*
rabbis
rabbit *noun*
rabbits
rabid
rabies
raccoon *noun*
raccoons
race *noun*
races
race *verb*
races
racing
raced
race *noun*
races
racecourse *noun*
racecourses
racer *noun*
racers
racial *adjective*
racially
racism
racist *noun*
racists
rack *noun*
racks
rack *verb*
racks
racking
racked
racket *noun*
rackets
radar
radial *adjective*
radially
radiance
radiant *adjective*
radiantly
radiate *verb*
radiates
radiating
radiated
radiation
radiator *noun*
radiators
radical *adjective*
radically
radical *noun*
radicals
radii see **radius**
radio *noun*
radios
radioactive
radioactivity
radish *noun*
radishes
radium
radius *noun*
radii
raffle *noun*
raffles
raffle *verb*
raffles
raffling
raffled

raft *noun*
rafts
rafter *noun*
rafters
rag *noun*
rags
rage *noun*
rages
rage *verb*
rages
raging
raged
ragged
ragtime
raid *noun*
raids
raid *verb*
raids
raiding
raided
raider *noun*
raiders
rail *noun*
rails
railings *plural noun*
railway *noun*
railways
rain *verb*
rains
raining
rained
rain *noun*
rains
rainbow *noun*
rainbows
raincoat *noun*
raincoats
raindrop *noun*
raindrops
rainfall
rainforest *noun*
rainforests
raise *verb*
raises
raising
raised
raisin *noun*
raisins
rake *verb*
rakes
raking
raked
rake *noun*
rakes
rally *verb*
rallies
rallying
rallied
rally *noun*
rallies
ram *verb*
rams
ramming
rammed
ram *noun*
rams
Ramadan
ramble *noun*
rambles
ramble *verb*
rambles
rambling
rambled
rambler *noun*
ramblers
ramp *noun*
ramps
rampage *verb*
rampages
rampaging
rampaged
rampage *noun*
ran see **run**
ranch *noun*
ranches
random
rang see **ring**
range *noun*
ranges
range *verb*
ranges
ranging
ranged
★ **ranger** *noun*
rangers
rank *noun*
ranks
rank *verb*
ranks
ranking
ranked
ransack *verb*
ransacks
ransacking
ransacked
ransom *verb*
ransoms
ransoming
ransomed
ransom *noun*
ransoms
☆ **rap** *verb*
raps
rapping
rapped
rap *noun*
raps
rapid *adjective*
rapidly
rapidity
rapids *plural noun*

★ You use a capital R when you mean a senior Guide.
☆ To **rap** is to knock loudly. ! **wrap**.

rare *adjective*
rarer
rarest
rarely
rarity *noun*
rarities
rascal *noun*
rascals
rash *adjective*
rasher
rashest
rashly
rash *noun*
rashes
rasher *noun*
rashers
raspberry *noun*
raspberries
Rastafarian *noun*
Rastafarians
rat *noun*
rats
rate *noun*
rates
rate *verb*
rates
rating
rated
rather
ratio *noun*
ratios
ration *noun*
rations
ration *verb*
rations
rationing
rationed
rational *adjective*
rationally
rationalize *verb*
rationalizes
rationalizing
rationalized

rattle *verb*
rattles
rattling
rattled
rattle *noun*
rattles
rattlesnake *noun*
rattlesnakes
rave *verb*
raves
raving
raved
rave *noun*
raves
raven *noun*
ravens
ravenous *adjective*
ravenously
ravine *noun*
ravines
raw *adjective*
rawer
rawest
ray *noun*
rays
razor *noun*
razors

re-

re- makes words meaning 'again', e.g. **reproduce**. These words are normally spelt joined up, but a few need a hyphen so you don't confuse them with other words, e.g. **re-cover** (= to put a new cover on); **recover** has another meaning. You also need a hyphen in words beginning with e, e.g. **re-enter**.

reach *verb*
reaches
reaching
reached
reach *noun*
reaches
react *verb*
reacts
reacting
reacted
reaction *noun*
reactions
reactor *noun*
reactors
★ **read** *verb*
reads
reading
read
readable
reader *noun*
readers
readily
readiness
reading *noun*
readings
ready *adjective*
readier
readiest
☆ **real** *adjective*
realism
realist *noun*
realists
realistic *adjective*
realistically
reality *noun*
realities
realization
realize *verb*
realizes
realizing
realized

★ To **read** is to look at something written or printed. ! **reed**.
☆ **Real** means 'true' or 'existing'. ! **reel**.

really
realm *noun*
realms
reap *verb*
reaps
reaping
reaped
reaper *noun*
reapers
reappear *verb*
reappears
reappearing
reappeared
reappearance *noun*
reappearances
rear *adjective* and *noun*
rears
rear *verb*
rears
rearing
reared
rearrange *verb*
rearranges
rearranging
rearranged
rearrangement *noun*
rearrangements
reason *noun*
reasons
reason *verb*
reasons
reasoning
reasoned
reasonable *adjective*
reasonably
reassurance *noun*
reassurances
reassure *verb*
reassures
reassuring
reassured
rebel *verb*
rebels
rebelling
rebelled
rebel *noun*
rebels
rebellion *noun*
rebellions
rebellious *adjective*
rebelliously
rebound *verb*
rebounds
rebounding
rebounded
rebuild *verb*
rebuilds
rebuilding
rebuilt
recall *verb*
recalls
recalling
recalled
recap *verb*
recaps
recapping
recapped
recapture *verb*
recaptures
recapturing
recaptured
recede *verb*
recedes
receding
receded
receipt *noun*
receipts
receive *verb*
receives
receiving
received
receiver *noun*
receivers
recent *adjective*
recently
receptacle *noun*
receptacles
reception *noun*
receptions
receptionist *noun*
receptionists
recess *noun*
recesses
recession *noun*
recessions
recipe *noun*
recipes
reciprocal *adjective*
reciprocally
reciprocal *noun*
reciprocals
recital *noun*
recitals
recitation *noun*
recitations
recite *verb*
recites
reciting
recited
reckless *adjective*
recklessly
recklessness
reckon *verb*
reckons
reckoning
reckoned
reclaim *verb*
reclaims
reclaiming
reclaimed

reclamation *noun*
reclamations
recline *verb*
reclines
reclining
reclined
recognition
recognizable *adjective*
recognizably
recognize *verb*
recognizes
recognizing
recognized
recoil *verb*
recoils
recoiling
recoiled
recollect *verb*
recollects
recollecting
recollected
recollection *noun*
recollections
recommend *verb*
recommends
recommending
recommended
recommendation *noun*
recommendations
reconcile *verb*
reconciles
reconciling
reconciled
reconciliation *noun*
reconciliations
reconstruction *noun*
reconstructions
record *noun*
records
record *verb*
records
recording
recorded
recorder *noun*
recorders
recover *verb*
recovers
recovering
recovered
recovery *noun*
recoveries
recreation *noun*
recreations
recreational *adjective*
recreationally
recruit *noun*
recruits
recruit *verb*
recruits
recruiting
recruited
rectangle *noun*
rectangles
rectangular
recur *verb*
recurs
recurring
recurred
recurrence *noun*
recurrences
recycle *verb*
recycles
recycling
recycled
red *adjective*
redder
reddest
red *noun*
reds
redden *verb*
reddens
reddening
reddened
reddish
redeem *verb*
redeems
redeeming
redeemed
redeemer *noun*
redeemers
redemption *noun*
redemptions
redhead *noun*
redheads
reduce *verb*
reduces
reducing
reduced
reduction *noun*
reductions
redundancy *noun*
redundancies
redundant *adjective*
redundantly
★ **reed** *noun*
reeds
reedy
reef *noun*
reefs
reef knot *noun*
reef knots
reek *verb*
reeks
reeking
reeked
☆ **reel** *noun*
reels
reel *verb*
reels
reeling
reeled

★ A **reed** is a plant or a thin strip. ! **read**.
☆ A **reel** is a cylinder on which something is wound. ! **real**.

refer *verb*
refers
referring
referred
referee *noun*
referees
referee *verb*
referees
refereeing
refereed
reference *noun*
references
referendum *noun*
referendums
refill *verb*
refills
refilling
refilled
refill *noun*
refills
refine *verb*
refines
refining
refined
refinement *noun*
refinements
refinery *noun*
refineries
reflect *verb*
reflects
reflecting
reflected
reflective *adjective*
reflectively
reflex *noun*
reflexes
reflexive *adjective*
reflexively
reform *verb*
reforms
reforming
reformed
reform *noun*
reforms
reformation *noun*
reformations
★ **Reformation**
reformer *noun*
reformers
refract *verb*
refracts
refracting
refracted
refraction
refrain *verb*
refrains
refraining
refrained
refrain *noun*
refrains
refresh *verb*
refreshes
refreshing
refreshed
refreshment *noun*
refreshments
refrigerate *verb*
refrigerates
refrigerating
refrigerated
refrigeration
refrigerator *noun*
refrigerators
refuel *verb*
refuels
refuelling
refuelled
refuge *noun*
refuges
refugee *noun*
refugees
refund *verb*
refunds
refunding
refunded
refund *noun*
refunds
refusal
refuse *verb*
refuses
refusing
refused
refuse
regain *verb*
regains
regaining
regained
regard *verb*
regards
regarding
regarded
regard *noun*
regards
regarding *preposition*
regardless
regatta *noun*
regattas
reggae
regiment *noun*
regiments
regimental
region *noun*
regions
regional *adjective*
regionally
register *noun*
registers
register *verb*
registers
registering
registered
registration *noun*
registrations

★ You use a capital R when you mean the historical religious movement.

regret *noun*
regrets
regret *verb*
regrets
regretting
regretted
regretful *adjective*
regretfully
regrettable *adjective*
regrettably
regular *adjective*
regularly
regularity
regulate *verb*
regulates
regulating
regulated
regulation *noun*
regulations
regulator *noun*
regulators
rehearsal *noun*
rehearsals
rehearse *verb*
rehearses
rehearsing
rehearsed
★ **reign** *verb*
reigns
reigning
reigned
reign *noun*
reigns
☆ **rein** *noun*
reins
reindeer *noun*
reindeer
reinforce *verb*
reinforces
reinforcing
reinforced
reinforcement *noun*
reinforcements
reject *verb*
rejects
rejecting
rejected
reject *noun*
rejects
rejection *noun*
rejections
rejoice *verb*
rejoices
rejoicing
rejoiced
relate *verb*
relates
relating
related
relation *noun*
relations
relationship *noun*
relationships
relative *adjective*
relatively
relative *noun*
relatives
relax *verb*
relaxes
relaxing
relaxed
relaxation
relay *verb*
relays
relaying
relayed
relay *noun*
relays
release *verb*
releases
releasing
released
release *noun*
releases
relegate *verb*
relegates
relegating
relegated
relegation
relent *verb*
relents
relenting
relented
relentless *adjective*
relentlessly
relevance
relevant *adjective*
relevantly
reliability
reliable *adjective*
reliably
reliance
reliant
relic *noun*
relics
relief *noun*
reliefs
relieve *verb*
relieves
relieving
relieved
religion *noun*
religions
religious *adjective*
religiously
reluctance
reluctant *adjective*
reluctantly
rely *verb*
relies
relying
relied

★ To **reign** is to rule as a king or queen. ! **rein**.
☆ A **rein** is a strap used to guide a horse. ! **reign**.

remain *verb*
remains
remaining
remained
remainder *noun*
remainders
remains
remark *verb*
remarks
remarking
remarked
remark *noun*
remarks
remarkable *adjective*
remarkably
remedial *adjective*
remedially
remedy *noun*
remedies
remember *verb*
remembers
remembering
remembered
remembrance
remind *verb*
reminds
reminding
reminded
reminder *noun*
reminders
reminisce *verb*
reminisces
reminiscing
reminisced
reminiscence *noun*
reminiscences
reminiscent
remnant *noun*
remnants
remorse
remorseful *adjective*
remorsefully
remorseless *adjective*
remorselessly
remote *adjective*
remoter
remotest
remotely
remoteness
removal *noun*
removals
remove *verb*
removes
removing
removed
★ **Renaissance**
render *verb*
renders
rendering
rendered
rendezvous *noun*
rendezvous
renew *verb*
renews
renewing
renewed
renewable
renewal *noun*
renewals
renown
renowned
rent *noun*
rents
rent *verb*
rents
renting
rented
repair *verb*
repairs
repairing
repaired
repair *noun*
repairs
repay *verb*
repays
repaying
repaid
repayment *noun*
repayments
repeat *verb*
repeats
repeating
repeated
repeat *noun*
repeats
repeatedly
repel *verb*
repels
repelling
repelled
repellent
repent *verb*
repents
repenting
repented
repentance
repentant
repetition *noun*
repetitions
repetitive *adjective*
repetitively
replace *verb*
replaces
replacing
replaced
replacement *noun*
replacements
replay *noun*
replays
replica *noun*
replicas

★ You use a capital R when you mean the historical period.

reply *verb*
replies
replying
replied
reply *noun*
replies
report *verb*
reports
reporting
reported
report *noun*
reports
reporter *noun*
reporters
repossess *verb*
repossesses
repossessing
repossessed
represent *verb*
represents
representing
represented
representation *noun*
representations
representative *adjective* and *noun*
representatives
repress *verb*
represses
repressing
repressed
repression *noun*
repressions
repressive *adjective*
repressively
reprieve *verb*
reprieves
reprieving
reprieved
reprieve *noun*
reprieves
reprimand *verb*
reprimands
reprimanding
reprimanded
reprisal *noun*
reprisals
reproach *verb*
reproaches
reproaching
reproached
reproduce *verb*
reproduces
reproducing
reproduced
reproduction *noun*
reproduction
reproductive *adjective*
reproductively
reptile *noun*
reptiles
republic *noun*
republics
republican *adjective* and *noun*
republicans
★ **Republican** *adjective* and *noun*
Republicans
repulsion
repulsive *adjective*
repulsively
reputation *noun*
reputations
request *verb*
requests
requesting
requested
request *noun*
requests
require *verb*
requires
requiring
required
requirement *noun*
requirements
reread *verb*
rereads
rereading
reread
rescue *verb*
rescues
rescuing
rescued
rescue *noun*
rescues
rescuer *noun*
rescuers
research *noun*
researches
researcher *noun*
researchers
resemblance *noun*
resemblances
resemble *verb*
resembles
resembling
resembled
resent *verb*
resents
resenting
resented
resentful *adjective*
resentfully
resentment
reservation *noun*
reservations
reserve *verb*
reserves
reserving
reserved

★ You use a capital R when you mean the political party in the USA.

reserve *noun*
reserves
reservoir *noun*
reservoirs
reshuffle *noun*
reshuffles
reside *verb*
resides
residing
resided
residence *noun*
residences
resident *noun*
residents
resign *verb*
resigns
resigning
resigned
resignation *noun*
resignations
resin *noun*
resins
resinous
resist *verb*
resists
resisting
resisted
resistance *noun*
resistances
resistant
resolute *adjective*
resolutely
resolution *noun*
resolutions
resolve *verb*
resolves
resolving
resolved
resort *noun*
resorts
resort *verb*
resorts
resorting
resorted
resound *verb*
resounds
resounding
resounded
resource *noun*
resources
respect *verb*
respects
respecting
respected
respect *noun*
respects
respectability
respectable *adjective*
respectably
respectful *adjective*
respectfully
respective *adjective*
respectively
respiration
respirator *noun*
respirators
respiratory
respond *verb*
responds
responding
responded
response *noun*
responses
responsibility *noun*
responsibilities
responsible *adjective*
responsibly
rest *verb*
rests
resting
rested
rest *noun*
rests
restaurant *noun*
restaurants
restful *adjective*
restfully
restless *adjective*
restlessly
restlessness
restoration *noun*
restorations
restore *verb*
restores
restoring
restored
restrain *verb*
restrains
restraining
restrained
restraint *noun*
restraints
restrict *verb*
restricts
restricting
restricted
restriction *noun*
restrictions
restrictive *adjective*
restrictively
result *verb*
results
resulting
resulted
result *noun*
results
resume *verb*
resumes
resuming
resumed
resumption *noun*
resumptions

resuscitate *verb*
resuscitates
resuscitating
resuscitated
retail *verb*
retails
retailing
retailed
retail *noun*
retain *verb*
retains
retaining
retained
retina *noun*
retinas
retire *verb*
retires
retiring
retired
retirement
retort *verb*
retorts
retorting
retorted
retort *noun*
retorts
retrace *verb*
retraces
retracing
retraced
retreat *verb*
retreats
retreating
retreated
retrievable *adjective*
retrievably
retrieval *noun*
retrievals
retrieve *verb*
retrieves
retrieving
retrieved
retriever *noun*
retrievers
return *verb*
returns
returning
returned
return *noun*
returns
reunion *noun*
reunions
rev *verb*
revs
revving
revved
rev *noun*
revs
reveal *verb*
reveals
revealing
revealed
revelation *noun*
revelations
revenge
revenue *noun*
revenues
revere *verb*
reveres
revering
revered
reverence
★ **Reverend**
★ **reverent** *adjective*
reverently
reversal *noun*
reversals
reverse *verb*
reverses
reversing
reversed
reverse *noun*
reverses
reversible *adjective*
reversibly
review *verb*
reviews
reviewing
reviewed
☆ **review** *noun*
reviews
reviewer *noun*
reviewers
revise *verb*
revises
revising
revised
revision *noun*
revisions
revival *noun*
revivals
revive *verb*
revives
reviving
revived
revolt *verb*
revolts
revolting
revolted
revolt *noun*
revolts
revolution *noun*
revolutions
revolutionary *adjective* and *noun*
revolutionaries
revolutionize *verb*
revolutionizes
revolutionizing
revolutionized

★ You use **Reverend** as a title of a member of the clergy, and **reverent** as an ordinary word meaning 'showing respect'.
☆ A **review** is a piece of writing about a film, play, etc. ! **revue**.

revolve *verb*
revolves
revolving
revolved
revolver *noun*
revolvers
★ **revue** *noun*
revues
reward *verb*
rewards
rewarding
rewarded
reward *noun*
rewards
rewind *verb*
rewinds
rewinding
rewound
rewrite *verb*
rewrites
rewriting
rewrote
rewritten
rheumatic
rheumatism
rhinoceros *noun*
rhinoceroses *or*
rhinoceros
rhododendron *noun*
rhododendrons
rhombus *noun*
rhombuses
rhubarb
rhyme *verb*
rhymes
rhyming
rhymed
rhyme *noun*
rhymes
rhythm *noun*
rhythms
rhythmic *or*
rhythmical *adjective*
rhythmically
rib *noun*
ribs
ribbon *noun*
ribbons
rice
rich *adjective*
richer
richest
richly
riches *plural noun*
richness
rick *noun*
ricks
rickety
rickshaw *noun*
rickshaws
ricochet *verb*
ricochets
ricocheting
ricocheted
rid *verb*
rids
ridding
rid
riddance
riddle *noun*
riddles
ride *verb*
rides
riding
rode
ridden
ride *noun*
rides
rider *noun*
riders
ridge *noun*
ridges
ridicule *verb*
ridicules
ridiculing
ridiculed
ridiculous *adjective*
ridiculously
rifle *noun*
rifles
rift *noun*
rifts
rig *verb*
rigs
rigging
rigged
rigging
right *adjective*
rightly
☆ **right** *noun*
rights
✪ **right** *verb*
rights
righting
righted
righteous *adjective*
righteously
righteousness
rightful *adjective*
rightfully
right-handed
rightness
rigid *adjective*
rigidly
rigidity
rim *noun*
rims
rind *noun*
rinds
ring *noun*
rings

★ A **revue** is an entertainment of short sketches. ! **review**.
☆ A **right** is something you are entitled to. ! **rite**, **write**.
✪ To **right** something is to make it right. ! **rite**, **write**.

★ **ring** *verb*
rings
ringing
rang
rung

☆ **ring** *verb*
rings
ringing
ringed

ring *noun*
rings

ringleader *noun*
ringleaders

ringlet *noun*
ringlets

ringmaster *noun*
ringmasters

rink *noun*
rinks

rinse *verb*
rinses
rinsing
rinsed

rinse *noun*
rinses

riot *verb*
riots
rioting
rioted

riot *noun*
riots

riotous *adjective*
riotously

rip *verb*
rips
ripping
ripped

rip *noun*
rips

ripe *adjective*
riper
ripest

ripen *verb*
ripens
ripening
ripened

ripeness

rip-off *noun*
rip-offs

ripple *noun*
ripples

ripple *verb*
ripples
rippling
rippled

rise *verb*
rises
rising
rose
risen

rise *noun*
rises

risk *verb*
risks
risking
risked

risk *noun*
risks

risky *adjective*
riskier
riskiest
riskily

risotto *noun*
risottos

rissole *noun*
rissoles

✪ **rite** *noun*
rites

ritual *noun*
rituals

rival *noun*
rivals

rival *verb*
rivals
rivalling
rivalled

rivalry *noun*
rivalries

river *noun*
rivers

rivet *noun*
rivets

rivet *verb*
rivets
riveting
riveted

✲ **road** *noun*
roads

roadroller *noun*
roadrollers

roadside *noun*
roadsides

roadway *noun*
roadways

roam *verb*
roams
roaming
roamed

roar *verb*
roars
roaring
roared

roar *noun*
roars

roast *verb*
roasts
roasting
roasted

rob *verb*
robs
robbing
robbed

★ The past tense is **rang** and the past participle is **rung** when you mean 'to make a sound like a bell'. ! **wring**.

☆ The past tense and past participle is **ringed** when you mean 'to put a ring round something'. ! **wring**.

✪ A **rite** is a ceremony or ritual. ! **right**, **write**.

✲ A **road** is a hard surface for traffic to use. ! **rode**.

robber *noun*
robbers
robbery *noun*
robberies
robe *noun*
robes
robin *noun*
robins
robot *noun*
robots
robust *adjective*
robustly
rock *verb*
rocks
rocking
rocked
rock *noun*
rocks
rocker *noun*
rockers
rockery *noun*
rockeries
rocket *noun*
rockets
rocky *adjective*
rockier
rockiest
rockily
rod *noun*
rods
★ **rode** see **ride**
rodent *noun*
rodents
rodeo *noun*
rodeos
rogue *noun*
rogues
roguish *adjective*
roguishly
☆ **role** *noun*
roles
roll *verb*
rolls
rolling
rolled
✪ **roll** *noun*
rolls
roller *noun*
rollers
Roman *adjective* and *noun*
Romans
Roman Catholic *noun*
Roman Catholics
romance *noun*
romances
Roman numeral
romantic *adjective*
romantically
Romany
romp *verb*
romps
romping
romped
romp *noun*
romps
rompers *plural noun*
roof *noun*
roofs
rook *noun*
rooks
room *noun*
rooms
roomful *adjective*
roomfuls
roomy *adjective*
roomier
roomiest
roomily
roost *noun*
roosts
✲ **root** *noun*
roots
root *verb*
roots
rooting
rooted
rope *noun*
ropes
rose *noun*
roses
rose see **rise**
rosette *noun*
rosettes
rosy *adjective*
rosier
rosiest
rosily
rot *verb*
rots
rotting
rotted
rot *noun*
rota *noun*
rotas
rotary
rotate *verb*
rotates
rotating
rotated
rotation *noun*
rotations
rotor *noun*
rotors
rotten
rottenness
rottweiler *noun*
rottweilers

★ **Rode** is the past tense of **ride**. ! **road**.
☆ A **role** is a part in a play or film. ! **roll**.
✪ A **roll** is a small loaf of bread or an act of rolling. ! **role**.
✲ A **root** is the part of a plant that grows underground. ! **route**.

rough *adjective*
rougher
roughest
roughly
roughness
roughage
roughen *verb*
roughens
roughening
roughened
round *adjective, adverb,* and *preposition*
rounder
roundest
roundly
round *noun*
rounds
round *verb*
rounds
rounding
rounded
roundabout *adjective* and *noun*
roundabouts
rounders *noun*
Roundhead *noun*
Roundheads
rouse *verb*
rouses
rousing
roused
rout *verb*
routs
routing
routed
rout *noun*
routs
★ **route** *noun*
routes
routine *noun*
routines
routine *adjective*
routinely
rove *verb*
roves
roving
roved
rover *noun*
rovers
☆ **row** *noun*
rows
✪ **row** *verb*
rows
rowing
rowed
rowdiness
rowdy *adjective*
rowdier
rowdiest
rowdily
rower *noun*
rowers
rowlock *noun*
rowlocks
royal *adjective*
royally
royalty
rub *verb*
rubs
rubbing
rubbed
rub *noun*
rubs
rubber *noun*
rubbers
rubbery
rubbish
rubble
ruby *noun*
rubies
rucksack *noun*
rucksacks
rudder *noun*
rudders
ruddy *adjective*
ruddier
ruddiest
rude *adjective*
ruder
rudest
rudely
rudeness
ruffian *noun*
ruffians
ruffle *verb*
ruffles
ruffling
ruffled
rug *noun*
rugs
✲ **rugby**
rugged *adjective*
ruggedly
rugger
ruin *verb*
ruins
ruining
ruined
ruin *noun*
ruins
ruinous *adjective*
ruinously
rule *noun*
rules
rule *verb*
rules
ruling
ruled
ruler *noun*
rulers
ruling *noun*
rulings

★ A **route** is the way you go to get to a place. ! **root**.
☆ A **row** is a line of people or things and rhymes with 'go'
. A **row** is also a noise or argument and rhymes with 'cow'.
✪ To **row** means to use oars to make a boat move and rhymes with 'go'.
✲ You can use a small r when you mean the game.

rum *noun*
rums
rumble *verb*
rumbles
rumbling
rumbled
rumble *noun*
rumbles
rummage *verb*
rummages
rummaging
rummaged
rummy
rumour *noun*
rumours
rump *noun*
rumps
run *verb*
runs
running
ran
run
run *noun*
runs
runaway *noun*
runaways
rung *noun*
rungs
rung see **ring**
runner *noun*
runners
runner-up *noun*
runners-up
runny *adjective*
runnier
runniest
runnily
runway *noun*
runways
rural
rush *verb*
rushes
rushing
rushed
rush *noun*
rushes
rusk *noun*
rusks
rust *noun*
rust *verb*
rusts
rusting
rusted
rustic
rustle *verb*
rustles
rustling
rustled
rustler *noun*
rustlers
rusty *adjective*
rustier
rustiest
rustily
rut *noun*
ruts
ruthless *adjective*
ruthlessly
ruthlessness
rutted
★ **rye** *noun*

Ss

sabbath *noun*
sabbaths
sabotage *noun*
sabotage *verb*
sabotages
sabotaging
sabotaged
saboteur *noun*
saboteurs
☆ **sac** *noun*
sacs
saccharin
sachet *noun*
sachets
✪ **sack** *noun*
sacks
sack *verb*
sacks
sacking
sacked
sacred
sacrifice *noun*
sacrifices
sacrificial *adjective*
sacrificially
sacrifice *verb*
sacrifices
sacrificing
sacrificed
sad *adjective*
sadder
saddest
sadly
sadness
sadden *verb*
saddens
saddening
saddened
saddle *noun*
saddles
saddle *verb*
saddles
saddling
saddled

★ **Rye** is a type of cereal or bread. ! **wry**.
☆ A **sac** is a bag-like part of an animal or plant. ! **sack**.
✪ A **sack** is a large bag. ! **sac**.

sadist *noun*
sadists
sadism
sadistic *adjective*
sadistically
safari *noun*
safaris
safe *adjective*
safer
safest
safely
safe *noun*
safes
safeguard *noun*
safeguards
safety
sag *verb*
sags
sagging
sagged
saga *noun*
sagas
sago
said see **say**
sail *verb*
sails
sailing
sailed
★ **sail** *noun*
sails
sailboard *noun*
sailboards
sailor *noun*
sailors
saint *noun*
saints
saintly *adjective*
saintlier
saintliest
sake
salaam *interjection*
salad *noun*
salads
salami *noun*
salamis
salary *noun*
salaries
☆ **sale** *noun*
sales
salesman *noun*
salesmen
salesperson *noun*
salespersons
saleswoman *noun*
saleswomen
saline
saliva
sally *verb*
sallies
sallying
sallied
salmon *noun*
salmon
salon *noun*
salons
saloon *noun*
saloons
salt *noun*
salt *verb*
salts
salting
salted
salty *adjective*
saltier
saltiest
salute *verb*
salutes
saluting
saluted
salute *noun*
salutes
salvage *verb*
salvages
salvaging
salvaged
salvation
same
samosa *noun*
samosas
sample *noun*
samples
sample *verb*
samples
sampling
sampled
sanctuary *noun*
sanctuaries
sand *noun*
sands
sand *verb*
sands
sanding
sanded
sander *noun*
sanders
sandal *noun*
sandals
sandbag *noun*
sandbags
sandpaper
sands *plural noun*
sandstone
sandwich *noun*
sandwiches
sandy *adjective*
sandier
sandiest
sane *adjective*
saner
sanest
sanely

★ A **sail** is a sheet that catches the wind to make a boat go. ! **sale**.
☆ You use **sale** in e.g. *The house is for sale.* ! **sail**.

sang see sing
sanitary
sanitation
sanity
sank see sink
Sanskrit
sap *noun*
sap *verb*
saps
sapping
sapped
sapling *noun*
saplings
sapphire *noun*
sapphires
sarcasm
sarcastic *adjective*
sarcastically
sardine *noun*
sardines
sari *noun*
saris
sash *noun*
sashes
sat see sit
satchel *noun*
satchels
satellite *noun*
satellites
satin
satire *noun*
satires
satirical *adjective*
satirically
satirist *noun*
satirists
satisfaction
satisfactory *adjective*
satisfactorily
satisfy *verb*
satisfies
satisfying
satisfied
saturate *verb*
saturates
saturating
saturated
saturation
Saturday *noun*
Saturdays
★ **sauce** *noun*
sauces
saucepan *noun*
saucepans
saucer *noun*
saucers
saucy *adjective*
saucier
sauciest
saucily
sauna *noun*
saunas
saunter *verb*
saunters
sauntering
sauntered
sausage *noun*
sausages
savage *adjective*
savagely
savage *noun*
savages
savage *verb*
savages
savaging
savaged
savagery
savannah *noun*
savannahs
save *verb*
saves
saving
saved
saver *noun*
savers
savings *plural noun*
saviour *noun*
saviours
savoury
saw *noun*
saws
saw *verb*
saws
sawing
sawed
sawn
saw see see
sawdust
saxophone *noun*
saxophones
say *verb*
says
saying
said
say *noun*
saying *noun*
sayings
scab *noun*
scabs
scabbard *noun*
scabbards
scaffold *noun*
scaffolds
scaffolding
scald *verb*
scalds
scalding
scalded

★ A **sauce** is a liquid you put on food. ! **source**.

scale *noun*
scales
scale *verb*
scales
scaling
scaled
scales *plural noun*
scaly *adjective*
scalier
scaliest
scalp *noun*
scalps
scalp *verb*
scalps
scalping
scalped
scamper *verb*
scampers
scampering
scampered
scampi *plural noun*
scan *verb*
scans
scanning
scanned
scan *noun*
scans
scandal *noun*
scandals
scandalous *adjective*
scandalous
scanner *noun*
scanners
scanty *adjective*
scantier
scantiest
scantily
scapegoat *noun*
scapegoats
scar *noun*
scars
scar *verb*
scars
scarring
scarred
scarce *adjective*
scarcer
scarcest
scarcely
scarcity *noun*
scarcities
scare *verb*
scares
scaring
scared
scare *noun*
scares
scarecrow *noun*
scarecrows
scarf *noun*
scarves
scarlet
scary *adjective*
scarier
scariest
scarily
scatter *verb*
scatters
scattering
scattered
★ **scene** *noun*
scenes
scenery
☆ **scent** *noun*
scents
scent *verb*
scents
scenting
scented
sceptic *noun*
sceptics
sceptical *adjective*
sceptically
scepticism
schedule *noun*
schedules
scheme *noun*
schemes
scheme *verb*
schemes
scheming
schemed
schemer *noun*
schemers
scholar *noun*
scholars
scholarly
scholarship *noun*
scholarships
school *noun*
schools
schoolboy *noun*
schoolboys
schoolchild *noun*
schoolchildren
schoolgirl *noun*
schoolgirls
schoolteacher *noun*
schoolteachers
schooner *noun*
schooners
science
scientific *adjective*
scientifically
scientist *noun*
scientists
scissors *plural noun*
scoff *verb*
scoffs
scoffing
scoffed

★ A **scene** is a place or part of a play. ! **seen**.
☆ A **scent** is a smell or perfume. ! **cent**, **sent**.

scold *verb*
scolds
scolding
scolded
scone *noun*
scones
scoop *noun*
scoops
scoop *verb*
scoops
scooping
scooped
scooter *noun*
scooters
scope
scorch *verb*
scorches
scorching
scorched
score *noun*
scores
score *verb*
scores
scoring
scored
scorer *noun*
scorers
scorn *noun*
scorn *verb*
scorns
scorning
scorned
scorpion *noun*
scorpions
Scot *noun*
Scots
scoundrel *noun*
scoundrels
scour *verb*
scours
scouring
scoured

★ **Scout** *noun*
Scouts
scout *noun*
scouts
scowl *verb*
scowls
scowling
scowled
scramble *verb*
scrambles
scrambling
scrambled
scramble *noun*
scrambles
scrap *verb*
scraps
scrapping
scrapped
scrap *noun*
scraps
scrape *verb*
scrapes
scraping
scraped
scrape *noun*
scrapes
scraper *noun*
scrapers
scrappy *adjective*
scrappier
scrappiest
scrappily
scratch *verb*
scratches
scratching
scratched
scratch *noun*
scratches
scrawl *verb*
scrawls
scrawling
scrawled

scrawl *noun*
scrawls
scream *verb*
screams
screaming
screamed
scream *noun*
screams
screech *verb*
screeches
screeching
screeched
screech *noun*
screeches
screen *noun*
screens
screen *verb*
screens
screening
screened
screw *noun*
screws
screw *verb*
screws
screwing
screwed
screwdriver *noun*
screwdrivers
scribble *verb*
scribbles
scribbling
scribbled
scribble *noun*
scribbles
scribbler *noun*
scribblers
script *noun*
scripts
scripture *noun*
scriptures

★ You use a capital S when you mean a member of the Scout Association.

scroll *noun*
scrolls
scrotum *noun*
scrotums *or* scrota
scrounge *verb*
scrounges
scrounging
scrounged
scrounger *noun*
scroungers
scrub *verb*
scrubs
scrubbing
scrubbed
scrub *noun*
scruffy *adjective*
scruffier
scruffiest
scruffily
scrum *noun*
scrums
scrummage *noun*
scrummages
scrutinize *verb*
scrutinizes
scrutinizing
scrutinized
scrutiny *noun*
scrutinies
scuba diving
scuffle *noun*
scuffles
scuffle *verb*
scuffles
scuffling
scuffled
scullery *noun*
sculleries
sculptor *noun*
sculptors
sculpture *noun*
sculptures
scum
scurry *verb*
scurries
scurrying
scurried
scurvy
scuttle *verb*
scuttles
scuttling
scuttled
scuttle *noun*
scuttles
scythe *noun*
scythes
★ **sea** *noun*
seas
seabed
seafarer *noun*
seafarers
seafaring
seafood
seagull *noun*
seagulls
sea horse *noun*
sea horses
seal *verb*
seals
sealing
sealed
seal *noun*
seals
sea lion *noun*
sea lions
☆ **seam** *noun*
seams
seaman *noun*
seamen
seamanship
seaplane *noun*
seaplanes
seaport *noun*
seaports
search *verb*
searches
searching
searched
search *noun*
searches
searcher *noun*
searchers
searchlight *noun*
searchlights
seashore *noun*
seashores
seasick
seasickness
seaside
season *noun*
seasons
season *verb*
seasons
seasoning
seasoned
seasonal *adjective*
seasonally
seasoning *noun*
seasonings
seat *noun*
seats
seat *verb*
seats
seating
seated
seat belt *noun*
seat belts
seaward *adjective* and *adverb*

★ A **sea** is an area of salt water. **! see.**
☆ A **seam** is a line of stitching in cloth. **! seem.**

seawards *adverb*
seaweed *noun*
seaweeds
secateurs *plural noun*
secluded
seclusion
second *adjective*
secondly
second *noun*
seconds
second *verb*
seconds
seconding
seconded
secondary
second-hand *adjective*
secrecy
secret *adjective*
secretly
secret *noun*
secrets
secretary *noun*
secretaries
secrete *verb*
secretes
secreting
secreted
secretion *noun*
secretions
secretive *adjective*
secretively
secretiveness
sect *noun*
sects
section *noun*
sections
sectional
sector *noun*
sectors

secure *adjective*
securer
securest
securely
secure *verb*
secures
securing
secured
security
sedate *adjective*
sedately
sedation
sedative *noun*
sedatives
sediment
sedimentary
★ **see** *verb*
sees
seeing
saw
seen
seed *noun*
seeds
seedling *noun*
seedlings
seek *verb*
seeks
seeking
sought
☆ **seem** *verb*
seems
seeming
seemed
seemingly
✪ **seen** see **see**
seep *verb*
seeps
seeping
seeped
seepage

see-saw *noun*
see-saws
seethe *verb*
seethes
seething
seethed
segment *noun*
segments
segmented
segregate *verb*
segregates
segregating
segregated
segregation
seismograph *noun*
seismographs
seize *verb*
seizes
seizing
seized
seizure *noun*
seizures
seldom
select *verb*
selects
selecting
selected
select *adjective*
self *noun*
selves
self-confidence
self-confident *adjective*
self-confidently
self-conscious *adjective*
self-consciously
self-contained
selfish *adjective*
selfishly

★ You use **see** in e.g. *I can't see anything.* ! **sea**.
☆ You use **seem** in e.g. *they seem tired.* ! **seam**.
✪ **Seen** is the past participle of **see**. ! **scene**.

selfishness
selfless *adjective*
selflessly
self-service
★ **sell** *verb*
sells
selling
sold
semaphore
semen

semi-
semi- makes words meaning 'half', e.g. **semi-automatic**, **semi-skimmed**. A few words are spelt joined up, e.g. **semicircle**, **semicolon**, but most of them have hyphens.

semibreve *noun*
semibreves
semicircle *noun*
semicircles
semicircular
semicolon *noun*
semicolons
semi-detached
semi-final *noun*
semi-finals
semi-finalist *noun*
semi-finalists
semitone *noun*
semitones
semolina
senate
senator *noun*
senators
send *verb*
sends
sending
sent
senior *adjective* and *noun*
seniors
seniority
sensation *noun*
sensations
sensational *adjective*
sensationally
sense *noun*
senses
sense *verb*
senses
sensing
sensed
senseless *adjective*
senselessly
sensible *adjective*
sensibly
sensitive *adjective*
sensitively
sensitivity *noun*
sensitivities
sensitize *verb*
sensitizes
sensitizing
sensitized
sensor *noun*
sensors
☆ **sent** see **send**
sentence *noun*
sentences
sentence *verb*
sentences
sentencing
sentenced
sentiment *noun*
sentiments
sentimental *adjective*
sentimentally
sentimentality
sentinel *noun*
sentinels
sentry *noun*
sentries
separable
separate *adjective*
separately
separate *verb*
separates
separating
separated
separation *noun*
separations
September *noun*
Septembers
septic
sequel *noun*
sequels
sequence *noun*
sequences
sequin *noun*
sequins
serene *adjective*
serenely
serenity
sergeant *noun*
sergeants
sergeant major *noun*
sergeant majors
✪ **serial** *noun*
serials
series *noun*
series
serious *adjective*
seriously

★ To **sell** something means 'to exchange it for money'. ! **cell**.
☆ You use **sent** in e.g. *he was sent home*. ! **cent**, **scent**.
✪ A **serial** is a story or programme in separate parts. ! **cereal**.

seriousness
sermon *noun*
sermons
serpent *noun*
serpents
servant *noun*
servants
serve *verb*
serves
serving
served
server *noun*
servers
serve *noun*
serves
service *noun*
services
service *verb*
services
servicing
serviced
serviette *noun*
serviettes
session *noun*
sessions
set *verb*
sets
setting
set
set *noun*
sets
set square *noun*
set squares
★ **sett** *noun*
setts
settee *noun*
settees
setting *noun*
settings
settle *verb*
settles
settling
settled
settlement *noun*
settlements
settler *noun*
settlers
set-up *noun*
set-ups
seven
seventeen
seventeenth
seventh *adjective* and *noun*
seventhly
seventieth
seventy *adjective* and *noun*
seventies
sever *verb*
severs
severing
severed
several *adjective*
severally
severe *adjective*
severer
severest
severely
severity
☆ **sew** *verb*
sews
sewing
sewed
sewn
sewage
sewer *noun*
sewers
sex *noun*
sexes
sexism
sexist *adjective* and *noun*
sexists
sextet *noun*
sextets
sexual *adjective*
sexually
sexuality
sexy *adjective*
sexier
sexiest
sexily
shabbiness
shabby *adjective*
shabbier
shabbiest
shabbily
shack *noun*
shacks
shade *noun*
shades
shade *verb*
shades
shading
shaded
shadow *noun*
shadows
shadow *verb*
shadows
shadowing
shadowed
shadowy
shady *adjective*
shadier
shadiest
shaft *noun*
shafts
shaggy *adjective*
shaggier
shaggiest
shaggily

★ A sett is a badger's burrow.
☆ To sew is to work with a needle and thread. ! sow.

shake *verb*
shakes
shaking
shook
shaken
★ **shake** *noun*
shakes
shaky *adjective*
shakier
shakiest
shakily
shall *verb*
should
shallow *adjective*
shallower
shallowest
shallowly
sham *noun*
shams
shamble *verb*
shambles
shambling
shambled
shambles *noun*
shame *verb*
shames
shaming
shamed
shame *noun*
shameful *adjective*
shamefully
shameless *adjective*
shamelessly
shampoo *noun*
shampoos
shampoo *verb*
shampoos
shampooing
shampooed
shamrock
shandy *noun*
shandies
shan't *verb*
shanty *noun*
shanties
shape *noun*
shapes
shape *verb*
shapes
shaping
shaped
shapeless *adjective*
shapelessly
shapely *adjective*
shapelier
shapeliest
share *noun*
shares
share *verb*
shares
sharing
shared
shark *noun*
sharks
sharp *adjective*
sharper
sharpest
sharply
sharp *noun*
sharps
sharpen *verb*
sharpens
sharpening
sharpened
sharpener *noun*
sharpeners
sharpness
shatter *verb*
shatters
shattering
shattered
shave *verb*
shaves
shaving
shaved
shave *noun*
shaves
shaver *noun*
shavers
shavings *plural noun*
shawl *noun*
shawls
she
sheaf *noun*
sheaves
☆ **shear** *verb*
shears
shearing
sheared
shorn
shearer *noun*
shearers
shears *plural noun*
sheath *noun*
sheaths
sheathe *verb*
sheathes
sheathing
sheathed
shed *noun*
sheds
shed *verb*
sheds
shedding
shed
she'd *verb*
sheen
sheep *noun*
sheep
sheepdog *noun*
sheepdogs

★ To **shake** is to tremble or quiver. ! **sheikh**.
☆ To **shear** is to cut wool from a sheep. ! **sheer**.

sheepish *adjective*
sheepishly
★ **sheer** *adjective*
sheerer
sheerest
sheet *noun*
sheets
sheikh *noun*
sheikhs
shelf *noun*
shelves
shell *noun*
shells
shell *verb*
shells
shelling
shelled
she'll *verb*
shellfish *noun*
shellfish
shelter *noun*
shelters
shelter *verb*
shelters
sheltering
sheltered
shelve *verb*
shelves
shelving
shelved
shepherd *noun*
shepherds
sherbet *noun*
sherbets
sheriff *noun*
sheriffs
sherry *noun*
sherries
she's *verb*
shield *noun*
shields
shield *verb*
shields
shielding
shielded
shift *noun*
shifts
shift *verb*
shifts
shifting
shifted
shilling *noun*
shillings
shimmer *verb*
shimmers
shimmering
shimmered
shin *noun*
shins
shine *verb*
shines
shining
shone
shined
shine *noun*
shingle
shiny *adjective*
shinier
shiniest

-ship
-ship makes nouns, e.g. **friendship**. Other noun suffixes are **-dom**, **-hood**, **-ment**, and **-ness**.

ship *noun*
ships
ship *verb*
ships
shipping
shipped
shipping
shipwreck *noun*
shipwrecks
shipwrecked
shipyard *noun*
shipyards
shire *noun*
shires
shirk *verb*
shirks
shirking
shirked
shirt *noun*
shirts
shiver *verb*
shivers
shivering
shivered
shiver *noun*
shivers
shivery
shoal *noun*
shoals
shock *verb*
shocks
shocking
shocked
shock *noun*
shocks
shoddy *adjective*
shoddier
shoddiest
shoddily
shoe *noun*
shoes
shoelace *noun*
shoelaces
shoestring *noun*
shoestrings
shone see **shine**
shook see **shake**

★ You use **sheer** in e.g. *sheer joy*. ! **shear**.

shoot *verb*
shoots
shooting
shot
★ **shoot** *noun*
shoots
shop *noun*
shops
shop *verb*
shops
shopping
shopped
shopkeeper *noun*
shopkeepers
shoplifter *noun*
shoplifters
shopper *noun*
shoppers
shopping
shore *noun*
shores
shorn see **shear**
short *adjective*
shorter
shortest
shortly
shortness
shortage *noun*
shortages
shortbread
shortcake *noun*
shortcakes
shortcoming *noun*
shortcomings
shorten *verb*
shortens
shortening
shortened
shorthand
short-handed
shortly
shorts *plural noun*
short-sighted
shot *noun*
shots
shot see **shoot**
shotgun *noun*
shotguns
should
shoulder *noun*
shoulders
shoulder *verb*
shoulders
shouldering
shouldered
shout *verb*
shouts
shouting
shouted
shout *noun*
shouts
shove *verb*
shoves
shoving
shoved
shovel *noun*
shovels
shovel *verb*
shovels
shovelling
shovelled
show *verb*
shows
showing
showed
shown
show *noun*
shows
shower *noun*
showers
shower *verb*
showers
showering
showered
showery
showjumper *noun*
showjumpers
showjumping
showman *noun*
showmen
showmanship
showroom *noun*
showrooms
showiness
showy *adjective*
showier
showiest
showily
shrank see **shrink**
shrapnel
shred *noun*
shreds
shred *verb*
shreds
shredding
shredded
shrew *noun*
shrews
shrewd *adjective*
shrewder
shrewdest
shrewdly
shrewdness
shriek *verb*
shrieks
shrieking
shrieked
shriek *noun*
shrieks

★ To **shoot** is to fire at someone with a gun. ! **chute**.

shrill *adjective*
shriller
shrillest
shrilly
shrillness
shrimp *noun*
shrimps
shrine *noun*
shrines
shrink *verb*
shrinks
shrinking
shrank
shrunk
shrinkage
shrivel *verb*
shrivels
shrivelling
shrivelled
shroud *noun*
shrouds
shroud *verb*
shrouds
shrouding
shrouded
Shrove Tuesday
shrub *noun*
shrubs
shrubbery *noun*
shrubberies
shrug *verb*
shrugs
shrugging
shrugged
shrug *noun*
shrugs
shrunk see **shrink**
shrunken *adjective*
shudder *verb*
shudders
shuddering
shuddered
shudder *noun*
shudders
shuffle *verb*
shuffles
shuffling
shuffled
shuffle *noun*
shuffles
shunt *verb*
shunts
shunting
shunted
shunter *noun*
shunters
shut *verb*
shuts
shutting
shut
shutter *noun*
shutters
shuttle *noun*
shuttles
shuttlecock *noun*
shuttlecocks
shy *adjective*
shyer
shyest
shyly
Siamese
sick *adjective*
sicker
sickest
sicken *verb*
sickens
sickening
sickened
sickly *adjective*
sicklier
sickliest
sickness *noun*
sicknesses
side *noun*
sides
side *verb*
sides
siding
sided
sideboard *noun*
sideboards
sidecar *noun*
sidecars
sideline *noun*
sidelines
sideshow *noun*
sideshows
sideways
siding *noun*
sidings
siege *noun*
sieges
sieve *noun*
sieves
sift *verb*
sifts
sifting
sifted
sigh *verb*
sighs
sighing
sighed
sigh *noun*
sighs
★ **sight** *noun*
sights
sight *verb*
sights
sighting
sighted
sightseer *noun*
sightseers
sightseeing

★ A **sight** is something you see. ! **site**.

sign *verb*
signs
signing
signed
sign *noun*
signs
signal *noun*
signals
signal *verb*
signals
signalling
signalled
signaller *noun*
signallers
signalman *noun*
signalmen
signature *noun*
signatures
★ **signet** *noun*
signets
significance
significant *adjective*
significantly
signify *verb*
signifies
signifying
signified
signing
signpost *noun*
signposts
Sikh *noun*
Sikhs
silence *noun*
silences
silence *verb*
silences
silencing
silenced
silencer *noun*
silencers
silent *adjective*
silently
silhouette *noun*
silhouettes
silicon
silk
silken
silkworm *noun*
silkworms
silky *adjective*
silkier
silkiest
silkily
sill *noun*
sills
silliness
silly *adjective*
sillier
silliest
sillily
silver
silvery
similar *adjective*
similarly
similarity
simile *noun*
similes
simmer *verb*
simmers
simmering
simmered
simple *adjective*
simpler
simplest
simplicity
simplification
simplify *verb*
simplifies
simplifying
simplified
simply
simulate *verb*
simulates
simulating
simulated
simulation *noun*
simulations
simulator *noun*
simulators
simultaneous *adjective*
simultaneously
sin *noun*
sins
sin *verb*
sins
sinning
sinned
since *preposition, adverb,* and *conjunction*
sincere *adjective*
sincerer
sincerest
sincerely
sincerity
sinew *noun*
sinews
sinful *adjective*
sinfully
sinfulness
sing *verb*
sings
singing
sang
sung
singer *noun*
singers
singe *verb*
singes
singeing
singed

★ A **signet** is a seal worn in a ring. ! **cygnet**.

single *adjective*
singly
single *noun*
singles
single *verb*
singles
singling
singled
single-handed
singular *adjective*
singularly
singular *noun*
singulars
sinister *adjective*
sinisterly
sink *verb*
sinks
sinking
sank *or* sunk
sunk
sink *noun*
sinks
sinner *noun*
sinners
sinus *noun*
sinuses
sip *verb*
sips
sipping
sipped
siphon *noun*
siphons
siphon *verb*
siphons
siphoning
siphoned
sir
siren *noun*
sirens
sister *noun*
sisters
sisterly
sister-in-law *noun*
sisters-in-law
sit *verb*
sits
sitting
sat
sitter *noun*
sitters
★ **site** *noun*
sites
site *verb*
sites
siting
sited
sit-in *noun*
sit-ins
situated
situation *noun*
situations
six *noun*
sixes
sixpence *noun*
sixpences
sixteen *noun*
sixteens
sixteenth
sixth
sixthly
sixtieth
sixty *noun*
sixties
size *noun*
sizes
size *verb*
sizes
sizing
sized
sizeable
sizzle *verb*
sizzles
sizzling
sizzled
skate *verb*
skates
skating
skated
☆ **skate** *noun*
skates *or* skate
skateboard *noun*
skateboards
skater *noun*
skaters
skeletal *adjective*
skeletally
skeleton *noun*
skeletons
sketch *noun*
sketches
sketch *verb*
sketches
sketching
sketched
sketchy *adjective*
sketchier
sketchiest
sketchily
skewer *noun*
skewers
ski *verb*
skis
skiing
skied
ski'd
ski *noun*
skis

★ A **site** is a place where something will be built. ! **sight**.
☆ The plural is **skate** when you mean the fish.

skid *verb*
skids
skidding
skidded
skid *noun*
skids
skier *noun*
skiers
skilful *adjective*
skilfully
skill *noun*
skills
skilled
skim *verb*
skims
skimming
skimmed
skimp *verb*
skimps
skimping
skimped
skimpy *adjective*
skimpier
skimpiest
skimpily
skin *noun*
skins
skin *verb*
skins
skinning
skinned
skinny *adjective*
skinnier
skinniest
skint
skip *verb*
skips
skipping
skipped
skip *noun*
skips
skipper *noun*
skippers
skirt *noun*
skirts
skirt *verb*
skirts
skirting
skirted
skirting *noun*
skirtings
skit *noun*
skits
skittish *adjective*
skittishly
skittle *noun*
skittles
skull *noun*
skulls
skunk *noun*
skunks
sky *noun*
skies
skylark *noun*
skylarks
skylight *noun*
skylights
skyscraper *noun*
skyscrapers
slab *noun*
slabs
slack *adjective*
slacker
slackest
slackly
slacken *verb*
slackens
slackening
slackened
slackness
slacks *plural noun*
slag heap *noun*
slag heaps
slain see **slay**
slam *verb*
slams
slamming
slammed
slang
slant *verb*
slants
slanting
slanted
slant *noun*
slants
slap *verb*
slaps
slapping
slapped
slap *noun*
slaps
slapstick
slash *verb*
slashes
slashing
slashed
slash *noun*
slashes
slat *noun*
slats
slate *noun*
slates
slaty *adjective*
slatier
slatiest
slaughter *verb*
slaughters
slaughtering
slaughtered
slaughter *noun*

slaughterhouse *noun*
slaughterhouses
slave *noun*
slaves
slave *verb*
slaves
slaving
slaved
slavery
★ **slay** *verb*
slays
slaying
slew
slain
sled *noun*
sleds
sledge *noun*
sledges
sledgehammer *noun*
sledgehammers
sleek *adjective*
sleeker
sleekest
sleekly
sleep *verb*
sleeps
sleeping
slept
sleep *noun*
sleeper *noun*
sleepers
sleepiness
sleepless
sleepwalker *noun*
sleepwalkers
sleepwalking
sleepy *adjective*
sleepier
sleepiest
sleepily
sleet
sleeve *noun*
sleeves
sleeveless
☆ **sleigh** *noun*
sleighs
slender *adjective*
slenderer
slenderest
slept see **sleep**
slew see **slay**
slice *noun*
slices
slice *verb*
slices
slicing
sliced
slick *adjective*
slicker
slickest
slickly
slick *noun*
slicks
slide *verb*
slides
sliding
slid
slide *noun*
slides
slight *adjective*
slighter
slightest
slightly
slim *adjective*
slimmer
slimmest
slimly
slim *verb*
slims
slimming
slimmed
slime
slimmer *noun*
slimmers
slimy *adjective*
slimier
slimiest
sling *verb*
slings
slinging
slung
sling *noun*
slings
slink *verb*
slinks
slinking
slunk
slip *verb*
slips
slipping
slipped
slip *noun*
slips
slipper *noun*
slippers
slippery
slipshod
slit *noun*
slits
slit *verb*
slits
slitting
slit
slither *verb*
slithers
slithering
slithered
sliver *noun*
slivers
slog *verb*
slogs
slogging
slogged

★ To **slay** people is to kill them. **! sleigh**.
☆ A **sleigh** is a vehicle for sliding on snow. **! slay**.

slog *noun*
slogs
slogan *noun*
slogans
slop *verb*
slops
slopping
slopped
slope *verb*
slopes
sloping
sloped
slope *noun*
slopes
sloppiness
sloppy *adjective*
sloppier
sloppiest
sloppily
slops *plural noun*
slosh *verb*
sloshes
sloshing
sloshed
slot *noun*
slots
sloth *noun*
sloths
slouch *verb*
slouches
slouching
slouched
slovenly
slow *adjective*
slower
slowest
slowly
slow *verb*
slows
slowing
slowed
slowcoach *noun*
slowcoaches
slowness
sludge
slug *noun*
slugs
slum *noun*
slums
slumber
slumber *verb*
slumbers
slumbering
slumbered
slump *verb*
slumps
slumping
slumped
slump *noun*
slumps
slung see **sling**
slunk see **slink**
slur *noun*
slurs
slush
slushy *adjective*
slushier
slushiest
slushily
sly *adjective*
slyer
slyest
slyly
slyness
smack *verb*
smacks
smacking
smacked
smack *noun*
smacks
small *adjective*
smaller
smallest
smallpox
smart *adjective*
smarter
smartest
smartly
smart *verb*
smarts
smarting
smarted
smarten *verb*
smartens
smartening
smartened
smartness
smash *verb*
smashes
smashing
smashed
smash *noun*
smashes
smashing
smear *verb*
smears
smearing
smeared
smear *noun*
smears
smell *verb*
smells
smelling
smelt *or* smelled
smell *noun*
smells
smelly *adjective*
smellier
smelliest
smelt *verb*
smelts
smelting
smelted

smile *noun*
smiles
smile *verb*
smiles
smiling
smiled
smith *noun*
smiths
smithereens *plural noun*
smock *noun*
smocks
smog
smoke *noun*
smoke *verb*
smokes
smoking
smoked
smokeless
smoker *noun*
smokers
smoky *adjective*
smokier
smokiest
smooth *adjective*
smoother
smoothest
smoothly
smooth *verb*
smooths
smoothing
smoothed
smoothness
smother *verb*
smothers
smothering
smothered
smoulder *verb*
smoulders
smouldering
smouldered
smudge *verb*
smudges
smudging
smudged
smudge *noun*
smudges
smuggle *verb*
smuggles
smuggling
smuggled
smuggler *noun*
smugglers
smut *noun*
smuts
smutty *adjective*
smuttier
smuttiest
smuttily
snack *noun*
snacks
snag *noun*
snags
snail *noun*
snails
snake *noun*
snakes
snaky *adjective*
snakier
snakiest
snap *verb*
snaps
snapping
snapped
snap *noun*
snaps
snappy *adjective*
snappier
snappiest
snappily
snapshot *noun*
snapshots
snare *noun*
snares
snare *verb*
snares
snaring
snared
snarl *verb*
snarls
snarling
snarled
snarl *noun*
snarls
snatch *verb*
snatches
snatching
snatched
snatch *noun*
snatches
sneak *verb*
sneaks
sneaking
sneaked
sneak *noun*
sneaks
sneaky *adjective*
sneakier
sneakiest
sneakily
sneer *verb*
sneers
sneering
sneered
sneeze *verb*
sneezes
sneezing
sneezed
sneeze *noun*
sneezes
sniff *verb*
sniffs
sniffing
sniffed

sniff *noun*
sniffs
snigger *verb*
sniggers
sniggering
sniggered
snigger *noun*
sniggers
snip *verb*
snips
snipping
snipped
snip *noun*
snips
snipe *verb*
snipes
sniping
sniped
sniper *noun*
snipers
snippet *noun*
snippets
snivel *verb*
snivels
snivelling
snivelled
snob *noun*
snobs
snobbery
snobbish *adjective*
snobbishly
snooker
snoop *verb*
snoops
snooping
snooped
snooper *noun*
snoopers
snore *verb*
snores
snoring
snored
snorkel *noun*
snorkels
snort *verb*
snorts
snorting
snorted
snort *noun*
snorts
snout *noun*
snouts
snow *noun*
snow *verb*
snows
snowing
snowed
snowball *noun*
snowballs
snowdrop *noun*
snowdrops
snowflake *noun*
snowflakes
snowman *noun*
snowmen
snowplough *noun*
snowploughs
snowshoe *noun*
snowshoes
snowstorm *noun*
snowstorms
snowy *adjective*
snowier
snowiest
snub *verb*
snubs
snubbing
snubbed
snuff
snug *adjective*
snugger
snuggest
snugly
snuggle *verb*
snuggles
snuggling
snuggled
soak *verb*
soaks
soaking
soaked
so-and-so *noun*
so-and-so's
soap *noun*
soaps
soapiness *noun*
soapy *adjective*
soapier
soapiest
soapily
⋆ **soar** *verb*
soars
soaring
soared
sob *verb*
sobs
sobbing
sobbed
sob *noun*
sobs
sober *adjective*
soberly
sobriety
so-called
soccer
sociability
sociable *adjective*
sociably
social *adjective*
socially
socialism
socialist *noun*
socialists

⋆ To **soar** is to rise or fly high. ! **sore**.

society *noun*
societies
sociological *adjective*
sociologically
sociologist *noun*
sociologists
sociology
sock *noun*
socks
sock *verb*
socks
socking
socked
socket *noun*
sockets
soda
sodium
sofa *noun*
sofas
soft *adjective*
softer
softest
softly
soften *verb*
softens
softening
softened
softness
software
soggy *adjective*
soggier
soggiest
soggily
soil *noun*
soil *verb*
soils
soiling
soiled
solar
sold see **sell**
solder *noun*
solder *verb*
solders
soldering
soldered
soldier *noun*
soldiers
★ **sole** *noun*
soles
sole *adjective*
solely
solemn *adjective*
solemnly
solemnity
solicitor *noun*
solicitors
solid *adjective*
solidly
solid *noun*
solids
solidify *verb*
solidifies
solidifying
solidified
solidity
soliloquy *noun*
soliloquies
solitary
solitude
solo *noun*
solos
soloist *noun*
soloists
solstice *noun*
solstices
solubility
soluble *adjective*
solubly
solution *noun*
solutions
solve *verb*
solves
solving
solved
solvent *adjective* and *noun*
solvents
sombre *adjective*
sombrely
☆ **some** *adjective* and *pronoun*
somebody
somehow
someone
somersault *noun*
somersaults
something
sometime
sometimes
somewhat
somewhere
✪ **son** *noun*
sons
sonar *noun*
sonars
song *noun*
songs
songbird *noun*
songbirds
sonic *adjective*
sonically
sonnet *noun*
sonnets

★ A **sole** is a fish or a part of a shoe. ! **soul**.
☆ You use **some** in e.g. *Have some cake.* ! **sum**.
✪ A **son** is a male child. ! **sun**.

soon *adverb*
sooner
soonest
soot
soothe *verb*
soothes
soothing
soothed
sooty *adjective*
sootier
sootiest
sophisticated
sophistication
sopping
soppy *adjective*
soppier
soppiest
soppily
soprano *noun*
sopranos
sorcerer *noun*
sorcerers
sorceress *noun*
sorceresses
sorcery
★ **sore** *adjective*
sorer
sorest
sorely
sore *noun*
sores
soreness
sorrow *noun*
sorrows
sorrowful *adjective*
sorrowfully
sorry *adjective*
sorrier
sorriest
sort *noun*
sorts
sort *verb*
sorts
sorting
sorted
sought see **seek**
☆ **soul** *noun*
souls
sound *noun*
sounds
sound *verb*
sounds
sounding
sounded
sound *adjective*
sounder
soundest
soundly
soundness
soundtrack *noun*
soundtracks
soup *noun*
soups
sour *adjective*
sourer
sourest
sourly
✪ **source** *noun*
sources
sourness
south *adjective* and *adverb*
✲ **south** *noun*
south-east *noun* and *adjective*
southerly *adjective* and *noun*
southerlies
southern *adjective*
southerner *noun*
southerners
southward *adjective* and *adverb*
southwards *adverb*
south-west *noun* and *adjective*
souvenir *noun*
souvenirs
sovereign *noun*
sovereigns
✸ **sow** *verb*
sows
sowing
sowed
sown
sow *noun*
sows
sower *noun*
sowers
soya bean *noun*
soya beans
space *noun*
spaces
space *verb*
spaces
spacing
spaced
spacecraft *noun*
spacecraft
spaceman *noun*
spacemen
spaceship *noun*
spaceships
spacewoman *noun*
spacewomen
spacious *adjective*
spaciously

★ You use **sore** in e.g. *I've got a sore tooth.* ! **soar.**
☆ A **soul** is a person's spirit. ! **sole.**
✪ The **source** is where something comes from. ! **sauce.**
✲ You use a capital S in **the South**, when you mean a particular region.
✸ To **sow** is to put seed in the ground. ! **sew.**

spaciousness
spade *noun*
spades
spaghetti
span *verb*
spans
spanning
spanned
span *noun*
spans
spaniel *noun*
spaniels
spank *verb*
spanks
spanking
spanked
spanner *noun*
spanners
spar *noun*
spars
spar *verb*
spars
sparring
sparred
spare *verb*
spares
sparing
spared
spare *adjective* and *noun*
spares
sparing *adjective*
sparingly
spark *noun*
sparks
spark *verb*
sparks
sparking
sparked
sparkle *verb*
sparkles
sparkling
sparkled
sparkler *noun*
sparklers
sparrow *noun*
sparrows
sparse *adjective*
sparser
sparsest
sparsely
sparseness
spastic *noun*
spastics
spat see **spit**
spatter *verb*
spatters
spattering
spattered
spawn *noun*
spawn *verb*
spawns
spawning
spawned
speak *verb*
speaks
speaking
spoke
spoken
speaker *noun*
speakers
spear *noun*
spears
spear *verb*
spears
spearing
speared
special *adjective*
specially
specialist *noun*
specialists
speciality *noun*
specialities
specialization
specialize *verb*
specializes
specializing
specialized
species *noun*
species
specific *adjective*
specifically
specification *noun*
specifications
specify *verb*
specifies
specifying
specified
specimen *noun*
specimens
speck *noun*
specks
speckled
spectacle *noun*
spectacles
spectacular *adjective*
spectacularly
spectator *noun*
spectators
spectre *noun*
spectres
spectrum *noun*
spectra
speech *noun*
speeches
speechless

speed *noun*
speeds
★ **speed** *verb*
speeds
speeding
sped *or* speeded
speedboat *noun*
speedboats
speedometer *noun*
speedometers
speedway *noun*
speedways
speedy *adjective*
speedier
speediest
speedily
spell *verb*
spells
spelling
spelt
spelled
spell *noun*
spells
spelling *noun*
spellings
spend *verb*
spends
spending
spent
sperm *noun*
sperms *or* sperm
sphere *noun*
spheres
spherical *adjective*
spherically
spice *noun*
spices
spicy *adjective*
spicier
spiciest
spider *noun*
spiders
spied see **spy**
spike *noun*
spikes
spiky *adjective*
spikier
spikiest
☆ **spill** *verb*
spills
spilling
spilt *or* spilled
spill *noun*
spills
spin *verb*
spins
spinning
spun
spin *noun*
spins
spinach
spindle *noun*
spindles
spin-drier *noun*
spin-driers
spine *noun*
spines
spinal
spin-off *noun*
spin-offs
spinster *noun*
spinsters
spiny *adjective*
spiniest
spiniest
spiral *adjective*
spirally
spire *noun*
spires
spirit *noun*
spirits
spiritual *adjective*
spiritually
spiritual *noun*
spirituals
spiritualism
spiritualist *noun*
spiritualists
spit *verb*
spits
spitting
spat
spit *noun*
spits
spite
spiteful *adjective*
spitefully
spittle
splash *verb*
splashes
splashing
splashed
splash *noun*
splashes
splashdown *noun*
splashdowns
splendid *adjective*
splendidly
splendour
splint *noun*
splints
splinter *noun*
splinters
splinter *verb*
splinters
splintering
splintered
split *verb*
splits
splitting
split
split *noun*
splits

★ You use **sped** in e.g. *Cars sped past* and **speeded** in e.g. *They speeded up the process.*
☆ You use **spilled** in e.g. *I spilled the milk.* You use **spilt** in e.g. *I can see spilt milk.* You use **spilled** or **spilt** in e.g. *I have spilled/spilt the milk.*

splutter *verb*
splutters
spluttering
spluttered

★ **spoil** *verb*
spoils
spoiling
spoilt *or* spoiled

spoils *plural noun*

spoilsport *noun*
spoilsports

spoke *noun*
spokes

spoke see **speak**

spoken see **speak**

spokesperson *noun*
spokespersons

sponge *noun*
sponges

sponge *verb*
sponges
sponging
sponged

sponger *noun*
spongers

sponginess *noun*

spongy *adjective*
spongier
spongiest
spongily

sponsor *noun*
sponsors

sponsorship *noun*
sponsorships

spontaneity

spontaneous *adjective*
spontaneously

spooky *adjective*
spookier
spookiest
spookily

spool *noun*
spools

spoon *noun*
spoons

spoon *verb*
spoons
spooning
spooned

spoonful *noun*
spoonfuls

sport *noun*
sports

sporting

sportsman *noun*
sportsmen

sportsmanship

sportswoman *noun*
sportswomen

spot *noun*
spots

spot *verb*
spots
spotting
spotted

spotless *adjective*
spotlessly

spotlight *noun*
spotlights

spotter *noun*
spotters

spotty *adjective*
spottier
spottiest
spottily

spout *noun*
spouts

spout *verb*
spouts
spouting
spouted

sprain *verb*
sprains
spraining
sprained

sprain *noun*
sprains

sprang see **spring**

sprawl *verb*
sprawls
sprawling
sprawled

spray *verb*
sprays
spraying
sprayed

spray *noun*
sprays

spread *verb*
spreads
spreading
spread

spread *noun*
spreads

spreadsheet *noun*
spreadsheets

sprightliness

sprightly *adjective*
sprightlier
sprightliest

spring *verb*
springs
springing
sprang
sprung

spring *noun*
springs

springboard *noun*
springboards

★ You use **spoiled** in e.g. *They spoiled the party*. You use **spoilt** in e.g. *a spoilt child*. You use **spoiled** or **spoilt** in e.g. *They have spoiled/spoilt the party*.

spring-clean *verb*
spring-cleans
spring-cleaning
spring-cleaned
springtime
springy *adjective*
springier
springiest
sprinkle *verb*
sprinkles
sprinkling
sprinkled
sprinkler *noun*
sprinklers
sprint *verb*
sprints
sprinting
sprinted
sprinter *noun*
sprinters
sprout *verb*
sprouts
sprouting
sprouted
sprout *noun*
sprouts
spruce *noun*
spruces
spruce *adjective*
sprucer
sprucest
sprung see **spring**
spud *noun*
spuds
spun see **spin**
spur *noun*
spurs
spur *verb*
spurs
spurring
spurred
spurt *verb*
spurts
spurting
spurted
spurt *noun*
spurts
spy *noun*
spies
spy *verb*
spies
spying
spied
squabble *verb*
squabbles
squabbling
squabbled
squabble *noun*
squabbles
squad *noun*
squads
squadron *noun*
squadrons
squalid *adjective*
squalidly
squall *noun*
squalls
squally *adjective*
squallier
squalliest
squalor
squander *verb*
squanders
squandering
squandered
square *adjective*
squarely
square *noun*
squares
square *verb*
squares
squaring
squared
squareness
squash *verb*
squashes
squashing
squashed
squash *noun*
squashes
squat *verb*
squats
squatting
squatted
squat *adjective*
squatter
squattest
squatly
squatter *noun*
squatters
squaw *noun*
squaws
squawk *verb*
squawks
squawking
squawked
squawk *noun*
squawks
squeak *verb*
squeaks
squeaking
squeaked
squeak *noun*
squeaks
squeaky *adjective*
squeakier
squeakiest
squeakily
squeal *verb*
squeals
squealing
squealed
squeal *noun*
squeals

squeeze *verb*
squeezes
squeezing
squeezed
squeeze *noun*
squeezes
squeezer *noun*
squeezers
squelch *verb*
squelches
squelching
squelched
squelch *noun*
squelches
squid *noun*
squid *or* squids
squint *verb*
squints
squinting
squinted
squint *noun*
squints
squire *noun*
squires
squirm *verb*
squirms
squirming
squirmed
squirrel *noun*
squirrels
squirt *verb*
squirts
squirting
squirted
stab *verb*
stabs
stabbing
stabbed
stab *noun*
stabs
stability

stabilize *verb*
stabilizes
stabilizing
stabilized
stabilizer *noun*
stabilizers
stable *adjective*
stabler
stablest
stably
stable *noun*
stables
stack *verb*
stacks
stacking
stacked
stack *noun*
stacks
stadium *noun*
stadiums *or* stadia
staff *noun*
staffs
stag *noun*
stags
stage *noun*
stages
stage *verb*
stages
staging
staged
stagecoach *noun*
stagecoaches
stagger *verb*
staggers
staggering
staggered
stagnant *adjective*
stagnantly
stain *noun*
stains

stain *verb*
stains
staining
stained
stainless
★ **stair** *noun*
stairs
staircase *noun*
staircases
☆ **stake** *noun*
stakes
stake *verb*
stakes
staking
staked
stalactite *noun*
stalactites
stalagmite *noun*
stalagmites
stale *adjective*
staler
stalest
stalk *noun*
stalks
stalk *verb*
stalks
stalking
stalked
stall *noun*
stalls
stall *verb*
stalls
stalling
stalled
stallion *noun*
stallions
stalls *plural noun*
stamen *noun*
stamens
stamina

★ A **stair** is one of a set of steps. ! **stare**.
☆ A **stake** is a pointed stick or post. ! **steak**.

stammer *verb*
stammers
stammering
stammered
stammer *noun*
stammers
stamp *noun*
stamps
stamp *verb*
stamps
stamping
stamped
stampede *noun*
stampedes
stand *verb*
stands
standing
stood
stand *noun*
stands
standard *adjective* and *noun*
standards
standardize *verb*
standardizes
standardizing
standardized
standby *noun*
standbys
standstill *noun*
standstills
stank see **stink**
stanza *noun*
stanzas
staple *noun*
staples
staple *adjective*
stapler *noun*
staplers

star *noun*
stars
starry *adjective*
starrier
starriest
starrily
star *verb*
stars
starring
starred
starboard
starch *noun*
starches
starchy *adjective*
starchier
starchiest
★ **stare** *verb*
stares
staring
stared
starfish *noun*
starfish *or* starfishes
starling *noun*
starlings
start *verb*
starts
starting
started
start *noun*
starts
starter *noun*
starters
startle *verb*
startles
startling
startled
starvation
starve *verb*
starves
starving
starved

state *noun*
states
state *verb*
states
stating
stated
stateliness
stately *adjective*
statelier
stateliest
statement *noun*
statements
statesman *noun*
statesmen
statesmanship
stateswoman *noun*
stateswomen
static *adjective*
statically
station *noun*
stations
station *verb*
stations
stationing
stationed
☆ **stationary** *adjective*
✪ **stationery** *noun*
stationmaster *noun*
stationmasters
statistic *noun*
statistics
statistical *adjective*
statistically
statistician *noun*
statisticians
statistics
statue *noun*
statues
status *noun*
statuses

★ To **stare** is to look at something without moving your eyes. **! stair.**
☆ **Stationary** means 'not moving'. **! stationery.**
✪ **Stationery** means 'paper and envelopes'. **! stationary.**

staunch *adjective*
stauncher
staunchest
staunchly
stave *noun*
staves
stave *verb*
staves
staving
staved
stove
stay *verb*
stays
staying
stayed
stay *noun*
stays
steadiness
steady *adjective*
steadier
steadiest
steadily
steady *verb*
steadies
steadying
steadied
★ **steak** *noun*
steaks
☆ **steal** *verb*
steals
stealing
stole
stolen
stealth
stealthy *adjective*
stealthier
stealthiest
stealthily
steam *noun*
steam *verb*
steams
steaming
steamed
steamy *adjective*
steamier
steamiest
steamily
steamer *noun*
steamers
steamroller *noun*
steamrollers
steamship *noun*
steamships
steed *noun*
steeds
steel *noun*
✪ **steel** *verb*
steels
steeling
steeled
steely *adjective*
steelier
steeliest
steep *adjective*
steeper
steepest
steeply
steepness
steeple *noun*
steeples
steeplechase *noun*
steeplechases
steeplejack *noun*
steeplejacks
steer *verb*
steers
steering
steered
steer *noun*
steers
stem *noun*
stems
stem *verb*
stems
stemming
stemmed
stench *noun*
stenches
stencil *noun*
stencils
✲ **step** *noun*
steps
step *verb*
steps
stepping
stepped
stepchild *noun*
stepchildren
stepfather *noun*
stepfathers
stepladder *noun*
stepladders
stepmother *noun*
stepmothers
✹ **steppe** *noun*
steppes
stereo *adjective* and *noun*
stereos
stereophonic *adjective*
stereophonically
sterile
sterility
sterilization
sterilize *verb*
sterilizes
sterilizing
sterilized
sterling

★ A **steak** is a thick slice of meat. ! **stake**.
☆ To **steal** is to take something that is not yours. ! **steel**.
✪ To **steel** yourself is to find courage to do something hard. ! **steal**.
✲ A **step** is a movement of the feet or part of a stair. ! **steppe**.
✹ A **steppe** is a grassy plain. ! **step**.

stern *noun*
sterns
stern *adjective*
sterner
sternest
sternly
sternness
stethoscope *noun*
stethoscopes
stew *verb*
stews
stewing
stewed
stew *noun*
stews
steward *noun*
stewards
stewardess *noun*
stewardesses
stick *verb*
sticks
sticking
stuck
stick *noun*
sticks
sticker *noun*
stickers
stickiness
stickleback *noun*
sticklebacks
sticky *adjective*
stickier
stickiest
stickily
stiff *adjective*
stiffer
stiffest
stiffly
stiffen *verb*
stiffens
stiffening
stiffened
stiffness
stifle *verb*
stifles
stifling
stifled
stile *noun*
stiles
still *adjective*
stiller
stillest
still *adverb*
still *verb*
stills
stilling
stilled
stillness
stilts
stimulant *noun*
stimulants
stimulate *verb*
stimulates
stimulating
stimulated
stimulation
stimulus *noun*
stimuli
sting *noun*
stings
sting *verb*
stings
stinging
stung
stingy *adjective*
stingier
stingiest
stingily
stink *noun*
stinks
stink *verb*
stinks
stinking
stank
stunk
stir *verb*
stirs
stirring
stirred
stir *noun*
stirs
stirrup *noun*
stirrups
stitch *noun*
stitches
stoat *noun*
stoats
stock *noun*
stocks
stock *verb*
stocks
stocking
stocked
stockade *noun*
stockades
stockbroker *noun*
stockbrokers
stocking *noun*
stockings
stockpile *noun*
stockpiles
stocks *plural noun*
stocky *adjective*
stockier
stockiest
stockily
stodgy *adjective*
stodgier
stodgiest
stodgily
stoke *verb*
stokes
stoking
stoked

stole *noun*
stoles
stole see **steal**
stolen see **steal**
stomach *noun*
stomachs
stomach *verb*
stomachs
stomaching
stomached
stone *noun*
stones *or* stone
stone *verb*
stones
stoning
stoned
stony *adjective*
stonier
stoniest
stood see **stand**
stool *noun*
stools
stoop *verb*
stoops
stooping
stooped
stop *verb*
stops
stopping
stopped
stop *noun*
stops
stoppage *noun*
stoppages
stopper *noun*
stoppers
stopwatch *noun*
stopwatches
storage
store *verb*
stores
storing
stored
store *noun*
stores
★ **storey** *noun*
storeys
stork *noun*
storks
storm *noun*
storms
storm *verb*
storms
storming
stormed
stormy *adjective*
stormier
stormiest
stormily
☆ **story** *noun*
stories
stout *adjective*
stouter
stoutest
stoutly
stoutness
stove *noun*
stoves
stove see **stave**
stow *verb*
stows
stowing
stowed
stowaway *noun*
stowaways
straddle *verb*
straddles
straddling
straddled
straggle *verb*
straggles
straggling
straggled
straggler *noun*
stragglers
straggly *adjective*
stragglier
straggliest
✪ **straight** *adjective*
straighter
straightest
straighten *verb*
straightens
straightening
straightened
straightforward *adjective*
straightforwardly
strain *verb*
strains
straining
strained
strain *noun*
strains
strainer *noun*
strainers
✲ **strait** *noun*
straits
✹ **straits** *plural noun*
strand *noun*
strands
stranded
strange *adjective*
stranger
strangest
strangely
strangeness
stranger *noun*
strangers

★ A **storey** is a floor of a building. ! **story**.
☆ You use **story** in e.g. *read me a story*. ! **storey**.
✪ **Straight** means 'not curving or bending'. ! **strait**.
✲ A **strait** is a narrow stretch of water. ! **straight**.
✹ You use **straits** in the phrase *in dire straits*.

strangle *verb*
strangles
strangling
strangled
strangler *noun*
stranglers
strangulation
strap *noun*
straps
strap *verb*
straps
strapping
strapped
strategic *adjective*
strategically
strategist *noun*
strategists
strategy *noun*
strategies
stratum *noun*
strata
straw *noun*
straws
strawberry *noun*
strawberries
stray *verb*
strays
straying
strayed
stray *adjective*
streak *noun*
streaks
streak *verb*
streaks
streaking
streaked
streaky *adjective*
streakier
streakiest
streakily
stream *noun*
streams
stream *verb*
streams
streaming
streamed
streamer *noun*
streamers
streamline *verb*
streamlines
streamlining
streamlined
street *noun*
streets
strength *noun*
strengths
strengthen *verb*
strengthens
strengthening
strengthened
strenuous *adjective*
strenuously
stress *noun*
stresses
stress *verb*
stresses
stressing
stressed
stretch *verb*
stretches
stretching
stretched
stretch *noun*
stretches
stretcher *noun*
stretchers
strew *verb*
strews
strewing
strewed
strewn
stricken
strict *adjective*
stricter
strictest
strictly
strictness
stride *verb*
strides
striding
strode
stridden
stride *noun*
strides
strife
strike *verb*
strikes
striking
struck
strike *noun*
strikes
striker *noun*
strikers
striking *adjective*
strikingly
string *noun*
strings
string *verb*
strings
stringing
strung
stringiness
stringy *adjective*
stringier
stringiest
stringily
strip *verb*
strips
stripping
stripped
strip *noun*
strips

stripe *noun*
stripes
striped
stripy *adjective*
stripier
stripiest
strive *verb*
strives
striving
strove
striven
strobe *noun*
strobes
strode see **stride**
stroke *noun*
strokes
stroke *verb*
strokes
stroking
stroked
stroll *verb*
strolls
strolling
strolled
stroll *noun*
strolls
strong *adjective*
stronger
strongest
strongly
stronghold *noun*
strongholds
strove see **strive**
struck see **strike**
structural *adjective*
structurally
structure *noun*
structures
struggle *verb*
struggles
struggling
struggled
struggle *noun*
struggles
strum *verb*
strums
strumming
strummed
strung see **string**
strut *verb*
struts
strutting
strutted
strut *noun*
struts
stub *verb*
stubs
stubbing
stubbed
stub *noun*
stubs
stubble
stubborn *adjective*
stubbornly
stubbornness
stuck see **stick**
stuck-up
stud *noun*
studs
student *noun*
students
studio *noun*
studios
studious *adjective*
studiously
study *verb*
studies
studying
studied
study *noun*
studies
stuff *noun*
stuff *verb*
stuffs
stuffing
stuffed
stuffiness
stuffing *noun*
stuffings
stuffy *adjective*
stuffier
stuffiest
stuffily
stumble *verb*
stumbles
stumbling
stumbled
stump *noun*
stumps
stump *verb*
stumps
stumping
stumped
stun *verb*
stuns
stunning
stunned
stung see **sting**
stunk see **stink**
stunt *noun*
stunts
stupendous *adjective*
stupendously
stupid *adjective*
stupider
stupidest
stupidly
stupidity
sturdiness
sturdy *adjective*
sturdier
sturdiest
sturdily

stutter *verb*
stutters
stuttering
stuttered
stutter *noun*
stutters
★ **sty** *noun*
sties
style *noun*
styles
style *verb*
styles
styling
styled
stylish *adjective*
stylishly
stylus *noun*
styluses
subcontinent *noun*
subcontinents
subdivide *verb*
subdivides
subdividing
subdivided
subdivision *noun*
subdivisions
subdue *verb*
subdues
subduing
subdued
subject *adjective* and *noun*
subjects
subject *verb*
subjects
subjecting
subjected
subjective *adjective*
subjectively
submarine *noun*
submarines
submerge *verb*
submerges
submerging
submerged
submersion
submission *noun*
submissions
submissive *adjective*
submissively
submit *verb*
submits
submitting
submitted
subordinate *adjective* and *noun*
subordinates
subordinate *verb*
subordinates
subordinating
subordinated
subordination
subscribe *verb*
subscribes
subscribing
subscribed
subscriber *noun*
subscribers
subscription *noun*
subscriptions
subsequent *adjective*
subsequently
subside *verb*
subsides
subsiding
subsided
subsidence
subsidize *verb*
subsidizes
subsidizing
subsidized
subsidy *noun*
subsidies
substance *noun*
substances
substantial *adjective*
substantially
substitute *verb*
substitutes
substituting
substituted
substitute *noun*
substitutes
substitution *noun*
substitutions
subtle *adjective*
subtler
subtlest
subtly
subtlety *noun*
subtleties
subtract *verb*
subtracts
subtracting
subtracted
subtraction *noun*
subtractions
suburb *noun*
suburbs
suburban
suburbia
subway *noun*
subways
succeed *verb*
succeeds
succeeding
succeeded
success *noun*
successes
successful *adjective*
successfully

★ A **sty** is a place for pigs or a swelling on the eye. In the second meaning you can also use *stye*, plural *styes*.

succession *noun*
successions
successive *adjective*
successively
successor *noun*
successors
such
suck *verb*
sucks
sucking
sucked
suck *noun*
sucks
suction
sudden *adjective*
suddenly
suddenness
suds *plural noun*
sue *verb*
sues
suing
sued
suede
suet
suffer *verb*
suffers
suffering
suffered
sufficiency
sufficient *adjective*
sufficiently
suffix *noun*
suffixes
suffocate *verb*
suffocates
suffocating
suffocated
suffocation
sugar
sugary
suggest *verb*
suggests
suggesting
suggested
suggestion *noun*
suggestions
suicidal *adjective*
suicidally
suicide *noun*
suicides
★ **suit** *noun*
suits
suit *verb*
suits
suiting
suited
suitability
suitable *adjective*
suitably
suitcase *noun*
suitcases
☆ **suite** *noun*
suites
suitor *noun*
suitors
sulk *verb*
sulks
sulking
sulked
sulkiness
sulky *adjective*
sulkier
sulkiest
sulkily
sullen *adjective*
sullenly
sullenness
sulphur
sulphuric acid
sultan *noun*
sultans
sultana *noun*
sultanas
✪ **sum** *noun*
sums
sum *verb*
sums
summing
summed
summarize *verb*
summarizes
summarizing
summarized
summary *noun*
summaries
summer *noun*
summers
summertime
summit *noun*
summits
summon *verb*
summons
summoning
summoned
summons *noun*
summonses
✲ **sun** *noun*
suns
sun *verb*
suns
sunning
sunned
sunbathe *verb*
sunbathes
sunbathing
sunbathed
sunburn
sunburned *or* **sunburnt**
✹ **sundae** *noun*
sundaes

★ A **suit** is a set of matching clothes. ! **suite**.
☆ A **suite** is a set of furniture or a group of rooms. ! **suit**.
✪ A **sum** is an amount or total. ! **some**.
✲ A **sun** is a large star. ! **son**.
✹ A **sundae** is a cocktail of fruit and ice cream. ! **Sunday**.

★ **Sunday** *noun*
Sundays
sundial *noun*
sundials
sunflower *noun*
sunflowers
sung see **sing**
sunglasses
sunk see **sink**
sunlight
sunlit
sunny *adjective*
sunnier
sunniest
sunnily
sunrise *noun*
sunrises
sunset *noun*
sunsets
sunshade *noun*
sunshades
sunshine
sunspot *noun*
sunspots
sunstroke
suntan *noun*
suntans
suntanned
super

super-
super- makes words meaning 'very good' or 'extra', e.g. **supermarket**, **supermodel**. They are normally spelt joined up.

superb *adjective*
superbly
superficial *adjective*
superficially
superfluous *adjective*
superfluously
superintend *verb*
superintends
superintending
superintended
superintendent *noun*
superintendents
superior *adjective* and *noun*
superiors
superiority
superlative *adjective*
superlatively
superlative *noun*
superlatives
supermarket *noun*
supermarkets
supernatural *adjective*
supernaturally
supersonic *adjective*
supersonically
superstition *noun*
superstitions
superstitious *adjective*
superstitiously
supervise *verb*
supervises
supervising
supervised
supervision
supervisor
supper *noun*
suppers
supple *adjective*
suppler
supplest
supplely
supplement *noun*
supplements
supplementary
suppleness
supply *verb*
supplies
supplying
supplied
supplier *noun*
suppliers
supply *noun*
supplies
support *verb*
supports
supporting
supported
support *noun*
supports
supporter *noun*
supporters
suppose *verb*
supposes
supposing
supposed
supposedly
supposition *noun*
suppositions
suppress *verb*
suppresses
suppressing
suppressed
suppression
supremacy
supreme *adjective*
supremely
sure *adjective*
surer
surest
surely
surf *noun*

★ **Sunday** is a day of the week. ! **sundae**.

surf *verb*
surfs
surfing
surfed
surface *noun*
surfaces
surface *verb*
surfaces
surfacing
surfaced
surfboard *noun*
surfboards
surfer *noun*
surfers
surge *verb*
surges
surging
surged
surge *noun*
surges
surgeon *noun*
surgeons
surgery *noun*
surgeries
surgical *adjective*
surgically
surname *noun*
surnames
surpass *verb*
surpasses
surpassing
surpassed
surplus *noun*
surpluses
surprise *verb*
surprises
surprising
surprised
surprise *noun*
surprises
surrender *verb*
surrenders
surrendering
surrendered
surrender *noun*
surrenders
surround *verb*
surrounds
surrounding
surrounded
surroundings *plural noun*
survey *noun*
surveys
survey *verb*
surveys
surveying
surveyed
surveyor *noun*
surveyors
survival
survive *verb*
survives
surviving
survived
survivor *noun*
survivors
suspect *verb*
suspects
suspecting
suspected
suspect *noun*
suspects
suspend *verb*
suspends
suspending
suspended
suspense
suspension *noun*
suspensions
suspicion *noun*
suspicions
suspicious *adjective*
suspiciously
sustain *verb*
sustains
sustaining
sustained
swagger *verb*
swaggers
swaggering
swaggered
swallow *verb*
swallows
swallowing
swallowed
swallow *noun*
swallows
swam see **swim**
swamp *verb*
swamps
swamping
swamped
swamp *noun*
swamps
swampy *adjective*
swampier
swampiest
swan *noun*
swans
swank *verb*
swanks
swanking
swanked
swap *verb*
swaps
swapping
swapped
swap *noun*
swaps
swarm *noun*
swarms

swarm *verb*
swarms
swarming
swarmed
swastika *noun*
swastikas
★ **swat** *verb*
swats
swatting
swatted
swatter *noun*
swatters
sway *verb*
sways
swaying
swayed
swear *verb*
swears
swearing
swore
sworn
sweat *verb*
sweats
sweating
sweated
sweat *noun*
sweater *noun*
sweaters
sweatshirt *noun*
sweatshirts
sweaty *adjective*
sweatier
sweatiest
sweatily
swede *noun*
swedes
sweep *verb*
sweeps
sweeping
swept
sweep *noun*
sweeps
sweeper *noun*
sweepers
sweet *adjective*
sweeter
sweetest
sweetly
sweet *noun*
sweets
sweetcorn
sweeten *verb*
sweetens
sweetening
sweetened
sweetener *noun*
sweeteners
sweetheart *noun*
sweethearts
sweetness
swell *verb*
swells
swelling
swelled
swollen
swell *noun*
swells
swelling *noun*
swellings
swelter *verb*
swelters
sweltering
sweltered
swept see **sweep**
swerve *verb*
swerves
swerving
swerved
swerve *noun*
swerves
swift *adjective*
swifter
swiftest
swiftly
swift *noun*
swifts
swiftness
swill *verb*
swills
swilling
swilled
swill *noun*
swim *verb*
swims
swimming
swam
swum
swim *noun*
swims
swimmer *noun*
swimmers
swimsuit *noun*
swimsuits
swindle *verb*
swindles
swindling
swindled
swindler *noun*
swindlers
swindle *noun*
swindles
swine *noun*
swine *or* swines
swing *verb*
swings
swinging
swung
swing *noun*
swings
swipe *verb*
swipes
swiping
swiped

★ To **swat** an insect is to hit it. ! **swot**.

swipe *noun*
swipes
swirl *verb*
swirls
swirling
swirled
swirl *noun*
swirls
swish *verb*
swishes
swishing
swished
swish *noun*
swishes
Swiss roll *noun*
Swiss rolls
switch *verb*
switches
switching
switched
switch *noun*
switches
switchboard *noun*
switchboards
swivel *verb*
swivels
swivelling
swivelled
swollen see swell
swoon *verb*
swoons
swooning
swooned
swoop *verb*
swoops
swooping
swooped
swoop *noun*
swoops
swop *verb*
swops
swopping
swopped
sword *noun*
swords
swore see swear
sworn see swear
★ **swot** *verb*
swots
swotting
swotted
swot *noun*
swots
swum see swim
swung see swing
sycamore *noun*
sycamores
syllabic *adjective*
syllabically
syllable *noun*
syllables
syllabus *noun*
syllabuses
symbol *noun*
symbols
symbolic *adjective*
symbolically
symbolism
symbolize *verb*
symbolizes
symbolizing
symbolized
symmetrical *adjective*
symmetrically
symmetry
sympathetic *adjective*
sympathetically
sympathize *verb*
sympathizes
sympathizing
sympathized
sympathy *noun*
sympathies
symphonic *adjective*
symphonically
symphony *noun*
symphonies
symptom *noun*
symptoms
symptomatic *adjective*
symptomatically
synagogue *noun*
synagogues
synchronization
synchronize *verb*
synchronizes
synchronizing
synchronized
syncopated
synonym *noun*
synonyms
synonymous *adjective*
synonymously
synthesis *noun*
syntheses
synthesize *verb*
synthesizes
synthesizing
synthesized
synthesizer *noun*
synthesizers
synthetic *adjective*
synthetically
syringe *noun*
syringes

★ To swot is to study hard. ! swat.

syrup *noun*
syrups
syrupy
system *noun*
systems
systematic *adjective*
systematically

Tt

-t
See the note at **-ed**.

tab *noun*
tabs
tabby *noun*
tabbies
table *noun*
tables
tablecloth *noun*
tablecloths
tablespoon *noun*
tablespoons
tablespoonful *noun*
tablespoonfuls
tablet *noun*
tablets
tack *noun*
tacks
tack *verb*
tacks
tacking
tacked
tackle *verb*
tackles
tackling
tackled
tackle *noun*
tackles
tacky *adjective*
tackier
tackiest
tackily
tact
tactful *adjective*
tactfully
tactical *adjective*
tactically
tactics *plural noun*
tactless *adjective*
tactlessly
tadpole *noun*
tadpoles
tag *noun*
tags
tag *verb*
tags
tagging
tagged
★ **tail** *noun*
tails
tail *verb*
tails
tailing
tailed
tailback *noun*
tailbacks
tailless
tailor *noun*
tailors
take *verb*
takes
taking
took
taken
takeaway *noun*
takeaways
takings *plural noun*
talc
talcum powder
☆ **tale** *noun*
tales
talent *noun*
talents
talented
talk *verb*
talks
talking
talked
talk *noun*
talks
talkative *adjective*
talkatively
talker *noun*
talkers
tall *adjective*
taller
tallest
tally *verb*
tallies
tallying
tallied
Talmud
talon *noun*
talons
tambourine *noun*
tambourines
tame *adjective*
tamer
tamest
tamely
tame *verb*
tames
taming
tamed
tameness
tamer *noun*
tamers

★ A **tail** is a part at the back of an animal. ! **tale**.
☆ A **tale** is a story. ! **tail**.

tamper *verb*
tampers
tampering
tampered
tampon *noun*
tampons
tan *noun*
tans
tan *verb*
tans
tanning
tanned
tandem *noun*
tandems
tang *noun*
tangs
tangent *noun*
tangents
tangerine *noun*
tangerines
tangle *verb*
tangles
tangling
tangled
tangle *noun*
tangles
tank *noun*
tanks
tankard *noun*
tankards
tanker *noun*
tankers
tanner *noun*
tanners
tantalize *verb*
tantalizes
tantalizing
tantalized
tantrum *noun*
tantrums
tap *noun*
taps
tap *verb*
taps
tapping
tapped
tap dance *noun*
tap dances
tap dancer *noun*
tap dancers
tap dancing
tape *noun*
tapes
tape *verb*
tapes
taping
taped
tape-measure *noun*
tape-measures
taper *verb*
tapers
tapering
tapered
taper *noun*
tapers
tape recorder *noun*
tape recorders
tapestry *noun*
tapestries
tapeworm *noun*
tapeworms
tapioca
tar *noun*
tar *verb*
tars
tarring
tarred
tarantula *noun*
tarantulas
target *noun*
targets
target *verb*
targets
targeting
targeted
tarmac
tarmacadam
tarnish *verb*
tarnishes
tarnishing
tarnished
tarpaulin *noun*
tarpaulins
tarry *adjective*
tarrier
tarriest
tart *noun*
tarts
tart *adjective*
tarter
tartest
tartly
tartan *noun*
tartans
task *noun*
tasks
tassel *noun*
tassels
taste *verb*
tastes
tasting
tasted
taste *noun*
tastes
tasteful *adjective*
tastefully
tasteless *adjective*
tastelessly
tasty *adjective*
tastier
tastiest
tastily
tattered

tatters *plural noun*
tattoo *noun*
tattoos
tattoo *verb*
tattoos
tattooing
tattooed
tatty *adjective*
tattier
tattiest
tattily
taught see **teach**
taunt *verb*
taunts
taunting
taunted
taunt *noun*
taunts
taut *adjective*
tauter
tautest
tautly
tautness
tavern *noun*
taverns
tawny *adjective*
tawnier
tawniest
tax *noun*
taxes
tax *verb*
taxes
taxing
taxed
taxable
taxation
taxi *noun*
taxis
taxi *verb*
taxis
taxiing
taxied
taxpayer *noun*
taxpayers
★ **tea** *noun*
teas
teabag *noun*
teabags
teacake *noun*
teacakes
teach *verb*
teaches
teaching
taught
teacher *noun*
teachers
tea cloth *or* **tea towel** *noun*
tea cloths *or* tea towels
teacup *noun*
teacups
teak
☆ **team** *noun*
teams
teapot *noun*
teapots
tear *verb*
tears
tearing
tore
torn
✪ **tear** *noun*
tears
tearful *adjective*
tearfully
tear gas
tease *verb*
teases
teasing
teased
teaspoon *noun*
teaspoons
teaspoonful *noun*
teaspoonfuls
teat *noun*
teats
tech *noun*
techs
technical *adjective*
technically
technicality *noun*
technicalities
technician *noun*
technicians
technique *noun*
techniques
technological *adjective*
technologically
technology *noun*
technologies
teddy bear *noun*
teddy bears
tedious *adjective*
tediously
tediousness
tedium
✲ **tee** *noun*
tees
✹ **teem** *verb*
teems
teeming
teemed
teenage
teenager *noun*
teenagers
teens
teeth see **tooth**
teetotal
teetotaller *noun*
teetotallers

★ **Tea** is a hot drink. ! **tee**.
☆ You use **team** in e.g. *a football team*. ! **team**.
✪ A **tear** is a drop of water from an eye and rhymes with 'here', or a split in something and rhymes with 'hair'.
✲ A **tee** is part of a golf course. ! **tea**.
✹ You use **teem** in e.g. *a place teeming with people*. ! **team**.

telecommunications *plural noun*
telegram *noun*
telegrams
telegraph *noun*
telegraphs
telegraphic *adjective*
telegraphically
telegraphy
telepathic *adjective*
telepathically
telepathy
telephone *noun*
telephones
telephone *verb*
telephones
telephoning
telephoned
telephonist *noun*
telephonists
telescope *noun*
telescopes
telescopic *adjective*
telescopically
teletext
televise *verb*
televises
televising
televised
television *noun*
televisions
tell *verb*
tells
telling
told
tell-tale *adjective* and *noun*
tell-tales
telly *noun*
tellies
temper *noun*
tempers
temperate
temperature *noun*
temperatures
tempest *noun*
tempests
tempestuous *adjective*
tempestuously
temple *noun*
temples
tempo *noun*
tempos
temporary *adjective*
temporarily
tempt *verb*
tempts
tempting
tempted
temptation *noun*
temptations
tempter *noun*
tempters
temptress *noun*
temptresses
ten *noun*
tens
tenancy *noun*
tenancies
tenant *noun*
tenants
tend *verb*
tends
tending
tended
tendency *noun*
tendencies
tender *adjective*
tenderer
tenderest
tenderly
tender *noun*
tenders
tender *verb*
tenders
tendering
tendered
tenderness
tendon *noun*
tendons
tendril *noun*
tendrils
tennis
tenor *noun*
tenors
tenpin bowling
tense *adjective*
tenser
tensest
tensely
tense *noun*
tenses
tension *noun*
tensions
tent *noun*
tents
tentacle *noun*
tentacles
tenth
tenthly
tepid
term *noun*
terms
term *verb*
terms
terming
termed
terminal *noun*
terminals
terminate *verb*
terminates
terminating
terminated

termination *noun*
terminations
terminus *noun*
termini
terrace *noun*
terraces
terrapin *noun*
terrapins
terrible *adjective*
terribly
terrier *noun*
terriers
terrific *adjective*
terrifically
terrify *verb*
terrifies
terrifying
terrified
territorial *adjective*
territorially
territory *noun*
territories
terror *noun*
terrors
terrorism
terrorist *adjective*
and *noun*
terrorists
terrorize *verb*
terrorizes
terrorizing
terrorized
tessellation *noun*
tessellations
test *noun*
tests
test *verb*
tests
testing
tested
testament *noun*
testaments
testicle *noun*
testicles
testify *verb*
testifies
testifying
testified
testimonial *noun*
testimonials
testimony *noun*
testimonies
testy *adjective*
testier
testiest
tether *verb*
tethers
tethering
tethered
tether *noun*
tethers
text *noun*
texts
textbook *noun*
textbooks
textile *noun*
textiles
texture *noun*
textures
than
thank *verb*
thanks
thanking
thanked
thankful *adjective*
thankfully
thankless *adjective*
thanklessly
thanks *plural noun*
that *adjective, pronoun,* and *conjunction*
thatch *noun*
thatch *verb*
thatches
thatching
thatched
thatcher *noun*
thatchers
thaw *verb*
thaws
thawing
thawed
theatre *noun*
theatres
theatrical *adjective*
theatrically
thee
theft *noun*
thefts
★ **their**
☆ **theirs**
them
theme *noun*
themes
theme park *noun*
theme parks
themselves
then
theologian *noun*
theologians
theological *adjective*
theologically
theology
theorem *noun*
theorems
theoretical *adjective*
theoretically
theory *noun*
theories
therapist *noun*
therapists

★ You use **their** in e.g. *this is their house.* ! **there, they're.**
☆ You use **theirs** in e.g. *the house is theirs.* Note that there is no apostrophe in this word.

therapy *noun*
therapies
★ **there** *adverb*
thereabouts
therefore
thermal *adjective*
thermally
thermometer *noun*
thermometers
Thermos *noun*
Thermoses
thermostat *noun*
thermostats
thermostatic *adjective*
thermostatically
thesaurus *noun*
thesauri *or* thesauruses
these
they
they'd *verb*
they'll *verb*
☆ **they're** *verb*
they've *verb*
thick *adjective*
thicker
thickest
thickly
thicken *verb*
thickens
thickening
thickened
thicket *noun*
thickets
thickness *noun*
thicknesses
thief *noun*
thieves
thigh *noun*
thighs
thimble *noun*
thimbles
thin *adjective*
thinner
thinnest
thinly
thin *verb*
thins
thinning
thinned
thine
thing *noun*
things
think *verb*
thinks
thinking
thought
thinker *noun*
thinkers
thinness
third
thirdly
Third World
thirst
thirsty *adjective*
thirstier
thirstiest
thirstily
thirteen
thirteenth
thirtieth
thirty *noun*
thirties
this
thistle *noun*
thistles
thorn *noun*
thorns
thorny *adjective*
thornier
thorniest
thorough *adjective*
thoroughly
thoroughness
those
thou
though
thought *noun*
thoughts
thought see **think**
thoughtful *adjective*
thoughtfully
thoughtfulness
thoughtless *adjective*
thoughtlessly
thoughtlessness
thousand *noun*
thousands
thousandth
✪ **thrash** *verb*
thrashes
thrashing
thrashed
thread *noun*
threads
thread *verb*
threads
threading
threaded
threadbare
threat *noun*
threats
threaten *verb*
threatens
threatening
threatened
three *noun*
threes

★ You use **there** in e.g. *Look over there*. ! **their**, **they're**.
☆ **They're** is short for *they are*. ! **their**, **there**.
✪ To **thrash** someone is to beat them. ! **thresh**.

three-dimensional *adjective*
three-dimensionally
★ **thresh** *verb*
threshes
threshing
threshed
threshold *noun*
thresholds
threw see **throw**
thrift
thrifty *adjective*
thriftier
thriftiest
thriftily
thrill *noun*
thrills
thrill *verb*
thrills
thrilling
thrilled
thriller *noun*
thrillers
thrive *verb*
thrives
thriving
thrived *or* throve *or* thriven
throat *noun*
throats
throb *verb*
throbs
throbbing
throbbed
throb *noun*
throbs
throne *noun*
thrones
throng *noun*
throngs
throttle *verb*
throttles
throttling
throttled
throttle *noun*
throttles
through
throughout
throve see **thrive**
throw *verb*
throws
throwing
threw
thrown
throw *noun*
throws
thrush *noun*
thrushes
thrust *verb*
thrusts
thrusting
thrust
thud *noun*
thuds
thud *verb*
thuds
thudding
thudded
thumb *noun*
thumbs
thump *verb*
thumps
thumping
thumped
thump *noun*
thumps
thunder *noun*
thunder *verb*
thunders
thundering
thundered
thunderous *adjective*
thunderously
thunderstorm *noun*
thunderstorms
Thursday *noun*
Thursdays
thus
thy
tick *verb*
ticks
ticking
ticked
tick *noun*
ticks
ticket *noun*
tickets
tickle *verb*
tickles
tickling
tickled
ticklish *adjective*
ticklishly
tidal
tiddler *noun*
tiddlers
tiddlywink *noun*
tiddlywinks
tide *noun*
tides
tide *verb*
tides
tiding
tided
tidiness
tidy *adjective*
tidier
tidiest
tidily
tie *verb*
ties
tying
tied

★ To **thresh** corn is to beat it to separate the grain. ! **thrash**

tie *noun*
ties
tie-break *noun*
tie-breaks
tiger *noun*
tigers
tight *adjective*
tighter
tightest
tightly
tighten *verb*
tightens
tightening
tightened
tightness
tightrope *noun*
tightropes
tights *plural noun*
tigress *noun*
tigresses
tile *noun*
tiles
tiled
till *preposition* and *conjunction*
till *noun*
tills
till *verb*
tills
tilling
tilled
tiller *noun*
tillers
tilt *verb*
tilts
tilting
tilted
tilt *noun*
tilts
timber *noun*
timbers
time *noun*
times
time *verb*
times
timing
timed
timer *noun*
timers
times
timetable *noun*
timetables
timid *adjective*
timidly
timidity
timing
timpani *plural noun*
tin *noun*
tins
tin *verb*
tins
tinning
tinned
tingle *verb*
tingles
tingling
tingled
tingle *noun*
tingles
tinker *verb*
tinkers
tinkering
tinkered
tinker *noun*
tinkers
tinkle *verb*
tinkles
tinkling
tinkled
tinkle *noun*
tinkles
tinny *adjective*
tinnier
tinniest
tinnily
tinsel
tint *noun*
tints
tint *verb*
tints
tinting
tinted
tiny *adjective*
tinier
tiniest
tip *verb*
tips
tipping
tipped
tip *noun*
tips
tiptoe *verb*
tiptoes
tiptoeing
tiptoed
tiptoe *noun*
★ **tire** *verb*
tires
tiring
tired
tired
tireless *adjective*
tirelessly
tiresome *adjective*
tiresomely
tissue *noun*
tissues
tit *noun*
tits
titbit *noun*
titbits

★ To **tire** is to become tired. **! tyre.**

title *noun*
titles
titter *verb*
titters
tittering
tittered
★ **to** *preposition*
toad *noun*
toads
toadstool *noun*
toadstools
toast *verb*
toasts
toasting
toasted
toast *noun*
toasts
toaster *noun*
toasters
tobacco *noun*
tobaccos
tobacconist *noun*
tobacconists
toboggan *noun*
toboggans
tobogganing
today
toddler *noun*
toddlers
☆ **toe** *noun*
toes
toffee *noun*
toffees
toga *noun*
togas
together
toil *verb*
toils
toiling
toiled
toilet *noun*
toilets
token *noun*
tokens
told see tell
tolerable *adjective*
tolerably
tolerance
tolerant *adjective*
tolerantly
tolerate *verb*
tolerates
tolerating
tolerated
toll *noun*
tolls
toll *verb*
tolls
tolling
tolled
tomahawk *noun*
tomahawks
tomato *noun*
tomatoes
tomb *noun*
tombs
tomboy *noun*
tomboys
tombstone *noun*
tombstones
tomcat *noun*
tomcats
tommy-gun *noun*
tommy-guns
tomorrow
tom-tom *noun*
tom-toms
✪ **ton** *noun*
tons
tonal *adjective*
tonally
tone *noun*
tones
tone *verb*
tones
toning
toned
tone-deaf
tongs *plural noun*
tongue *noun*
tongues
tonic *noun*
tonics
tonight
✲ **tonne** *noun*
tonnes
tonsillitis
tonsils *plural noun*
✸ **too** *adverb*
took see take
tool *noun*
tools
tooth *noun*
teeth
toothache
toothbrush *noun*
toothbrushes
toothed
toothpaste *noun*
toothpastes
top *noun*
tops
top *verb*
tops
topping
topped
topic *noun*
topics
topical *adjective*
topically
topicality

★ You use **to** in e.g. *go to bed* or *I want to stay.* ! too, two.
☆ A **toe** is a part of a foot. ! tow.
✪ A **ton** is a non-metric unit of weight. ! tonne.
✲ A **tonne** is a metric unit of weight. ! ton.
✸ You use **too** in e.g. *it's too late* or *I want to come too.* ! to, two.

topless
topmost
topping *noun*
toppings
topple *verb*
topples
toppling
toppled
topsy-turvy
torch *noun*
torches
tore see **tear**
toreador *noun*
toreadors
torment *verb*
torments
tormenting
tormented
torment *noun*
torments
tormentor *noun*
tormentors
torn see **tear**
tornado *noun*
tornadoes
torpedo *noun*
torpedoes
torpedo *verb*
torpedoes
torpedoing
torpedoed
torrent *noun*
torrents
torrential *adjective*
torrentially
torso *noun*
torsos
tortoise *noun*
tortoises
torture *verb*
tortures
torturing
tortured
torture *noun*
tortures
torturer *noun*
torturers
Tory *noun*
Tories
toss *verb*
tosses
tossing
tossed
toss *noun*
tosses
total *noun*
totals
total *adjective*
totally
total *verb*
totals
totalling
totalled
totalitarian
totem pole *noun*
totem poles
totter *verb*
totters
tottering
tottered
touch *verb*
touches
touching
touched
touch *noun*
touches
touchy *adjective*
touchier
touchiest
touchily
tough *adjective*
tougher
toughest
toughly
toughen *verb*
toughens
toughening
toughened
toughness
tour *noun*
tours
tourism
tourist *noun*
tourists
tournament *noun*
tournaments
★ **tow** *verb*
tows
towing
towed
tow *noun*
toward *or* **towards**
towel *noun*
towels
towelling
tower *noun*
towers
tower *verb*
towers
towering
towered
town *noun*
towns
towpath *noun*
towpaths
toxic *adjective*
toxically
toy *noun*
toys

★ To **tow** something is to pull it along. ! **toe**.

toy *verb*
toys
toying
toyed
toyshop *noun*
toyshops
trace *noun*
traces
trace *verb*
traces
tracing
traced
traceable
track *noun*
tracks
track *verb*
tracks
tracking
tracked
tracker *noun*
trackers
tracksuit *noun*
tracksuits
tract *noun*
tracts
traction
tractor *noun*
tractors
trade *noun*
trades
trade *verb*
trades
trading
traded
trademark *noun*
trademarks
trader *noun*
traders
tradesman *noun*
tradesmen
trade union *noun*
trade unions
tradition *noun*
traditions
traditional *adjective*
traditionally
traffic *noun*
traffic *verb*
traffics
trafficking
trafficked
tragedy *noun*
tragedies
tragic *adjective*
tragically
trail *noun*
trails
trail *verb*
trails
trailing
trailed
trailer *noun*
trailers
train *noun*
trains
train *verb*
trains
training
trained
trainer *noun*
trainers
traitor *noun*
traitors
tram *noun*
trams
tramp *noun*
tramps
tramp *verb*
tramps
tramping
tramped
trample *verb*
tramples
trampling
trampled
trampoline *noun*
trampolines
trance *noun*
trances
tranquil *adjective*
tranquilly
★ **tranquillity**
tranquillizer *noun*
tranquillizers
transact *verb*
transacts
transacting
transacted
transaction *noun*
transactions
transatlantic
transfer *verb*
transfers
transferring
transferred
transfer *noun*
transfers
transferable
transference
transform *verb*
transforms
transforming
transformed
transformation *noun*
transformations
transformer *noun*
transformers
transfusion *noun*
transfusions
transistor *noun*
transistors

★ Note that there are two ls in this word.

transition *noun*
transitions
transitional *adjective*
transitionally
transitive *adjective*
transitively
translate *verb*
translates
translating
translated
translation *noun*
translations
translator *noun*
translators
translucent
transmission *noun*
transmissions
transmit *verb*
transmits
transmitting
transmitted
transmitter *noun*
transmitters
transparency *noun*
transparencies
transparent *adjective*
transparently
transpire *verb*
transpires
transpiring
transpired
transplant *verb*
transplants
transplanting
transplanted
transplant *noun*
transplants
transplantation *noun*
transplantations
transport *verb*
transports
transporting
transported
transportation
transport
transporter *noun*
transporters
trap *verb*
traps
trapping
trapped
trap *noun*
traps
trapdoor *noun*
trapdoors
trapeze *noun*
trapezes
trapezium *noun*
trapeziums
trapezoid *noun*
trapezoids
trapper *noun*
trappers
trash
trashy *adjective*
trashier
trashiest
trashily
travel *verb*
travels
travelling
travelled
travel *noun*
traveller *noun*
travellers
traveller's cheque *noun*
traveller's cheques
trawler *noun*
trawlers
tray *noun*
trays
treacherous *adjective*
treacherously
treachery
treacle
tread *verb*
treads
treading
trod
trodden
tread *noun*
treads
treason
treasure *noun*
treasures
treasure *verb*
treasures
treasuring
treasured
treasurer *noun*
treasurers
treasury *noun*
treasuries
treat *verb*
treats
treating
treated
treat *noun*
treats
treatment *noun*
treatments
treaty *noun*
treaties

treble *adjective* and *noun*
trebles
treble *verb*
trebles
trebling
trebled
tree *noun*
trees
trek *verb*
treks
trekking
trekked
trek *noun*
treks
trellis *noun*
trellises
tremble *verb*
trembles
trembling
trembled
tremble *noun*
trembles
tremendous *adjective*
tremendously
tremor *noun*
tremors
trench *noun*
trenches
trend *noun*
trends
trendiness
trendy *adjective*
trendier
trendiest
trendily
trespass *verb*
trespasses
trespassing
trespassed
trespasser *noun*
trespassers
trestle *noun*
trestles
trial *noun*
trials
triangle *noun*
triangles
triangular
tribal *adjective*
tribally
tribe *noun*
tribes
tribesman *noun*
tribesmen
tributary *noun*
tributaries
tribute *noun*
tributes
trick *noun*
tricks
trick *verb*
tricks
tricking
tricked
trickery
trickster *noun*
tricksters
trickle *verb*
trickles
trickling
trickled
trickle *noun*
trickles
tricky *adjective*
trickier
trickiest
trickily
tricycle *noun*
tricycles
tried see **try**
trifle *noun*
trifles
trifle *verb*
trifles
trifling
trifled
trifling
trigger *noun*
triggers
trigger *verb*
triggers
triggering
triggered
trillion *noun*
trillions
trim *adjective*
trimmer
trimmest
trimly
trim *verb*
trims
trimming
trimmed
trim *noun*
trims
★ **Trinity**
trio *noun*
trios
trip *verb*
trips
tripping
tripped
trip *noun*
trips
tripe
triple *adjective*
triply
triple *noun*
triples

★ You use a capital T when you mean the three persons of God in Christianity.

triple *verb*
triples
tripling
tripled
triplet *noun*
triplets
tripod *noun*
tripods
triumph *noun*
triumphs
triumphant *adjective*
triumphantly
trivial *adjective*
trivially
triviality *noun*
trivialities
trod see **tread**
trodden see **tread**
troll *noun*
trolls
trolley *noun*
trolleys
trombone *noun*
trombones
troop *noun*
troops
troop *verb*
troops
trooping
trooped
troops *plural noun*
trophy *noun*
trophies
tropic *noun*
tropics
tropical *adjective*
trot *verb*
trots
trotting
trotted
trot *noun*
trots
trouble *noun*
troubles
trouble *verb*
troubles
troubling
troubled
troublesome
trough *noun*
troughs
trousers *plural noun*
trout *noun*
trout
trowel *noun*
trowels
truancy *noun*
truancies
truant *noun*
truants
truce *noun*
truces
truck *noun*
trucks
trudge *verb*
trudges
trudging
trudged
true *adjective*
truer
truest
truly
trump *noun*
trumps
trump *verb*
trumps
trumping
trumped
trumpet *noun*
trumpets
trumpet *verb*
trumpets
trumpeting
trumpeted
trumpeter *noun*
trumpeters
truncheon *noun*
truncheons
trundle *verb*
trundles
trundling
trundled
trunk *noun*
trunks
trunks *plural noun*
trust *verb*
trusts
trusting
trusted
trust
trustful *adjective*
trustfully
trustworthy *adjective*
trustworthily
trusty *adjective*
trustier
trustiest
trustily
truth *noun*
truths
truthful *adjective*
truthfully
truthfulness
try *verb*
tries
trying
tried
try *noun*
tries
T-shirt *noun*
T-shirts
tub *noun*
tubs

tuba *noun*
tubas
tube *noun*
tubes
tuber *noun*
tubers
tubing
tubular
tuck *verb*
tucks
tucking
tucked
tuck *noun*
tucks
Tuesday *noun*
Tuesdays
tuft *noun*
tufts
tug *noun*
tugs
tug *verb*
tugs
tugging
tugged
tulip *noun*
tulips
tumble *verb*
tumbles
tumbling
tumbled
tumble *noun*
tumbles
tumble-drier *noun*
tumble-driers
tumbler *noun*
tumblers
tummy *noun*
tummies
tumour *noun*
tumours
tumult
tumultuous *adjective*
tumultuously
tuna *noun*
tuna *or* tunas
tundra
tune *noun*
tunes
tune *verb*
tunes
tuning
tuned
tuneful *adjective*
tunefully
tunic *noun*
tunics
tunnel *noun*
tunnels
tunnel *verb*
tunnels
tunnelling
tunnelled
turban *noun*
turbans
turbine *noun*
turbines
turbulence
turbulent *adjective*
turbulently
turf *noun*
turfs *or* turves
turkey *noun*
turkeys
Turkish bath *noun*
Turkish baths
Turkish delight
turmoil
turn *verb*
turns
turning
turned
turn
noun
turns
turncoat *noun*
turncoats
turnip *noun*
turnips
turnover *noun*
turnovers
turnstile *noun*
turnstiles
turntable *noun*
turntables
turpentine
turquoise
turret *noun*
turrets
turtle *noun*
turtles
tusk *noun*
tusks
tussle *verb*
tussles
tussling
tussled
tussle *noun*
tussles
tutor *noun*
tutors
tweak *verb*
tweaks
tweaking
tweaked
tweak *noun*
tweaks
tweed
tweezers *plural noun*

twelve *noun*
twelves
twelfth
twentieth
twenty *noun*
twenties
twice
twiddle *verb*
twiddles
twiddling
twiddled
twiddle *noun*
twiddles
twig *noun*
twigs
twig *verb*
twigs
twigging
twigged
twilight
twin *noun*
twins
twin *verb*
twins
twinning
twinned
twine
twinkle *verb*
twinkles
twinkling
twinkled
twinkle *noun*
twinkles
twirl *verb*
twirls
twirling
twirled
twirl *noun*
twirls
twist *verb*
twists
twisting
twisted
twist *noun*
twists
twister *noun*
twisters
twitch *verb*
twitches
twitching
twitched
twitch *noun*
twitches
twitter *verb*
twitters
twittering
twittered
★ **two** *adjective* and *noun*
twos
tying see **tie**
type *noun*
types
type *verb*
types
typing
typed
typewriter *noun*
typewriters
typewritten
typhoon *noun*
typhoons
typical *adjective*
typically
typist *noun*
typists
tyranny *noun*
tyrannies
tyrannical *adjective*
tyrannically
tyrant *noun*
tyrants
☆ **tyre** *noun*
tyres

Uu

udder *noun*
udders
ugliness
ugly *adjective*
uglier
ugliest
ulcer *noun*
ulcers
ultimate *adjective*
ultimately
ultraviolet
umbilical cord *noun*
umbilical cords
umbrella *noun*
umbrellas
umpire *noun*
umpires

un-
un- makes words meaning 'not', e.g. **unable**, **unhappiness**. Some of these words have special meanings, e.g. **unprofessional**. See the note at **non-**.

unable
unaided
unanimity
unanimous *adjective*
unanimously
unavoidable *adjective*
unavoidably
unaware

★ You use **two** in e.g. *two people* or *there are two of them*. ! **to**, **too**.
☆ A **tyre** is a rubber cover for a wheel. ! **tire**.

unawares
unbearable *adjective*
unbearably
unbelievable *adjective*
unbelievably
unblock *verb*
unblocks
unblocking
unblocked
unborn
uncalled for
uncanny *adjective*
uncannier
uncanniest
uncertain *adjective*
uncertainly
uncertainty
uncle *noun*
uncles
uncomfortable *adjective*
uncomfortably
uncommon *adjective*
uncommonly
unconscious *adjective*
unconsciously
unconsciousness
uncontrollable *adjective*
uncontrollably
uncountable
uncouth
uncover *verb*
uncovers
uncovering
uncovered
undecided
undeniable *adjective*
undeniably
under
underarm *adjective*
underclothes *plural noun*
underdeveloped
underdone
underfoot
undergo *verb*
undergoes
undergoing
underwent
undergone
undergraduate *noun*
undergraduates
underground *adjective* and *noun*
undergrounds
undergrowth
underhand
underlie *verb*
underlies
underlying
underlay
underlain
underline *verb*
underlines
underlining
underlined
undermine *verb*
undermines
undermining
undermined
underneath *preposition*
underpants *plural noun*
underpass *noun*
underpasses
underprivileged
understand *verb*
understands
understanding
understood
understandable *adjective*
understandably
understanding
undertake *verb*
undertakes
undertaking
undertook
undertaken
undertaker *noun*
undertakers
undertaking *noun*
undertakings
underwater
underwear
underworld
undesirable *adjective*
undesirably
undeveloped
undo *verb*
undoes
undoing
undid
undone
undoubted *adjective*
undoubtedly
undress *verb*
undresses
undressing
undressed
unearth *verb*
unearths
unearthing
unearthed
unearthly

unease
uneasiness
uneasy *adjective*
uneasier
uneasiest
uneasily
uneatable
unemployed
unemployment
uneven *adjective*
unevenly
unevenness
unexpected *adjective*
unexpectedly
unfair *adjective*
unfairly
unfairness
unfaithful *adjective*
unfaithfully
unfamiliar
unfamiliarity
unfasten *verb*
unfastens
unfastening
unfastened
unfavourable *adjective*
unfavourably
unfinished
unfit
unfold *verb*
unfolds
unfolding
unfolded
unforgettable *adjective*
unforgettably
unforgivable *adjective*
unforgivably
unfortunate *adjective*
unfortunately
unfreeze *verb*
unfreezes
unfreezing
unfroze
unfrozen
unfriendliness
unfriendly
ungrateful *adjective*
ungratefully
unhappiness
unhappy *adjective*
unhappier
unhappiest
unhappily
unhealthy *adjective*
unhealthier
unhealthiest
unhealthily
unheard-of
unicorn *noun*
unicorns
unification
uniform *noun*
uniforms
uniform *adjective*
uniformly
uniformed
uniformity
unify *verb*
unifies
unifying
unified
unimportance
unimportant
uninhabited
unintentional *adjective*
unintentionally
uninterested
uninteresting
union *noun*
unions
unique *adjective*
uniquely
uniqueness
unisex
unison
unit *noun*
units
unite *verb*
unites
uniting
united
unity *noun*
unities
universal *adjective*
universally
universe
university *noun*
universities
unjust *adjective*
unjustly
unkind *adjective*
unkinder
unkindest
unkindly
unkindness
unknown
unleaded
unless
unlike
unlikely *adjective*
unlikelier
unlikeliest

unload *verb*
unloads
unloading
unloaded
unlock *verb*
unlocks
unlocking
unlocked
unlucky *adjective*
unluckier
unluckiest
unluckily
unmistakable *adjective*
unmistakably
unnatural *adjective*
unnaturally
unnecessary *adjective*
unnecessarily
unoccupied
unpack *verb*
unpacks
unpacking
unpacked
unpleasant *adjective*
unpleasantly
unpleasantness
unplug *verb*
unplugs
unplugging
unplugged
unpopular *adjective*
unpopularly
unpopularity
unravel *verb*
unravels
unravelling
unravelled
unreal
unreasonable *adjective*
unreasonably
unrest
unroll *verb*
unrolls
unrolling
unrolled
unruliness
unruly *adjective*
unrulier
unruliest
unscrew *verb*
unscrews
unscrewing
unscrewed
unseemly
unseen
unselfish *adjective*
unselfishly
unselfishness
unsightly
unskilled
unsound *adjective*
unsoundly
unsteadiness
unsteady *adjective*
unsteadier
unsteadiest
unsteadily
unsuccessful *adjective*
unsuccessfully
unsuitable *adjective*
unsuitably
unthinkable *adjective*
unthinkably
untidiness
untidy *adjective*
untidier
untidiest
untidily
untie *verb*
unties
untying
untied
until
untimely
unto
untold
untoward
untrue *adjective*
untruly
untruthful *adjective*
untruthfully
unused
unusual *adjective*
unusually
unwanted
unwell
unwilling *adjective*
unwillingly
unwillingness
unwind *verb*
unwinds
unwinding
unwound
unwrap *verb*
unwraps
unwrapping
unwrapped
unzip *verb*
unzips
unzipping
unzipped
update *verb*
updates
updating
updated

upgrade *verb*
upgrades
upgrading
upgraded
upheaval *noun*
upheavals
uphill
uphold *verb*
upholds
upholding
upheld
upholstery
upkeep
uplands *plural noun*
upon
upper
upright *adjective*
uprightly
upright *noun*
uprights
uprising *noun*
uprisings
uproar *noun*
uproars
upset *verb*
upsets
upsetting
upset
upset *noun*
upsets
upshot
upside down
upstairs
upstart *noun*
upstarts
upstream *adjective*
uptake
uptight
upward *adjective* and *adverb*
upwards *adverb*
uranium
urban
urbanization
urbanize *verb*
urbanizes
urbanizing
urbanized
urchin *noun*
urchins
Urdu
urge *verb*
urges
urging
urged
urge *noun*
urges
urgency
urgent *adjective*
urgently
urinary
urinate *verb*
urinates
urinating
urinated
urination
urine
urn *noun*
urns

-us
Most nouns ending in *-us* come from Latin words, e.g. **bonus** and **terminus**. They normally have plurals ending in *-uses*, e.g. **bonuses** and **terminuses**. Some more technical words have plurals ending in *-i*, e.g. **nucleus** - **nuclei**.

usable
usage *noun*
usages
use *verb*
uses
using
used
use *noun*
uses
useful *adjective*
usefully
usefulness
useless *adjective*
uselessly
uselessness
user *noun*
users
user-friendly *adjective*
user-friendlier
user-friendliest
usher *noun*
ushers
usher *verb*
ushers
ushering
ushered
usherette *noun*
usherettes
usual *adjective*
usually
usurp *verb*
usurps
usurping
usurped
usurper *noun*
usurpers
utensil *noun*
utensils
uterus *noun*
uteri

utilization
utilize *verb*
utilizes
utilizing
utilized
utmost
utter *adjective*
utter *verb*
utters
uttering
uttered
utterance *noun*
utterances
utterly *adverb*
U-turn *noun*
U-turns

Vv

vacancy *noun*
vacancies
vacant *adjective*
vacantly
vacate *verb*
vacates
vacating
vacated
vacation *noun*
vacations
vaccinate *verb*
vaccinates
vaccinating
vaccinated
vaccination *noun*
vaccinations
vaccine *noun*
vaccines
vacuum *noun*
vacuums
vagina *noun*
vaginas
vague *adjective*
vaguer
vaguest
vaguely
vagueness
★ **vain** *adjective*
vainer
vainest
vainly
☆ **vale** *noun*
vales
valentine *noun*
valentines
valiant *adjective*
valiantly
valid *adjective*
validly
validity
valley *noun*
valleys
valour
valuable *adjective*
valuably
valuables *plural noun*
valuation *noun*
valuations
value *noun*
values
value *verb*
values
valuing
valued
valueless
valuer *noun*
valuers
valve *noun*
valves
vampire *noun*
vampires
van *noun*
vans
vandal *noun*
vandals
vandalism
✪ **vane** *noun*
vanes
vanilla
vanish *verb*
vanishes
vanishing
vanished
vanity
vanquish *verb*
vanquishes
vanquishing
vanquished
vaporize *verb*
vaporizes
vaporizing
vaporized
vapour *noun*
vapours
variable *adjective*
variably
variable *noun*
variables
variation *noun*
variations
varied
variety *noun*
varieties
various *adjective*
variously
varnish *noun*
varnishes

★ **Vain** means 'conceited' or 'proud'. ! **vane, vein.**
☆ A **vale** is a valley. ! **veil.**
✪ A **vane** is a pointer that shows which way the wind is blowing. ! **vain, vein.**

varnish *verb*
varnishes
varnishing
varnished
vary *verb*
varies
varying
varied
vase *noun*
vases
vast *adjective*
vastly
vastness
vat *noun*
vats
vault *verb*
vaults
vaulting
vaulted
vault *noun*
vaults
veal
vector *noun*
vectors
Veda
veer *verb*
veers
veering
veered
vegan *noun*
vegans
vegetable *noun*
vegetables
vegetarian *noun*
vegetarians
vegetate *verb*
vegetates
vegetating
vegetated
vegetation
vehicle *noun*
vehicles
★ **veil** *noun*
veils
veil *verb*
veils
veiling
veiled
☆ **vein** *noun*
veins
velocity *noun*
velocities
velvet
velvety
vendetta *noun*
vendettas
vendor *noun*
vendors
venerable *adjective*
venerably
venereal disease *noun*
venereal diseases
venetian blind *noun*
venetian blinds
vengeance
venison
Venn diagram *noun*
Venn diagrams
venom
venomous *adjective*
venomously
vent *noun*
vents
ventilate *verb*
ventilates
ventilating
ventilated
ventilation
ventilator *noun*
ventilators
ventriloquism
ventriloquist *noun*
ventriloquists
venture *verb*
ventures
venturing
ventured
venture *noun*
ventures
veranda *noun*
verandas
verb *noun*
verbs
verdict *noun*
verdicts
verge *verb*
verges
verging
verged
verge *noun*
verges
verification
verify *verb*
verifies
verifying
verified
vermin
verruca *noun*
verrucas
versatile
versatility
verse *noun*
verses
version *noun*
versions
versus
vertebra *noun*
vertebrae
vertebrate *noun*
vertebrates
vertex *noun*
vertices

★ A **veil** is a covering for the face. ! **vale**.
☆ A **vein** carries blood to the heart. ! **vain**, **vane**.

vertical *adjective*
vertically
very
Vesak
vessel *noun*
vessels
vest *noun*
vests
vested *adjective*
vested
vestment *noun*
vestments
vestry *noun*
vestries
vet *noun*
vets
veteran *noun*
veterans
veterinary
veto *verb*
vetoes
vetoing
vetoed
veto *noun*
vetoes
vex *verb*
vexes
vexing
vexed
vexation
via
viaduct *noun*
viaducts
vibrate *verb*
vibrates
vibrating
vibrated
vibration *noun*
vibrations
vicar *noun*
vicars
vicarage *noun*
vicarages
vice *noun*
vices
vice-president *noun*
vice-presidents
vice versa
vicinity *noun*
vicinities
vicious *adjective*
viciously
viciousness
victim *noun*
victims
victimize *verb*
victimizes
victimizing
victimized
victor *noun*
victors
Victorian *adjective*
and *noun*
Victorians
victorious *adjective*
victoriously
victory *noun*
victories
video *noun*
videos
video *verb*
videoes
videoing
videoed
videotape *noun*
videotapes
view *noun*
views
view *verb*
views
viewing
viewed
viewer *noun*
viewers
vigilance
vigilant *adjective*
vigilantly
vigorous *adjective*
vigorously
vigour
Viking *noun*
Vikings
vile *adjective*
viler
vilest
vilely
villa *noun*
villas
village *noun*
villages
villager *noun*
villagers
villain *noun*
villains
villainous *adjective*
villainously
villainy
vine *noun*
vines
vinegar
vineyard *noun*
vineyards
vintage *noun*
vintages
vinyl
viola *noun*
violas
violate *verb*
violates
violating
violated

violation *noun*
violations
violator *noun*
violators
violence
violent *adjective*
violently
violet *noun*
violets
violin *noun*
violins
violinist *noun*
violinists
viper *noun*
vipers
virgin *noun*
virgins
virginity
virtual *adjective*
virtually
virtue *noun*
virtues
virtuous *adjective*
virtuously
virus *noun*
viruses
visa *noun*
visas
visibility
visible *adjective*
visibly
vision *noun*
visions
visit *verb*
visits
visiting
visited
visit *noun*
visits
visitor *noun*
visitors
visor *noun*
visors
visual *adjective*
visually
visualize *verb*
visualizes
visualizing
visualized
vital *adjective*
vitally
vitality
vitamin *noun*
vitamins
vivid *adjective*
vividly
vividness
vivisection *noun*
vivisections
vixen *noun*
vixens
vocabulary *noun*
vocabularies
vocal *adjective*
vocally
vocalist *noun*
vocalists
vocation *noun*
vocations
vocational *adjective*
vocationally
vodka *noun*
vodkas
voice *noun*
voices
voice *verb*
voices
voicing
voiced
volcanic
volcano *noun*
volcanoes
vole *noun*
voles
volley *noun*
volleys
volleyball
volt *noun*
volts
voltage *noun*
voltages
volume *noun*
volumes
voluntary *adjective*
voluntarily
volunteer *verb*
volunteers
volunteering
volunteered
volunteer *noun*
volunteers
vomit *verb*
vomits
vomiting
vomited
vote *verb*
votes
voting
voted
vote *noun*
votes
voter *noun*
voters
vouch *verb*
vouches
vouching
vouched
voucher *noun*
vouchers
vow *noun*
vows

vow *verb*
vows
vowing
vowed
vowel *noun*
vowels
voyage *noun*
voyages
voyager *noun*
voyagers
vulgar *adjective*
vulgarly
vulnerable *adjective*
vulnerably
vulture *noun*
vultures
vulva *noun*
vulvas

Ww

wad *noun*
wads
waddle *verb*
waddles
waddling
waddled
waddle *noun*
waddles
wade *verb*
wades
wading
waded
wafer *noun*
wafers
wag *verb*
wags
wagging
wagged
wag *noun*
wags
wage *noun*
wages
wage *verb*
wages
waging
waged
wager *noun*
wagers
wager *verb*
wagers
wagering
wagered
waggle *verb*
waggles
waggling
waggled
wagon *noun*
wagons
wagtail *noun*
wagtails
wail *verb*
wails
wailing
wailed
★ **wail** *noun*
wails
☆ **waist** *noun*
waists
waistcoat *noun*
waistcoats
✪ **wait** *verb*
waits
waiting
waited
wait *noun*
waits
waiter *noun*
waiters
waitress *noun*
waitresses
✲ **waive** *verb*
waives
waiving
waived
wake *verb*
wakes
waking
woke
woken
wake *noun*
wakes
waken *verb*
wakens
wakening
wakened
walk *verb*
walks
walking
walked
walk *noun*
walks
walkabout *noun*
walkabouts
walker *noun*
walkers
walkie-talkie *noun*
walkie-talkies
Walkman *noun*
Walkmans
wall *noun*
walls
wall *verb*
walls
walling
walled
wallaby *noun*
wallabies

★ A **wail** is a loud sad cry. ! **whale**.
☆ A person's **waist** is the narrow part around their middle. ! **waste**.
✪ To **wait** is to delay, pause, or rest. ! **weight**.
✲ To **waive** a right is to say you do not need it. ! **wave**.

wallet *noun*
wallets
wallflower *noun*
wallflowers
wallop *verb*
wallops
walloping
walloped
wallow *verb*
wallows
wallowing
wallowed
wallpaper *noun*
wallpapers
walnut *noun*
walnuts
walrus *noun*
walruses
waltz *noun*
waltzes
waltz *verb*
waltzes
waltzing
waltzed
wand *noun*
wands
wander *verb*
wanders
wandering
wandered
wanderer *noun*
wanderers
wane *verb*
wanes
waning
waned
wangle *verb*
wangles
wangling
wangled
want *verb*
wants
wanting
wanted
want *noun*
wants
war *noun*
wars
warble *verb*
warbles
warbling
warbled
warble *noun*
warbles
warbler *noun*
warblers
ward *noun*
wards
ward *verb*
wards
warding
warded
warden *noun*
wardens
warder *noun*
warders
wardrobe *noun*
wardrobes
★ **ware** *noun*
wares
warehouse *noun*
warehouses
warfare
warhead *noun*
warheads
wariness
warlike
warm *adjective*
warmer
warmest
warmly
warm *verb*
warms
warming
warmed
warmth
warn *verb*
warns
warning
warned
warning *noun*
warnings
warp *verb*
warps
warping
warped
warp *noun*
warps
warrant *noun*
warrants
warrant *verb*
warrants
warranting
warranted
warren *noun*
warrens
warrior *noun*
warriors
warship *noun*
warships
wart *noun*
warts
wary *adjective*
warier
wariest
warily
was
wash *verb*
washes
washing
washed
wash *noun*
washes

★ **Wares** are manufactured goods. ! **wear**, **where**.

washable
washbasin *noun*
washbasins
washer *noun*
washers
washing
washing-up
wash-out *noun*
wash-outs
wasn't *verb*
wasp *noun*
wasps
wastage
★ **waste** *verb*
wastes
wasting
wasted
waste *adjective* and *noun*
wastes
wasteful *adjective*
wastefully
watch *verb*
watches
watching
watched
watch *noun*
watches
watchdog *noun*
watchdogs
watcher *noun*
watchers
watchful *adjective*
watchfully
watchfulness
watchman *noun*
watchmen
water *noun*
waters
water *verb*
waters
watering
watered
watercolour *noun*
watercolours
watercress
waterfall *noun*
waterfalls
waterlogged
watermark *noun*
watermarks
waterproof
water-skiing
watertight
waterway *noun*
waterways
waterworks *noun*
waterworks
watery
☆ **watt** *noun*
watts
✪ **wave** *verb*
waves
waving
waved
wave *noun*
waves
waveband *noun*
wavebands
wavelength *noun*
wavelengths
waver *verb*
wavers
wavering
wavered
wavy *adjective*
wavier
waviest
wavily
wax *noun*
waxes
wax *verb*
waxes
waxing
waxed
waxwork *noun*
waxworks
waxy *adjective*
waxier
waxiest
✲ **way** *noun*
ways
✸ **weak** *adjective*
weaker
weakest
weakly
weakness
weaken *verb*
weakens
weakening
weakened
weakling *noun*
weaklings
wealth
wealthy *adjective*
wealthier
wealthiest
wealthily
weapon *noun*
weapons
❄ **wear** *verb*
wears
wearing
wore
worn
wear *noun*
wearer *noun*
wearers
weariness

★ To **waste** something is to use more of it than is needed. ! **waist**.
☆ A **watt** is a unit of electricity. ! **what**.
✪ To **wave** is to move your arm in greeting. ! **waive**.
✲ You use **way** in e.g. *can you tell me the way?* ! **weigh**, **whey**.
✸ **Weak** means 'not strong'. ! **week**.
❄ To **wear** clothes is to be dressed in them. ! **ware**, **where**.

weary *adjective*
wearier
weariest
wearily
weasel *noun*
weasels
weather *noun*
weather *verb*
weathers
weathering
weathered
weathercock *noun*
weathercocks
★ **weave** *verb*
weaves
weaving
weaved *or* wove
woven
weaver *noun*
weavers
web *noun*
webs
webbed
website *noun*
websites
wed *verb*
weds
wedding
wedded *or* wed
we'd *verb*
wedding *noun*
weddings
wedge *noun*
wedges
wedge *verb*
wedges
wedging
wedged
Wednesday *noun*
Wednesdays
weed *noun*
weeds
weed *verb*
weeds
weeding
weeded
weedy *adjective*
weedier
weediest
weedily
☆ **week** *noun*
weeks
weekday *noun*
weekdays
weekend *noun*
weekends
weekly *adjective* and *adverb*
weep *verb*
weeps
weeping
wept
weft
✪ **weigh** *verb*
weighs
weighing
weighed
✲ **weight** *noun*
weights
weightless
weightlifting
weighty *adjective*
weightier
weightiest
weightily
weir *noun*
weirs
weird *adjective*
weirder
weirdest
weirdly
weirdness
welcome *noun*
welcomes
welcome *verb*
welcomes
welcoming
welcomed
weld *verb*
welds
welding
welded
welder *noun*
welders
welfare
well *noun*
wells
well *adjective* and *adverb*
better
best
we'll *verb*
well-being
wellington boots *plural noun*
well-known
went see **go**
wept see **weep**
were see **are**
we're *verb*
werewolf *noun*
werewolves
west *adjective* and *adverb*
✸ **west** *noun*
westerly *adjective* and *noun*
westerlies
western *adjective*
western *noun*
westerns

★ The past tense is **weaved** in e.g. *she weaved her way through the crowd* and **wove** in e.g. *she wove a shawl.*
☆ A **week** is a period of seven days. ! **weak**
✪ You use **weigh** in e.g. *how much do you weigh?* ! **way**, **whey**.
✲ **Weight** is how heavy something is. ! **wait**
✸ You use a capital W in **the West**, when you mean a particular region.

westward *adjective* and *adverb*
westwards *adverb*
wet *adjective*
wetter
wettest
wet *verb*
wets
wetting
wetted
wetness
we've *abbreviation*
whack *verb*
whacks
whacking
whacked
whack *noun*
whacks
★ **whale** *noun*
whales
whaler *noun*
whalers
whaling
wharf *noun*
wharves *or* wharfs
☆ **what**
whatever
wheat
wheel *noun*
wheels
wheel *verb*
wheels
wheeling
wheeled
wheelbarrow *noun*
wheelbarrows
wheelchair *noun*
wheelchairs
wheeze *verb*
wheezes
wheezing
wheezed
whelk *noun*
whelks
when
whenever *conjunction*
✪ **where**
whereabouts
whereas
whereupon
wherever
whether *conjunction*
✲ **whey**
✹ **which**
whichever
whiff *noun*
whiffs
while *adjective* and *noun*
while *verb*
whiles
whiling
whiled
whilst *conjunction*
whimper *verb*
whimpers
whimpering
whimpered
whimper *noun*
whimpers
whine *verb*
whines
whining
whined
❄ **whine** *noun*
whines
whinny *verb*
whinnies
whinnying
whinnied
whip *noun*
whips
whip *verb*
whips
whipping
whipped
whirl *verb*
whirls
whirling
whirled
whirl *noun*
whirls
whirlpool *noun*
whirlpools
whirlwind *noun*
whirlwinds
whirr *verb*
whirrs
whirring
whirred
whirr *noun*
whirrs
whisk *verb*
whisks
whisking
whisked
whisk *noun*
whisks
whisker *noun*
whiskers
whisky *noun*
whiskies
whisper *verb*
whispers
whispering
whispered
whisper *noun*
whispers
whist

★ A **whale** is a large sea mammal. ! **wail**.
☆ You use **what** in e.g. *what are they doing?* or *I don't know what you mean.* ! **watt**.
✪ You use **where** in e.g. *where are you?* ! **ware**, **wear**.
✲ **Whey** is a watery liquid from milk. ! **way**, **weigh**.
✹ You use **which** in e.g. *which one is that?* ! **witch**.
❄ A **whine** is a high piercing sound. ! **wine**.

whistle *verb*
whistles
whistling
whistled
whistle *noun*
whistles
whistler *noun*
whistlers
white *adjective*
whiter
whitest
whiteness
whitish
white *noun*
whites
whiten *verb*
whitens
whitening
whitened
whitewash *noun*
whitewash *verb*
whitewashes
whitewashing
whitewashed
Whitsun
Whit Sunday
whiz *verb*
whizzes
whizzing
whizzed
who
whoever
★ **whole** *adjective*
wholly
whole *noun*
wholes
wholefood *noun*
wholefoods
wholemeal
wholesale *adjective*
wholesome
wholly
whom
whoop *noun*
whoops
whoopee *interjection*
whooping cough
☆ **who's** *verb*
✪ **whose** *adjective*
why
wick *noun*
wicks
wicked *adjective*
wickeder
wickedest
wickedly
wickedness
wicker
wickerwork
wicket *noun*
wickets
wicketkeeper *noun*
wicketkeepers
wide *adjective* and *adverb*
wider
widest
widely
widen *verb*
widens
widening
widened
widespread
widow *noun*
widows
widower *noun*
widowers
width *noun*
widths
wield *verb*
wields
wielding
wielded
wife *noun*
wives
wig *noun*
wigs
wiggle *verb*
wiggles
wiggling
wiggled
wiggle *noun*
wiggles
wigwam *noun*
wigwams
wild *adjective*
wilder
wildest
wildly
wilderness *noun*
wildernesses
wildness
wildlife
wilful *adjective*
wilfully
wilfulness
wiliness
will *verb*
would
will *noun*
wills
willing *adjective*
willingly
willingness
willow *noun*
willows
wilt *verb*
wilts
wilting
wilted

★ You use **whole** in e.g. *I saw the whole film.* ! **hole**.
☆ You use **who's** in *who's* (= who is) *that?* and *I don't know who's* (= who has) *done it.* ! **whose**.
✪ You use **whose** in *whose is this?* and *I don't know whose it is.* ! **who's**.

wily *adjective*
wilier
wiliest
wimp *noun*
wimps
win *verb*
wins
winning
won
win *noun*
wins
wince *verb*
winces
wincing
winced
winch *noun*
winches
winch *verb*
winches
winching
winched
wind *noun*
winds
wind *verb*
winds
winding
wound
windfall *noun*
windfalls
windmill *noun*
windmills
window *noun*
windows
windpipe *noun*
windpipes
windscreen *noun*
windscreens
windsurfer
windsurfing
windward
windy *adjective*
windier
windiest
windily
★ **wine** *noun*
wines
wing *noun*
wings
wing *verb*
wings
winging
winged
winged
wingless
wingspan *noun*
wingspans
wink *verb*
winks
winking
winked
wink *noun*
winks
winkle *noun*
winkles
winkle *verb*
winkles
winkling
winkled
winner *noun*
winners
winnings *plural noun*
winter *noun*
winters
wintertime
wintry *adjective*
wintrier
wintriest
wipe *verb*
wipes
wiping
wiped
wipe *noun*
wipes
wiper *noun*
wipers
wire *noun*
wires
wire *verb*
wires
wiring
wired
wireless *noun*
wirelesses
wiring
wiry *adjective*
wirier
wiriest
wirily
wisdom
wise *adjective*
wiser
wisest
wisely
wish *verb*
wishes
wishing
wished
wish *noun*
wishes
wishbone *noun*
wishbones
wisp *noun*
wisps
wispy *adjective*
wispier
wispiest
wispily
wistful *adjective*
wistfully
wistfulness
wit *noun*
wits

★ **Wine** is a drink. **!** **whine**.

★ **witch** *noun*
witches
witchcraft
with
withdraw *verb*
withdraws
withdrawing
withdrew
withdrawn
withdrawal *noun*
withdrawals
wither *verb*
withers
withering
withered
withhold *verb*
withholds
withholding
withheld
within
without
withstand *verb*
withstands
withstanding
withstood
witness *noun*
witnesses
wittiness
witty *adjective*
wittier
wittiest
wittily
wizard *noun*
wizards
wizardry
wobble *verb*
wobbles
wobbling
wobbled
wobble *noun*
wobbles
wobbly *adjective*
wobblier
wobbliest
woe *noun*
woes
woeful *adjective*
woefully
wok *noun*
woks
woke see **wake**
woken see **wake**
wolf *noun*
wolves
woman *noun*
women
womb *noun*
wombs
☆ **won** see **win**
wonder *noun*
wonders
wonder *verb*
wonders
wondering
wondered
wonderful *adjective*
wonderfully
won't *verb*
✪ **wood** *noun*
woods
wooded
wooden
woodland *noun*
woodlands
woodlouse *noun*
woodlice
woodpecker *noun*
woodpeckers
woodwind
woodwork
woodworm *noun*
woodworm *or*
woodworms
woody *adjective*
woodier
woodiest
wool
woollen
woollens *plural noun*
woolliness
woolly *adjective*
woollier
woolliest
word *noun*
words
word *verb*
words
wording
worded
wording
wordy *adjective*
wordier
wordiest
wore see **wear**
work *noun*
works
work *verb*
works
working
worked
workable
worker *noun*
workers
workforce *noun*
workforces
workman *noun*
workmen
workmanship
workout *noun*
workouts

★ A **witch** is someone who uses witchcraft. ! **which**.
☆ You use **won** in e.g. *I won a prize*. ! **one**.
✪ **Wood** is material from trees or a lot of trees growing together. ! **would**.

works *plural noun*
worksheet *noun*
worksheets
workshop *noun*
workshops
world *noun*
worlds
worldliness
worldly *adjective*
worldlier
worldliest
worldwide *adjective*
worm *noun*
worms
worm *verb*
worms
worming
wormed
worn see **wear**
worry *verb*
worries
worrying
worried
worrier *noun*
worriers
worry *noun*
worries
worse *adjective* and *adverb*
worsen *verb*
worsens
worsening
worsened
worship *verb*
worships
worshipping
worshipped
worship *noun*
worshipper *noun*
worshippers
worst *adjective* and *adverb*
worth
worthiness
worthless *adjective*
worthlessly
worthwhile
worthy *adjective*
worthier
worthiest
worthily
★ **would** see **will**
wouldn't *verb*
wound *noun*
wounds
wound *verb*
wounds
wounding
wounded
wound see **wind**
wove see **weave**
woven see **weave**
☆ **wrap** *verb*
wraps
wrapping
wrapped
wrap *noun*
wraps
wrapper *noun*
wrappers
wrapping *noun*
wrappings
wrath
wrathful *adjective*
wrathfully
wreath *noun*
wreaths
wreathe *verb*
wreathes
wreathing
wreathed
wreck *verb*
wrecks
wrecking
wrecked
wreck *noun*
wrecks
wreckage *noun*
wreckages
wrecker *noun*
wreckers
wren *noun*
wrens
wrench *verb*
wrenches
wrenching
wrenched
wrench *noun*
wrenches
wrestle *verb*
wrestles
wrestling
wrestled
wrestler *noun*
wrestlers
wretch *noun*
wretches
wretched *adjective*
wretchedly
wriggle *verb*
wriggles
wriggling
wriggled
wriggle *noun*
wriggles
wriggly *adjective*
wrigglier
wriggliest
✪ **wring** *verb*
wrings
wringing
wrung

★ You use **would** in e.g. *would you like to come to tea?* ! **wood**.
☆ To **wrap** something is to cover it in paper etc. ! **rap**.
✪ To **wring** something is to squeeze it hard. ! **ring**.

wrinkle *noun*
wrinkles
wrinkle *verb*
wrinkles
wrinkling
wrinkled
wrist *noun*
wrists
wristwatch *noun*
wristwatches
★ **write** *verb*
writes
writing
wrote
written
writer *noun*
writers
writhe *verb*
writhes
writhing
writhed
writing *noun*
writings
written see **write**
wrong *adjective* and *adverb*
wrongly
wrong *noun*
wrongs
wrong *verb*
wrongs
wronging
wronged
wrote see **write**
wrung see **wring**
☆ **wry** *adjective*
wryer
wryest

Xx

xenophobia
Xmas *noun*
Xmases
X-ray *noun*
X-rays
X-ray *verb*
X-rays
X-raying
X-rayed
xylophone *noun*
xylophones

Yy

-y and -ey
Nouns ending in *-y* following a consonant, e.g. **story**, make plurals ending in *-ies*, e.g. **stories**, and verbs, e.g. **try**, make forms in *-ies* and *-ied*, e.g. **tries**, **tried**. Nouns ending in *-ey*, e.g. **journey**, make plurals ending in *-eys*, e.g. **journeys**.

yacht *noun*
yachts
yachtsman *noun*
yachtsmen
yachtswoman *noun*
yachtswomen
yam *noun*
yams
yank *verb*
yanks
yanking
yanked
yap *verb*
yaps
yapping
yapped
yap *noun*
yaps
yard *noun*
yards
yard *noun*
yards
yarn *noun*
yarns
yawn *verb*
yawns
yawning
yawned
yawn *noun*
yawns
year *noun*
years
yearly *adjective* and *adverb*
yearn *verb*
yearns
yearning
yearned
yeast
yell *noun*
yells
yell *verb*
yells
yelling
yelled
yellow *adjective* and *noun*
yellower
yellowest

★ You use **write** in e.g. *to write a letter*. ! **right**, **rite**.
☆ You use **wry** in e.g. *a wry smile*. ! **rye**.

yelp *verb*
yelps
yelping
yelped
yelp *noun*
yelps
★ **yen** *noun*
yens *or* yen
yeoman *noun*
yeomen
yesterday *adjective* and *noun*
yesterdays
yet
yeti *noun*
yetis
☆ **yew** *noun*
yews
yield *verb*
yields
yielding
yielded
yield *noun*
yields
yippee
yodel *verb*
yodels
yodelling
yodelled
yodeller *noun*
yodellers
yoga
yoghurt *noun*
yoghurts
✪ **yoke** *noun*
yokes
yoke *verb*
yokes
yoking
yoked
✲ **yolk** *noun*
yolks
Yom Kippur
yonder
✸ **you**
you'd *verb*
you'll *verb*
young *adjective*
younger
youngest
young *plural noun*
youngster *noun*
youngsters
your
you're *abbreviation*
yours
yourself *pronoun*
yourselves
youth *noun*
youths
youthful *adjective*
youthfully
you've *abbreviation*
yo-yo *noun*
yo-yos
yuppie *noun*
yuppies

Zz

zany *adjective*
zanier
zaniest
zanily
zap *verb*
zaps
zapping
zapped
zeal
zealous *adjective*
zealously
zebra *noun*
zebras
zenith *noun*
zeniths
zero *noun*
zeros
zest
zigzag *noun*
zigzags
zigzag *verb*
zigzags
zigzagging
zigzagged
zinc
zip *noun*
zips
zip *verb*
zips
zipping
zipped
zodiac
zombie *noun*
zombies
zone *noun*
zones
zoo *noun*
zoos
zoological *adjective*
zoologically
zoologist *noun*
zoologists
zoology
zoom *verb*
zooms
zooming
zoomed

★ The plural is **yens** when you mean 'a longing' and **yen** for Japanese money.
☆ A **yew** is a tree. ! **ewe, you**
✪ A **yoke** is a piece of wood put across animals pulling a cart. ! **yolk**
✲ A **yolk** is the yellow part of an egg. ! **yoke**
✸ You use **you** in e.g. *I love you*. ! **ewe, yew**